McFarlin Library
WITHDRAWN

Farlin Library
THDRAWN

FORGED DOCUMENTS

FORGED DOCUMENTS
PROCEEDINGS OF THE 1989 HOUSTON CONFERENCE

ORGANIZED BY THE UNIVERSITY OF HOUSTON LIBRARIES
EDITED BY PAT BOZEMAN

OAK KNOLL BOOKS
NEW CASTLE, DELAWARE
1990

Published by
OAK KNOLL BOOKS
*414 Delaware Street
New Castle, Delaware 19720*

© 1990 The University of Houston,
on behalf of the Libraries
ISBN 0-938768-22-0

*Typeset in 10 point Baskerville and
printed in the United States of America by
The Pioneer Press, Terra Alta, West Virginia
on 70lb. Mohawk Vellum acid-free paper*

Library of Congress Cataloging-in-Publication Data

Forged documents : proceedings of the 1989 Houston conference /
organized by the University of Houston Libraries : edited by Pat
Bozeman.
   p. cm.
  "The Houston Conference on Forged Documents"—Prelim. p.
Includes bibliographical references.
ISBN 0-938768-22-0
  1. Libraries—Security measures—Congresses. 2. Antiquarian
booksellers—Security measures—Congresses. 3. Printed ephemera—
Forgeries—Congresses. 4. Rare books—Forgeries—Congresses.
5. Book collecting—Congresses. 6. Forgery—Congresses.
I. Bozeman, Pat. II. University of Houston. Libraries.
III. Houston Conference (1989)
Z679.6.F67   1990
025.2—dc20
                                                    90-42701
                                                        CIP

Contents

CONTRIBUTORS	vi
CONFERENCE ATTENDEES	vii
ACKNOWLEDGMENTS	xii
PREFACE	xiii
W. THOMAS TAYLOR *Provenance and Lore of the Trade*	1
NICOLAS BARKER *The Forgery of Printed Documents*	7
FLOOR DISCUSSION I: *Forgery Detection*	19
ELLEN S. DUNLAP *Administrative Concerns*	25
SCOTT CHAFIN *Institutional Legal Considerations*	31
WILLIAM L. JOYCE *The Scholarly Implications of Documentary Forgeries*	37
MARCUS A. McCORISON *The Routine Handling of Forgeries in Research Libraries: or, Can Dishonesty Ever Be Routine?*	49
FLOOR DISCUSSION II: *Inter-related Institutional Factors*	55
TOM M. DAVIS, JR. *Authenticity: The Duty to Investigate*	65
DONALD J. MALOUF *Tax Donations and Appraisals*	73
MARIE C. MALARO *Legal and Ethical Levels of Responsibility*	99
FLOOR DISCUSSION III: *Tax and Legal Implications*	109
JENKINS GARRETT *Forged Documents: Considerations of the Collector/Donor*	119
GEORGE A. MILES *Dealer/Donor/Institutional Relations: Expectations of the Institution*	123
JENNIFER S. LARSON *Obligations of the Dealer: The U.S. Perspective*	133
ANTHONY ROTA *The Texas Forgeries. Obligations of the Dealer: The International Perspective*	153
FLOOR DISCUSSION IV: *Dealer/Donor/Institutional Relations*	159

Contributors

NICOLAS BARKER is Head of Select Materials at the British Library and serves as editor of *The Book Collector*. He is a leading authority on printed forgery, from those of Thomas J. Wise to the recent Mormon forgeries of Mark Hofmann.

SCOTT CHAFIN is General Counsel for the University of Houston System. He serves as an adjunct faculty member in the University of Houston's College of Education.

TOM M. DAVIS, JR. is a partner in the Houston law firm of Davis and Shank. He is a collector of Texana.

ELLEN S. DUNLAP is Director of the Rosenbach Museum and Library, Philadelphia. She serves as chair of the Steering Committee for the Research Libraries Group's Archives, Manuscripts, and Special Collections Program.

JENKINS GARRETT is an attorney with Harris, Finley, Creel & Bogle of Fort Worth, Texas. A life-long collector of Texana, he and his wife gave their book and manuscript collection to the University of Texas at Arlington, which became the nucleus of the Special Collections Division.

WILLIAM L. JOYCE is Associate University Librarian for Rare Books and Special Collections, Princeton University. He is an adjunct faculty member in the School of Library Service, Columbia University.

JENNIFER S. LARSON is the proprietor of Yerba Buena Books in San Francisco. She serves as Archivist for the Questioned Imprints Committee of the Antiquarian Booksellers Association of America, Inc.

MARIE C. MALARO is Director of the Museum Studies Program at George Washington University. Prior to holding this position she was Associate General Counsel at the Smithsonian Institution.

DONALD J. MALOUF is a partner in the law firm of Malouf, Lynch, Jackson, Kessler & Collins of Dallas, Texas. He has chaired the Colophon-Friends of the SMU Libraries book auction.

MARCUS A. McCORISON is President and Librarian of the American Antiquarian Society. He is a lecturer at Clark University, Worcester, Massachusetts.

GEORGE A. MILES is the Curator of Western Americana at the Beinecke Rare Book and Manuscript Library, Yale University. He is an instructor at Columbia University's summer Rare Book School.

ANTHONY ROTA is the head of Bertram Rota Ltd., Booksellers, London. He is President of the International League of Antiquarian Booksellers.

W. THOMAS TAYLOR is the owner of W. Thomas Taylor, Printers-Publishers-Antiquarian Booksellers, located in Austin, Texas. His extensive research on early nineteenth century Texas imprints led to the discovery of several forgeries, including copies of the 1836 Texas Declaration of Independence.

List of Participants

HOUSTON CONFERENCE ON FORGED DOCUMENTS
HOUSTON, TEXAS • NOVEMBER 2-4, 1989

Katherine Adams
Barker History Center
Richardson Hall 2, 101
University of Texas
Austin, TX 78713

Grant Anderson
50 E. North Temple St.
Salt Lake City, UT 84150
   LDS Church Historical Dept.

Jerome E. Anderson
101 Newbury Street
Boston, MA 02116
   New England Historic
   Genealogical Society

Nicolas Barker
The British Library
Great Russell Street
London WC1B 3DG
England

Barbara Barkley
2134 Dunstan
Houston, TX 77004

Lisa Belkin
The New York Times
4750 Republic Bank Center
700 Louisiana
Houston, TX 77002
   National Correspondent

Paul G. Bell
3800 Park Rd. 1836
LaPorte, TX 77571
   San Jacinto Museum of
   History

Artis Bernard
Special Collections
Univ. of Houston Libraries
Houston, TX 77204-2091

Kent Biffle
Dallas Morning News
Communications Center
Dallas, TX 75265

Annette Cheek Bishop
1022 South Shepherd
Houston, TX 77019

Anthony Bliss
Bancroft Library
Univ. of California
Berkeley, CA 94720

Curt Bohling
P.O. Box 204
Decatur, MI 49045
   Bohling Book Company

Stephen Bonario
Special Collections
Univ. of Houston Libraries
Houston, TX 77204-2091

Nancy L. Boothe
2135 University Blvd.
Houston, TX 77030
   Woodson Research Center,
   Rice University

Ann Bowden
2109B Exposition Blvd.
Austin, TX 78703
   University of Texas at
   Austin

Pat Bozeman
Special Collections
Univ. of Houston Libraries
Houston, TX 77204-2091

Peter Briscoe
12740 Wilmac Avenue
Grand Terrace, CA 92324
   University of California at
   Riverside

Roger L. Brooks
715 Center Hill Drive
Houston, TX 77079
   Armstrong Browning
   Library,
   Baylor University

Mrs. Roger L. Brooks
715 Center Hill Drive
Houston, TX 77079

J.P. Bryan
3 Shadowlawn
Houston, TX 77005
   Torch Energy

Mary Jon Bryan
3 Shadowlawn
Houston, TX 77005

Cynthia Buffington
P.O. Box 9536
Philadelphia, PA 19124
   Philadelphia Rare Books

Alfred L. Bush
Princeton University Library
One Washington Road
Princeton, NJ 08544
   Princeton Collections of
   Western Americana

Patrick H. Butler III
P.O. Box 1300
Galveston, TX 77553
   Moody Museum

Robert T. Buttweiler
Box 721793
Houston, TX 77272
   R.T. Buttweiler Ltd.

Antonio A. Cantu
U. S. Secret Service
Technical Security Division
1800 G Street NW
Washington, DC 20233

Don E. Carleton
Barker History Center
University of Texas
Austin, TX 78712

J. Scott Chafin
Univ. of Houston System
4600 Gulf Freeway, #421
Houston, TX 77023

John P. Chalmers
Humanities Research Center
University of Texas
P.O. Drawer 7219
Austin, TX 78713-7219

David L. Chapman
1803 Sabine Ct.
College Station, TX 77840
   Texas A&M University
   Archives

Robert Chapman
711 Studewood
Houston, TX 77007
  Booked Up

Jake Chernofsky
AB Bookman's Weekly
P.O. Box AB
Clifton, NJ 07015

M. Chomel de Coelho
Apartado Postal No. 41659
11000 Mexico, D.F.
Mexico

Betty A. Coley
Baylor University
Box 7152
Armstrong Browning
  Library
Waco, TX 76798-7044

Sharon R. Crutchfield
13743 Wilderness Point Dr.
San Antonio, TX 78231

Gregory Curtis
Texas Monthly
P.O. Box 1569
Austin, TX 78767

Susan Danforth
P.O. Box 1894
Providence, RI 02912
  John Carter Brown Library,
  Brown University

Elisabeth F. Darst
1601 Sealy
Galveston, TX 77550

Donald G. Davis, Jr.
Graduate School of Library
and Information Science
University of Texas
Austin, TX 78712-1276

Tom M. Davis, Jr.
Davis & Shank
1415 Louisiana
Suite 400
Houston, TX 77002

Muir Dawson
Dawson's Book Shop
535 North Larchmont Blvd.
Los Angeles, CA 90004

Chester Doby
1305 S. Shepherd
Houston, TX 77019
  A Book Buyer's Shop

Christine Doby
1305 S. Shepherd
Houston, TX 77019
  A Book Buyer's Shop

Robin Downes
Univ. of Houston Libraries
Houston, TX 77204-2091

Ellen S. Dunlap
Rosenbach Museum &
  Library
2010 DeLancy Place
Philadelphia, PA 19103

Donald H. Dyal
Sterling C. Evans Library
Texas A&M University
College Station, TX 77843

Lori Ely
c/o Bernice Moore
3801 19th Street
Suite 119
Lubbock, TX 79410-1016

Robert A. Erickson
1313 Vermont Ave. NW #14
Washington, DC 20005

Nancy Escher
9538 Brighton Way #332
Beverly Hills, CA 90210
  Nancy Escher, Inc.

David Farmer
DeGolyer Library
Southern Methodist
  University
Dallas, TX 75275

Carol Farmer
3223 Woodland Drive
Southlake, TX 76092

Donald Farren
Special Collections
University of Maryland
College Park, MD 20742

Robert C. Findlay
1000 North Bowen Rd.
Arlington, TX 76012

Carole D. Findlay
1000 North Bowen Rd.
Arlington, TX 76012

Mary Ann K. Folter
16 East 46th Street
New York, NY 10017
  H. P. Kraus Rare Books

Roland Folter
16 East 46th Street
New York, NY 10017
  H. P. Kraus Rare Books

Stuart M. Frank
P.O. Box 297
Sharon, MA 02067
  The Kendall Whaling
  Museum

Jenkins Garrett
Harris, Finley, Creel
  & Bogle
3100 Continental Plaza
Fort Worth, TX 76102

Mrs. Jenkins Garrett
Harris, Finley, Creel
  & Bogle
3100 Continental Plaza
Fort Worth, TX 76102

Jenkins Garrett, Jr.
3100 Continental Plaza
Ft. Worth, TX 76102
  University of Texas at
  Arlington

Marcia Garrett
3100 Continental Plaza
Ft. Worth, TX 76102

Gerard W. Gawalt
Manuscript Division
Library of Congress
Washington, D.C. 20540

Franklin Gilliam
112 Fourth St. NE
Charlottesville, VA 22901
  Franklin Gilliam:
  Rare Books

Mary Cooper Gilliam
Law Library
University of Virginia
Charlottesville, VA 22901

James Gilreath
2616 Key Boulevard
Arlington, VA 22201
  Library of Congress

Doris Glasser
Houston Public Library,
Texas Room
500 McKinney
Houston, TX 77002

John S. Gorajczyk
1049 Washington Court
Bartlett, IL 60103
  DuPage County Sheriff's
  Crime Lab

David B. Gracy II
EDB 564
University of Texas
Austin, TX 78712-1276
  Graduate School
  of Library
  & Information Science

Oscar Graham
Detering Book Gallery
2311 Bissonnet
Houston, TX 77005

Steven T. Granger
Carleton College
1 North College Street
Northfield, MN 55057

Barry A. Greenlaw
P.O. Box 870
Columbus, TX 78934

Alan Gribben
Department of English
University of Texas at Austin
Austin, TX 78712-1164

James P. Grizzard
2018 N. Memorial Way
Houston, TX 77007

Kathleen Gunning
Univ. of Houston Libraries
Houston, TX 77204-2091

Mihai H. Handrea
337 East 88th Street, 2A
New York, NY 10128
   The New York Public Library

Claude S. Harkins
P.O. Box 16514
Kansas City, MO 64133

Charles B. Harrell
Box 194248
University of Texas at Arlington
Arlington, TX 76019-0248

Henry J. Hauschild
P.O. Box 1129
210 E. Forrest
Victoria, TX 77901-1129
   Cognoscente di
   Eccellentissimo

James L. Hayes
221 No. LaSalle Street
Suite 1254
Chicago, IL 60601
   James L. Hayes & Assoc.
   Forensic Document Examiner

Michael V. Hazel
Dallas Historical Society
P.O. Box 26038
Dallas, TX 75206

Michael D. Heaston
5614 Wagon Train Rd.
Austin, TX 78749
   Michael D. Heaston Rare
   Books & Manuscripts

John H. Herbert
Historical Collections
P.O. Box 31623
Houston, TX 77231

Diana E. Herzog
26 Broadway
New York, N.Y. 10004
   R. M. Smythe Company, Inc.

David E. Hewett
6 Cherry Street
Brattleboro, VT 05301
   Maine Antique Digest

Janna Hewett
6 Cherry Street
Brattleboro, VT 05301
   Maine Antique Digest

Karen Hewitt
1601 Elm #4343
Dallas, TX 75201
   Hewitt & Jerome,
   Attorneys & Counselors

Nancy Hixon
Blaffer Gallery
University of Houston
Houston, TX 77002-4891

Richard Holland
309 Moore Blvd.
Austin, TX 78705
   Southwest Texas State
   University

Henry Hornblower III
176 Court Street
Dedham, MA 02026
   Advisor, Kendall Whaling
   Museum

Cathleen Huck
Hilton College of Hotel
& Restaurant Management
University of Houston
Houston, TX 77204-3902

Milan R. Hughston
P.O. Box 2365
Fort Worth, TX 76113-2365
   Amon Carter Museum Library

Marcelle Hull
3833 Heywood Ave.
Fort Worth, TX 76109
   University of Texas at
   Arlington Libraries

Sidney F. Huttner
University of Tulsa Library
600 South College
Tulsa, OK 74104

Ann Hyde
2720 Stratford Road
Lawrence, KS 66045
   Spencer Library, University
   of Kansas

Steve Ivy
311 Market St.
Dallas, TX 75202

Blandin Jones
2135 University Blvd.
Houston, TX 77030

William L. Joyce
Rare Books & Spec. Col.
Princeton University Library
Princeton, NJ 08544

Biruta Celmins Kearl
P.O. Box 2287
Austin, TX 78768

Kent Keeth
The Texas Collection
Baylor University
BU Box 7142
Waco, TX 76798-7142

David V. Koch
Morris Library
Southern Illinois University
Carbondale, IL 62901

Marie Korey
Rare Book Department
Free Library of Philadelphia
Logan Square
Philadelphia, PA 19107

Eric Korn
47 Tetherdown
London, N10
England
   Times Literary Supplement

Ruth Lamb
2423 Keats Way
Waterloo, Ontario N2L 5S7
Canada
   University of Waterloo

Lisa Shippee Lambert
Rosenberg Library
2310 Sealy Avenue
Galveston, TX 77550

Richard Landon
37 Coulson Avenue
Toronto M4V 1Y3
   University of Toronto

Thomas V. Lange
1151 Oxford Road
San Marino, CA 91108
   Huntington Library

Jennifer S. Larson
Yerba Buena Books
882 Bush Street
San Francisco, CA 94108

Kenneth Lavender
1102 Edinburg Lane
Denton, TX 76201
   University of North Texas

Kathleen Lazare
P.O. Box 117
Sherman, CT 06784
   Scarlet Letter Books

Michael Lazare
P.O. Box 117
Sherman, CT 06784
  Scarlet Letter Books

Glen Nolan Lewis
The Houston Post
P.O. Box 4747
Houston, TX 77210-4747

David Light
9406 West Broadview Drive
Bay Harbor Islands, FL 33154

Mrs. David Light
9406 West Broadview Drive
Bay Harbor Islands, FL 33154

Alan N. Livingston
7531 Olympia
Houston, TX 77063

James Lorson
Lorson's Books & Prints
116 West Wilshire Avenue
Fullerton, CA 92632

Rufus Lund
1746 Channel Road
Austin, TX 78746

Marcus McCorison
American Antiquarian Society
185 Salisbury Street
Worcester, MA 01609

Kevin MacDonnell
MacDonnell Rare Books
9307 Glen Lake Drive
Austin, TX 78730

Tania McKnight
8540 Melrose Avenue
Los Angeles, CA 90069
  Heritage Book Shop, Inc.

Larry McMurtry
Booked Up
1209 31st Street
Washington, DC 20007

Estela Madis
Box 381700
Duncanville, TX 75138

Franklin Madis
Box 381700
Duncanville, TX 75138

Marie C. Malaro
Museum Studies Program
George Washington University
Academic Center, Room 215
Washington, DC 20052

Donald J. Malouf
Malouf, Lynch, Jackson,
Kessler & Collins
8117 Preston Road, #700
Dallas, TX 75225

David Margolis
P. O. Box 2042
Santa Fe, NM 87504
  Moss and Margolis Book Shop

Lynn Wilson Marks
P.O. Box 690526
San Antonio, TX 78269
  Forensic Document
  Examination Associates

James C. Martin
3800 Park Rd. 1836
LaPorte, TX 77571
  San Jacinto Museum of
  History

Robert S. Martin
5968 Arden Place
Baton Rouge, LA 70806
  Hill Memorial Library,
  Louisiana State University

Alexandra Mason
Kenneth Spencer
  Research Library
University of Kansas
Lawrence, KS 66045

Janet Masson
5900 Memorial Drive
Suite 304
Houston, TX 77007
  Forensic Document Examiner

Bob Medlar
7115 Blanco Road
San Antonio, TX 78216
  Medlar Historical Gallery

George A. Miles
Beinecke Library
Yale University Station
P. O. Box 1603
New Haven, CT 06520
  Yale Collection of Western
  Americana

William A. Moffett
Oberlin College Library
Oberlin, OH 44074

Bernice Moore
4605 22nd Street
Lubbock, TX 79407

Mrs. George More
c/o Jane Owen
4615 Southwest Freeway
Suite 860E
Houston, TX 77027

Caroline S. Morris
1553 Schiavello Drive
Swarthmore, PA 19081
  Archivist, Pennsylvania
  Hospital

Charles T. Morrissey
One Baylor Plaza
Houston, TX 77030
  Oral History Project,
  Baylor College of Medicine

Dennis J. Moser
317 S. Division
Suite 213
Ann Arbor, MI 48104
  Guild of Bookworkers,
  University of Michigan

William Myers
1985 Velma Avenue
Columbus, OH 43211
  Ohio Historical Society

Kenneth Nebenzahl
P.O. Box 370
Glencoe, IL 60022
  Kenneth Nebenzahl, Inc.

Jane B. Owen
4615 Southwest Fwy.
Suite 860E
Houston, TX 77027

Betty A. Parker
P.O. Box 8390
Santa Fe, NM 87504
  Parker Books of the West

Riley G. Parker
P.O. Box 8390
Santa Fe, NM 87504
  Parker Books of the West

C.O. Patterson
715 Park Place
College Station, TX 77840

John R. Payne
2205 Bridle Path
Austin, TX 78703
  Library Consultant and
  Appraiser

Loretta J. Pitts
Univ. of Houston Law Library
Houston, TX 77204-6390

Lee Pryor
English Department
University of Houston
Houston, TX 77204-3012

Irving W. Robbins, Jr.
81 Ridgeview Dr.
Atherton, CA 94027
  Stanford University

Van W. Robinson
6933 Lyre Lane
Dallas, TX 75214
  Southern Methodist
  University

Anthony Rota
Bertram Rota Ltd.
911 Langley Court
Covent Garden
London WC2E 9RX
England

Glenn N. Rowe
50 E. North Temple St.
Salt Lake City, UT 84150
　LDS Church Historical Dept.

John Runnells
c/o Kenneth Nebenzahl
P.O. Box 370
Glencoe, IL 60022

Duane Runnels
Box 1776
La Porte, TX 77572-1776
　Louisiana Purchase Rare
　Books

Patricia Runnels
Box 1776
La Porte, TX 77572-1776
　Louisiana Purchase Rare
　Books

Barbara Ruppert
Ruppert Books
5909 Darnell
Houston, TX 77074

Betty Ruppert
Ruppert Books
5909 Darnell
Houston, TX 77074

Gerald D. Saxon
3409 Sheffield
Arlington, TX 76013
　University of Texas at
　Arlington

Kathryn Schadewald
2117 Woodhead
Houston, TX 77019
　Heritage Society

Alice Schreyer
101 Red Pine Circle
Newark, DE 19711
　University of Delaware
　Library

Pat Shaer
KUHF Radio
University of Houston
Houston, TX 77204-4061

A.J. Simmonds
Utah State University
Logan, UT 84322-3000
　Utah State University

Ray Simpson
4001 Main
Houston, TX 77002
　Simpson's Antiques

Dorothy Sloan
P.O. Box 49670
Austin, TX 78765
　Dorothy Sloan Rare Books

Michael Smith
Dallas Public Library
1515 Young Street
Dallas, TX 75201

Mickey M. Sparkman
P.O. Box 10370
Beaumont, TX 77710
　Lamar University

Sam Streit
Special Collections
John Hay Library
Brown University
Providence, RI 02912

Mitch Strucinski
155 Yale Road
Menlo Park, CA 94025

David Szewczyk
P.O. Box 9536
Philadelphia, PA 19124
　Philadelphia Rare Books

W. Thomas Taylor
1906 Miriam
Austin, TX 78722
　W. Thomas Taylor, Inc.

Russ Todd
28605 N. 63rd Street
Cave Creek, AZ 85331
　Russ Todd Books

William B. Todd
Department of English
University of Texas
Austin, TX 78712

Ludd A. Trozpek
4141 Via Padova
Claremont, CA 91711
　Ludd A. Trozpek Books

Ron Tyler
2/306 Richardson Hall
Austin, TX 78712
　Texas State Historical
　Association

Dianne Vaughan
Bank One, P.O. Box 900
San Antonio, TX 78293
　University of Texas at
　Arlington

Jim Veninga
100 Neches
Austin, TX 78701
　Texas Committee for the
　Humanities

Thomas Verich
1012 Harlan Drive
Oxford, MS 38655
　University of Mississippi

Elizabeth Wachendorfer
Univ. of Houston Libraries
Houston, TX 77204-2091

Clyde C. Walton
Library Administration, CB 184
University of Colorado
Boulder, CO 80309

Michael Whalon
Humanities Research Center
University of Texas
P.O. Drawer 7219
Austin, TX 78713-7219

Elizabeth White
HAMTMC Library
1133 M.D. Anderson Blvd.
Houston, TX 77030

David J. Whittaker
5030 Harold B. Lee Library
Brigham Young University
Provo, UT 84602

Mary Ann Willey
2602 Bandelier
Houston, TX 77080
　Abbiamo Books

Ron Williamson
P.O. Box 33245
Kerrville, TX 78029

Elicia I. Wolf
6300 Waterway Dr.
Falls Church, VA 22044
　Fiat Lux Library

Eric W. Wolf
6300 Waterway Dr.
Falls Church, VA 22044
　Fiat Lux Library

James Yarnell
1233 N. River Blvd.
Wichita, KS 67203
　Oak Park Press

Acknowledgments

THE HOUSTON CONFERENCE ON FORGED DOCUMENTS
WAS SPONSORED BY THE UNIVERSITY OF
HOUSTON LIBRARIES AND ROCKWELL FUND, INC.

Participating sponsors included Antiquarian Booksellers Association of America, Inc., Bibliographical Society of America, Friends of the University of Houston Libraries, Maine Antique Digest, and Texas Committee for the Humanities. Mid-Conference Reception Sponsors included A Book Buyer's Shop, Detering Book Gallery, Michael D. Heaston Rare Books & Manuscripts, The Jenkins Company, and Dorothy Sloan—Books. Conference Planning Committee consisted of Pat Bozeman, Chair, Don Carleton, Robin Downes, David Farmer, Kathleen Gunning, J.C. Martin, Dorothy Sloan, Tom Taylor, Ron Tyler, and Liz Wachendorfer, Co-chair. Planning and execution of the conference was aided by University of Houston Libraries staff members Cindy Barrett, Artis Bernard, Stephen Bonario, Jane Hays, and Kristin Jacobsen. Conference volunteer staff included Ann Foreman, Kathleen Hartt, and Peggy Shiffick.

Publication of the proceedings of the Houston Conference on Forged Documents was made possible by a significant contribution from Rockwell Fund, Inc., as well as by contributions from Antiquarian Booksellers Association of America, Inc., Dorothy Sloan—Books, Friends of the University of Houston Libraries, and Society of Southwest Archivists.

Assistance in readying these proceedings for publication was provided by Artis Bernard, Stephen Bonario, and Barbara Nytes-Baron.

Preface

When the existence of forged historical Texas documents was revealed through the work of Austin printer and rare book dealer W. Thomas Taylor, issues were raised of profoundly serious concern. They were of concern for libraries, for the antiquarian book trade, and for private collectors of these historical documents. Most critical, of course, was a concern for the ultimate users of historical records, the scholars who must rely on their authenticity.

As we considered what action to take, it quickly became evident that few benchmarks existed. Professional associations in librarianship and the book trade had not systematically addressed the issue of forged documents. Legal issues had not systematically been investigated and codified. Institutional policies were virtually non-existent.

In an ideal situation, the University of Houston Libraries could have turned, in this instance, to a set of standards, policies, and guidelines which had been established by professional organizations representing librarians, the book trade and collectors, museum professionals, and other affected professional groups. In the absence of such professional standards, the most responsible action was to begin the process of discovery and discussion out of which such standards might eventually emerge. That was the reason for the Houston Conference on Forged Documents.

Two persons from the University of Houston Libraries deserve special thanks for their key roles in planning and organizing the conference. They are Pat Bozeman, Head of Special Collections, and Liz Wachendorfer, Library Development Officer. Special thanks go also to the Rockwell Fund, and specifically to Joe M. Green, Jr. for a very generous grant to support publication of the conference proceedings. Special recognition goes also to all of the individuals and groups who contributed to the success of the conference and who have helped to make possible the publication of the proceedings.

Robin Downes, *Director*
University of Houston Libraries

Session I:
Forgery Detection

PAT BOZEMAN, Chair
University of Houston Libraries

W. THOMAS TAYLOR, W. Thomas Taylor, Inc.
Provenance and Lore of the Trade

NICOLAS BARKER, The British Library
Technical Aspects of Forgery: Printed Documents

ANTONIO A. CANTU, U.S. Secret Service
Technical Aspects of Detecting Manuscript Forgeries*

Discussion from the Floor

*Dr. Cantu's presentation was not available
for publication in these proceedings.

Provenance and Lore of the Trade

W. Thomas Taylor

If the truth be known, it feels a bit peculiar to give the first talk at this conference on forgeries. Despite my involvement with some dubious Texas documents, and the attendant publicity which has made me out to be an expert sleuth, I am, in fact, nothing of the sort. I possess an eighteen-year accumulation of odds and ends of useful information about old books and their histories, and some specific knowledge about printing types and practices. But I am not an expert in document authentication, and I have been somewhat amused by the odd assortment of artifacts that have been brought to me for examination—old land deeds, West Virginia Confederate imprints, Republic of Texas judicial decrees, and countless old newspapers—about which I know next to nothing. In fact, I became involved with forgeries through an unfortunate accident of commerce: I sold four of them some ten years ago. My investigations into these documents were simply an effort to satisfy myself that my customers had gotten what they paid for. They had not; but figuring this out required not so much expertise as a simple willingness to be clear and truthful about what I was seeing.

I must also confess to a weariness with the subject of forgery, brought on by having to repeat time and again the same story to many different people. At one time I suffered from the delusion that the exposure of the Texas forgeries and the overwhelming evidence that could be brought to light regarding their origins would result in the criminals—and they are criminals, however fascinating and charming they may be—being held accountable for their actions. This is not going to happen. There are a variety of reasons for this, and I do not want to dwell on them here. Suffice it to say that being responsible for one's own actions and holding others accountable for theirs are not things we value much in this society. A sign reading "The Buck Stops Here" has not been seen on a president's desk since Mr. Truman's day, and where there is a government by poll there is likely to be administration by avoidance as well, at all levels.

Unfortunately, when swindlers are not held accountable because it might be troublesome, the rest of us usually are forced to suffer in their stead. It has become more and more tedious for ordinary folk to make good use of materials in libraries because of increasingly stringent security measures, yet thefts continue unabated. In part this is because, as often as not, it is a librarian rather than a reader who is looting the collection, and in part because it is still unusual for a library to take strong action against an apprehended thief. Likewise, in the case of forgeries, I was told in stern tones by one librarian who has a few in his collection that, from now on, any dealer will have to provide veritable abstract of title to sell him a document. Yet this same librarian blithely continues buying materials from the very firm which sold him the forgeries.

What troubles me about this lack of will to hold a few people accountable for betraying our trust is that it makes it seem prudent to mistrust everyone, in self defense. This is nowhere more evident than in the area of provenance, the topic of this talk.

When I began as a bookseller, things were somewhat different. The history of ownership of the books that went through my hands was a constant source of fascination and pleasure to me, and an occasional source of profit as well. One of the first reference books I coveted was *A Sentimental Library*, the catalogue of the collection of Harry B. Smith, "comprising books formerly owned by famous writers, presentation copies, manuscripts, and drawings." Described were books such as *The Ring and the Book*, inscribed from Robert Browning to Alfred Tennyson, John Keats' *Endymion*, inscribed to his brother George, and page after page of Dickens and Thackeray letters and presentation copies. Not a great library, really, but faithful to the collector's intention and a wonderful source of fantasy for the neophyte bookseller. A few years later, I went on a little pilgrimage up the East Coast to visit and get to know some notable collectors and their collections. All of them—Robert Pirie, Bob Taylor, Bradley Martin—were remarkably friendly and open with their collections, and I was privileged to hold in my hands some truly evocative books: John Keats' first book, inscribed to William Wordsworth, in Bob Taylor's collection, and the matchless copy of *The Federalist Papers*, presented to George Washington from Alexander Hamilton, in the library of Bradley Martin, among many others of like quality.

After these heady experiences, my own stock seemed a pauper's portion, but I had acquired a fascination with provenance that has remained with me. Perhaps a weakness for provenance would be a better expression, because I have always been willing to pay more than I should for books with an interesting history. Some of my favorites have been Eric Gill's copy of the *Rhemes New Testament*,[1] with approving remarks in Gill's hand about the naked satyrs prancing around in the decorated initials; a fifteenth century edition of St. Augustine from the library of Hildebrand Brandenberg, the first collector to have a book plate; and a copy of John Locke's *Some Thoughts Concerning Education*, inscribed to his close friend William Molyneux, purchased by coincidence within two months of acquiring all of the extant autograph letters from Locke to Molyneux. Finally, I must mention a volume of trials from the library of John Brand, the eighteenth century English antiquary. It featured an account of the famous trial and beheading of Mervyn, Lord Audley, for "Rapine and Sodomy" in 1631. Brand's ownership inscription on the title page read "E Libris rariss.: J. Brand 1792/The head is in my collection."

Those were fine days. I remember vividly an evening in my office during the Grolier Club's visit to Texas in 1976. Charles Ryskamp, then director of the Morgan Library, Bob Taylor (mentioned earlier), and Mike Papantonio, proprietor of Seven Gables Bookshop, were going through the items in my safe with considerable gusto. I recall my bemused astonishment as Ryskamp and Taylor flipped a coin to see who would take home the manuscript account book for Queen Elizabeth's household in 1593, while Taylor clutched tightly under his arm a copy of W. B. Yeats' *The Shadowy Waters*, inscribed to John Masefield, as if to indicate there would be no discussion whatever of who got that. Of course, I did not care which way the coin fell; I was having the time of my life.

Times have changed. Bookselling is not so much fun anymore. I am still interested in provenance, but the nature of my curiosity is different. If an interesting item walks through my door, my speculations about its origins produce more apprehension than pleasure. Most of the time, of course, my concern is with the possibility, very real these days, that the item being offered is stolen. In that case, it is the provenance of the item immediately before me that is in question—a narrow, specific, definable area for investigation. In the case of forgery, however, the provenance of a single item generally will not be of much use; it is a pattern of provenance, including several copies of a particular document, that leads one to be suspicious. The pattern of provenance, with regard to the Texas forgeries, have several characteristics which have been shared by other forgeries as well. The insidious problem for the collector or librarian is that the pieces of the pattern are widely dispersed, and may reveal themselves only over a long period of time.

The first piece in the pattern is a realization that an item that has been, and by rights should be, extremely rare is suddenly, shall we say, less rare. It is a matter of instinct and judgment to determine where the line should be drawn between the merely unusual and the highly improbable. An example of the former would be William Butler Yeats' first book, *Mosada*. This is a genuinely rare book. I am not aware of a single copy being sold publicly between about 1950 and 1980. In the last ten years, however, I know of four copies that have appeared and changed hands. Even if *Mosada* were the sort of thing that could be easily forged, which it is not, this sudden flurry of copies would be merely unusual, because it is clearly the result of several well-known collections, formed over many years, being coincidentally dispersed at roughly the same time.

A dramatic example of the second category—the suspiciously improbable—is the printed broadside version of William Barret Travis' "Victory or Death" letter from the Alamo. In 1955, when Thomas Streeter compiled his *Bibliography of Texas, 1795-1845*, only two copies were recorded (No. 185): one in his own collection, and one at the Texas State Library. Streeter's copy had itself come by exchange from that library's Lamar Papers, which had been acquired in 1909. The other copy in the State Library was in the Public Printing Papers, which had been in the state's archive from a much earlier date. No copy of this document had ever been offered for sale, anywhere, before a copy appeared at a Sotheby's sale in October 1973. I was sitting next to Ray Walton in the auction room when he bought that copy on behalf of the collector John Peace. Since that time, eleven more copies have appeared, or about one every sixteen months. There is obviously something amiss here— some mammals have longer gestation periods. But if you were a collector in 1983, being offered a copy of this document, there is little likelihood that you would know of all those other copies. On the contrary, the bookseller's description would have undoubtedly said, "Only two copies recorded by Streeter," and you would have imagined yourself possessed of a great rarity.

This is a fairly obvious example. More complicated is a situation in which there are now three copies, of which only one was known in 1955, as in the case of Streeter No. 11, an 1829 broadside stating Stephen F. Austin's terms for his colonists. Mere numbers offer nothing conclusive, and it becomes necessary to go a step further and investigate the origins of the documents in question. In the case of the Texas forgeries, regardless of which document you choose to check, two patterns appeared: (1) the copies which had appeared recently bore no physical evidence—a signature, a date, even a doodle—to suggest prior ownership, and (2) the trail of confirmable provenance almost always ended with one of three dealers: Dorman David, William Simpson, or John Jenkins. Again, however, if you are a librarian being offered such a document, how are you to know this? It is not inherently suspicious that any given document has no evidence of early provenance, or that it be offered to you by a given dealer. It becomes suspicious only when the pattern is revealed, and you probably will not be in a position to know that there even *is* a pattern.

To summarize, there are three characteristics of the provenance of the Texas forgeries which have some general application to other situations: (1) the number of copies able to be located will have increased in recent times, with no convincing explanation for this increase; (2) they will bear no direct evidence of prior ownership; and (3) the first traceable owner of those copies able to be located will be the same.

This is fairly obvious, of course. What is not so obvious, if you are sitting in your office with a choice document on the table before you, is how you are going to figure out if your document fits into any, or all, of these patterns.

You might begin by calling a dealer known to be expert in the field. A bookseller makes his living in no small part by keeping a good mental accounting of the movement of books in commerce: who sold what, when, where, and for how much. Of course, in Texas this would have been absurd, since the logical expert to call, Mr. John Jenkins, was possessed of this knowledge by virtue of having been himself the vendor of twenty-two of the questionable documents. In any case, booksellers are known to be a shady lot, so you might prefer to contact a distinguished bibliographer in the field. If, in 1920, you had bought a copy of A. C. Swinburne's *Cleopatra,* or Robert Browning's *The Statue and the Bust,* or John Ruskin's *The Queen's Gardens,* the natural person to contact would have been Mr. Thomas J. Wise, doyen of collectors and the bibliographer of all three of the authors just mentioned. If you had written to ask about the history of the little pamphlet in your hand, the story he would have told you might well have been convincing, but it would have been a lie since all are forgeries, and Wise himself the forger.

No matter. Bibliographers are not to be relied upon, their brains being addled by too many years of close collation. Perhaps it would be better to look for a solid, dependable librarian for advice. You are a collector in Texas and you have in front of you the previously described Travis broadside. You look in Streeter's bibliography and below the entry for the Travis piece are the location symbols Tx and TWS. TWS refers to Streeter, whose collection is now at Yale. Much more accessible is the Tx copy at the State Library in Austin. You drive to Austin, but at the library they tell you that Streeter is in error; they have no record of ever having had the document. What they do not tell you is that, in fact, there are a good many items with the Tx location code in Streeter's bibliography which the library "can't find" or which "they have no record of having ever had." In truth, there was a massive theft at the State Library

NOTICE.

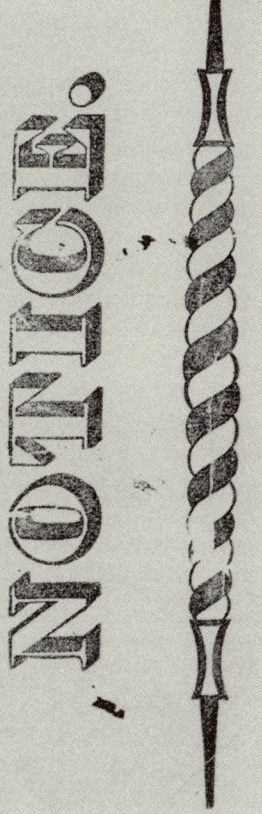

EACH Emigrant who has removed to this Colony, as a part of the Colonists, which I am authorized to settle, under my contracts with Government, as Empresario, and who has not received a title, is notified to present himself to me, after the 1st day of December next, in person, and hand in a list in writing, in conformity with the 3d article of the Colonization Law, containing the name and ages of the head of the family and his wife, the names and age and sex of each child, the number of dependants, or servants, his occupation or trade, where removed from, and the date of arrival in this colony with his family, which list must be signed by the applicant. Single men will also present themselves and hand, in the above list, so far as it is applicable to them. The said list must be made out before coming to the office, and the recommendations, accrediting the Christianity, morality and steady habits of the applicant, which are required by the 5th article of the said law, must be presented at the same time, in order that if the applicant should be received as a settler by me, his name may be registered, and the oath prescribed by the 3d article of the said law administered, and a certificate to that effect issued to him or her.

Two dollars must be paid to the Secretary on receipt of such certificate, fifty dollars must be paid to me, ten dollars of it on the receipt of title and the balance one year thereafter; and ten dollars must be paid to the Secretary, five of it on presenting the petition, in form, to the Commissioner, and five on receipt of title.—Notes for these sums must be executed before the above certificate will be issued in which notes all the benefits of law No. 70, approved 22d January 1829, (exempting lands, &c. from the payment of debts must be renounced. The above is a compensation for the labor of translating and attending to getting the title for the applicant, which I am not bound to do as Empresario, unless paid for it. This however, does not extend to locating land for the settler, each one must do that for himself, under such regulations as may hereafter be established by the Government Commissioner alone is authorized by law, to survey lands and issue titles; the above sums are independent of the Commissioner's legal fees.—Also, thirty dollars must be paid to the Government on each league in four, five and six years, from date of title, and quarter leagues in proportion, besides the stamp paper.

I am daily expecting the Commissioner, and therefore, wish all those who have removed and have their families in the country, to present themselves as above stated, as soon as possible, after the 1st of December next, in order that they may have their certificates of reception ready to present to him. None, who cannot present satisfactory recommendations and who have not actually removed with their families to this colony, need apply.

The certificate of reception may be declared null and void, any time before the title is issued, should it appear that the applicant had attempted to deceive me by false recommendations or false statements of any kind, or should he remove out of this Colony, or fail to present himself to the Commissioner, within one month after public notice is given to that effect, or should he refuse to comply with the terms of payment herein stated.

I also reserve the right of changing or modifying the terms of payment above stated, any time after the 1st of February next. No attention will be paid to any application, unless made by the applicant in person, and in the manner above stated, for it is evident that no other can take the oath but the applicant.

In order to have uniformity, applicants will use the following form:—

To Mr. S. F. Austin, Empresario.—I have emigrated to this Colony, as one of the colonists; which you are authorised by Government to introduce; and I request that you will examine my recommendations, and if found to be agreeably to law, receive me and my family under your contracts with the Government. I agree to the terms published by you, on the 20th November, 1829; and am ready to take the oath prescribed by the Colonization Law.

(Date and Signature.)

S. F. AUSTIN.

Town of Austin, 20th November, 1829.

[Here the list and other particulars, stated in the first paragraph of the above notice, must be inserted in regular order, and also whether the applicant is married or single, widow or widower.]

Figure 1 Notice [to colonists in Austin's Colony]

around 1969, which decimated their holdings for the crucial years 1835-36. I can prove there was a copy of the Travis broadside (Streeter No. 185) in the Public Printing Papers, and could probably do the same for any number of other documents the library cannot find.

Disappointed, you call various libraries around the state to see if there are other copies available. You discover three, and are kindly provided with photocopies, which you find comforting because these copies look identical to yours. They should; they are all forgeries as well, almost certainly made from the missing State Library copy. But you do not worry much about the three additional, identical copies because they are, after all, in distinguished collections with expert curators to assure authenticity. Of course, the curators have not looked at all closely at the documents because they came as gifts, and one does not look gift horses in the mouth, especially when they come from prominent donors.

So who can you trust? Who can you call upon for reliable, honest information regarding the provenance of a document, or group of documents? Not the greedy bookseller, not the shady bibliographer, not the timorous librarian.

This is not a charming scenario; neither is it accurate. The vast majority of the people involved in the trade of rare books—as dealers, collectors, bibliographers, and librarians—are honest, trustworthy people pursuing an interesting, and generally harmless, occupation or avocation. The very worst thing that could come out of the mess of forgeries and thefts that afflicts our little world these days is that we might lose sight of this fact and behave toward each other with cynicism and mistrust.

I do not wish to continue making decisions predicated upon the possible dishonesty of the people I deal with. The strongest case I can make for dealing severely with those few who betray our trust is that it makes it safer to deal with the rest of the world with a measure of faith. But I am weary of being the local Cassandra. We have a longstanding habit in Texas of romanticizing our crooks—the highwayman is always more interesting than his victim. Beaten and dazed, stripped of your purse, you do not cut a very dashing figure. But as one who was robbed, I somehow do not mind casting my lot with the victims. In the end, you see, we will have the last laugh. G. K. Chesterton expressed this poignantly in a description of Mr. Pickwick, the odd hero of Dickens' first major work:

> Pickwick goes through life with that god-like gullibility which is the key to all adventures. The greenhorn is the ultimate victor in everything; it is he that gets the most out of life... The whole is unerringly expressed in one fortunate phrase—he will always be 'taken in.' To be taken in every-where is to see the inside of everything... With torches and trumpets, like a guest, the greenhorn is taken in by Life.[2]

References

1. *The New Testament of Jesus Christ, translated faithfully into English* ... Printed at Rhemes by John Fogny, 1582.
2. G.K. Chesterton, *Charles Dickens: A Critical Study* (New York: Dodd, Mead & Company, 1906), 98-99.

The Forgery of
Printed Documents*

NICOLAS BARKER

I begin with the observation, not on printed documents alone as such, but about the general context of the forensic examination of documents, in the widest sense: that is to say, including any kind of human artifact. I was reading in one of the papers the other day the assertion by a curator of such documents that an important aspect of his analysis was what he called "curator's eye." Now this, of course, sounds instantly suspect. It is our old friend subjective judgment: "I have seen more paintings by Rembrandt than anyone else in the world and I know." On the other hand, take what is too slackly called forensic evidence. "Forensic" means evidence that will stand up in a court of law, and only that. The point I want to make is not the superior accuracy of such evidence, but its extraordinary limitations. There is a great deal more evidence which is not forensic, but which is nonetheless evidence, and I see this *contrapposto* between "I see with my little eye, and my eye is better than yours," and "it fluoresces, therefore it must be wrong" as a kind of balance of evidence, a pendulum effect. At any period, faced with any particular concatenation of circumstances that leads to the question, Is this right or wrong? the pendulum will swing more in one direction than the other. But one class of evidence should not be despised because it is "subjective" any more than another body of evidence should be adhered to strongly because it is "objective."

In fact, the truth about the validity of any object, as indeed of any statement, is that it is a summary of all the facts about it, observable or discoverable: about its structure, about the materials of which it is comprised, the methods used to make it or, subsequently, to alter it. Beyond those physical facts there are beliefs, because obviously beliefs as to the genuineness or otherwise of an object are an important factor in their history. This brings me to the question of motive, which is that fraud was, or was not, intended. Real life is often more complicated than this. An object which started off as perfectly genuine, a pious imitation, perhaps, of another object, becomes, with the passage of time, the subject of deliberate fraud, so that when one is talking about forgery or non-forgery one has a complicating time continuum to consider.

I first got involved in the consideration of typographic forgery in 1972; in fact, to be absolutely exact, I think it was on May 8, 1972, because it was on May 1 that Sotheby's put up for sale a collection of pamphlets printed by Frederic

---

*A slightly altered version of this paper appears in *Fakes and Frauds: Varieties of Deception in Print & Manuscript*, edited by Robin Myers and Michael Harris (Winchester: St. Paul Bibliographies, 1989).

Prokosch, which were described as "the property of a gentleman" (a characteristic piece of anonymity which was perhaps itself a forgery on this occasion), and as "the only complete set of all the pamphlets produced by Frederic Prokosch," among them no less than fifty separate printed pamphlets. Frederic Prokosch, I later discovered, was a very interesting man: he had been admitted very early on to a kind of charmed circle of international distinction in literature; he introduced himself to Masefield, de la Mare, and Yeats in the late 1920s, and he had become the intimate friend of Auden and Spender, both more or less his own age; he had not been slow to make the acquaintance of T. S. Eliot, Thomas Mann, and others, and he had formed the agreeable habit of taking a poem recently sent to him by one of his friends and having a few—a very few—copies printed as a kind of glorified Christmas card. He would usually send all these copies with the request that their author would autograph one copy for himself and to please distribute the rest to his friends. Few authors are immune to flattery, and I think that, without exception, all the authors to whom he addressed these things took them in good part. I suppose it could be said that they were an act of literary piracy, but perhaps that would be taking an unnecessarily severe view of things.

I think no one in the sale room at Sotheby's had any idea that as many as fifty of these pamphlets might have been printed, but then they did not, in the nature of their rarity, come up for sale very often and when they did, because they were about the size of a book of postage stamps, they tended to be kept in envelopes into which people did not look very often. So I think that if not very many people had seen them (although they might have handled them), still fewer people had looked at them very hard. As luck would have it, the vast majority were bought by Bernard Quaritch, who almost immediately bundled up those by T. S. Eliot and took them to Harvard. Theirs is the world's best collection of Eliot, a punctual archivist of his own work, and includes copies of everything the poet wrote, given by Eliot himself. It was rather disconcerting, therefore, to find that a number of these little books by Eliot were not at Harvard. Arthur Freeman, for it was he who had undertaken this mission, committed the first and crucial step in the process that followed by actually taking the booklets out of their envelopes and arranging them in order. As he did so, he noticed that some of them lay flat, while others seemed oddly springy. They would open up as he laid them on the table. So I hasten to point out that Arthur made the first crucial jump between acceptance and suspicion.

When he came home with suspicion in his mind, he sent for me and very quickly these were the images, among others, that were presented to me. The first example is a book printed in 1935, set in the then still fairly new Perpetua type of the Cambridge University Press (Prokosch had a research scholarship at King's College, Cambridge, at the time). The second example is an object allegedly printed in Lisbon (he spent the last months of 1940, before returning to the United States, at Estoril in Portugal), but in a type which I had no hesitation in identifying as one called Aster which had been produced by the Italian typefoundry Simoncini s.p.a., in 1958. A quick check in the *Encyclopedia of Type Faces* confirmed this. One does not need to go too far into the intricacies of the Roman numeral system to work out that the date on the title page posed something of a problem.

A lot of other things followed. First of all, we tested the paper and found that before World War II, at the alleged date, what are now known as optical dyes, that is, the bluish fluorescent dyes that make your whites whiter than Mrs. X's, did not exist. We also found that, although the thread used was pure cotton thread, we could see, under an electron microscope, here and there the tiniest thread of man-made fiber spun in. It is virtually impossible to run a spinning mill in which pure cotton and pure man-made fibers are spun. One may advertise what is being sold as 100 percent pure cotton, but what is floating in the air will tend to get absorbed in the spinning process.

The marbled paper covers turned out to be interesting as well. Pre-war papers were marbled mostly by hand, and one of the main manufacturers on the continent, the firm of Keller, Dorian, Putois, had supplied some of the marbled papers used by Prokosch before the war and others with the same design after the war. However, their plant had been completely destroyed during the war and, instead of having the traditional hand-marbling baths, they had introduced a thermographic marbling machine. Thermographic marbling and hand-marbling are actually quite easy to tell apart, even if the effect is essentially the same to the lay person's eye.

The pamphlets had little labels on the covers, with the title printed on shiny gold or silver paper. These were one of our failures. I thought I recognized a very modern phenomenon here, the result of the application of vacuum extraction. Vacuum extracted foil was a product of war-time needs; the process was developed in 1940-41 to produce the strips of metal that were dropped from airplanes to deflect and confuse enemy radar. It turned out that we were entirely wrong, because the foils used were old-fashioned rolled gold and silver paper. What was so new about them was that they had been coated with nitro-cellulose varnish, which is very shiny and gives the effect of high gloss metal. Nitro-cellulose varnishing has been in existence since the late 1860s. The fact that this varnish was used only, as far as I can make out, in the making of high gloss foil paper from about 1960 onwards cannot be proved. But, finally, each pamphlet was enclosed in transparent plastic covers made of polyvinyl chloride, which definitely was not in existence before the war.

There are two immediate lessons to be drawn from this tale, both with rather larger implications. The first is that time is of the essence: that is to say, establishing that an object is, or is not, a forgery must be related to time. This is very important with printed books and the implications will become clearer, but if one piece of printed matter is produced in 1900 and another piece thirty years later bearing exactly the same words, set in the same type, printed on the same paper, and also dated 1900, one has committed piracy (unless the printer is the author). But has forgery been committed? There is the sub-issue of the wording of the imprint on the title page. If it says by Messrs. G. Redwood and indeed the parties in question are not Messrs. G. Redwood, then, presumably, again forgery has been committed. If this were all, forgery would be easy to define and easy to do. But this is where the time factor comes in. Within this time continuum, huge human upheavals—war, vast expansions in economic demand for some commodity—will lead to changes which leave their mark on the way people make things. These marks are not charted, nor will they be recognized by a potential forger, unless he is very clever indeed. (I shall come, in a moment, to an example of a forger who is very clever.) Finally, I must repeat, in the context of this time continuum, that one can be as clever as he or she likes and still not spot the most innocent of imitations.

I will assume the knowledge of the basic outlines of the story of Thomas J. Wise and his accomplice, H. Buxton Forman, arch-forgers of printed books and, arguably, the inventors of this branch of human wickedness. It was the subject of that great classic of detection, *An Enquiry in the Nature of Certain Nineteenth Century Pamphlets* by John Carter and Graham Pollard, and it rocked not only the bibliographical world but made national headlines in 1934. It was a compound of negative and positive evidence. The negative evidence— no signed copies, no copies in early bindings, no mention in the author's correspondence—is suggestive but not compelling. The positive evidence is absolute. Paper was made of pure rag until 1861, when esparto was first used; wood pulp came into use about 1880. If, like the celebrated Reading *Sonnets* by Elizabeth Barrett Browning, the date on the title page is 1847, these elements in the paper condemn it. The use of an anachronistic text—Ruskin's *The Queen's Gardens*, purporting to be printed in 1864, is as revised by Ruskin in 1871 — is equally damning. Finally, type can give the forger away. Like paper, it can be anachronistic. Or, like the famous Long Primer No. 3, it may be unique to one printer, in this case to Richard Clay & Company, and therefore datable not before 1877 when they put it in: books with other imprints or earlier dates stand as guilty.

Here are some examples. First, *Siena*. This is interesting because the forgery is an imitation of a genuine original, a pamphlet by A. C. Swinburne. One will hardly credit the fact, barely visible, that every line in the forgery is in a different type from those in the original; however, it can be seen that the drop initial, which fits in the original, is a poor fit in the forgery.

Secondly, *Two Poems* is a quite genuine pamphlet containing two pieces by Elizabeth and Robert Browning and was originally printed for sale at a charity bazaar in 1854; *The Runaway Slave* is a forgery based upon it. There is no "original" here, but the similarity makes it clear that *Two Poems* provided the idea for the layout of *The Runaway Slave*, which nominally precedes it by five years. In fact, it is betrayed by the semi-romanesque ornament which was first advertised for sale by the typefounders in 1860, eleven years after the alleged date on the title page.

Not all the forgeries were printed by Clay. *The Books of William Morris*, one of Forman's curious essays in bibliography, for which he developed the interesting and unusual tactic of reproducing title pages in virtual type-fac-simile, led to the source of another group of forgeries,*The Manifesto of the Socialist League* of 1885 which exists in two forms. One is genuine, the other is false. There are a number of interesting features about this from a purely typographical point: the two wavy rules are quite different, as are the two black-letter types for "Socialist League Office." It is also noticeable that the types used for the forgery are exactly the same as the types used in the description of the pamphlet in Forman's book: there again the types used for forgery revealed the printer, Messrs. Billing of Guildford, who printed *The Books of William Morris*. The title block, an original wood block cut from a design by Walter Crane, has some rough marks left in to give an antique appearance. The

Figure 2 E.B. Browning, *The Runaway Slave*, '1849'; creative forgery based on *Fig. 1*

Figure 1 E. & R. Browning, *Two Poems*, 1854; genuine

forgery has the block reproduced by photo-engraving, and the process engraver, seeing these unsightly marks, decided he could do a good deal better and removed most of them, a piece of craftsman-like tidiness that further betrays the forgery.

Next is what may be called an extension of the Clay's Long Primer No. 3 theory; the type is important because it was a type peculiar to Richard Clay. Nobody has found any other printer with that particular combination of types in use at that time. *The God of the Poor* presents a similar problem. It purports to be printed in 1884, but there is another pamphlet, *How I Became a Socialist* by William Morris, which was printed after his death in 1896 by a firm called the Twentieth Century Press, and it is set in the same type. This press actually was founded to print the first edition of the Socialist *Manifesto* in 1893. At first I could not identify the type in which the two little books were set. Eventually, after a great deal of rummaging, I discovered that it was a long primer cut by Vincent Figgins, though neither their Long Primer No. 11 nor the Long Primer No. 15, but a *mélange* of both. I do not believe that a similar mixture of the two types exists elsewhere, and that is why I am convinced it was made up for the Twentieth Century Press when it was started in 1893. Therefore it cannot have been available in 1884 when *The God of the Poor* was alleged to have been printed.

All this, to paraphrase Marlowe, is long ago and in another land and, besides the wench is dead—or, rather, the two old rogues are dead. This brings me to a crime far graver than Wise and Forman's, which we may be thankful had a shorter run before it was detected. *The Oath of a Freeman* was the centerpiece of the activity of Mark Hofmann. Now in his mid-thirties and a native of Salt Lake City, Utah, Hofmann is the son of an extremely devout Mormon who was secretary of his local branch of the Church of Latter Day Saints. The father was noted for the beauty, accuracy and neatness with which he kept the handwritten records of the church's business. His son, like most Mormons, did his standard two years' service as a missionary, in Bristol, England. The tracing of ancestors for retrospective baptism is a regular feature of the Mormon missionaries' work. This involves looking up old church registers, going to record offices and anywhere else where large lists of names of people who existed in times past can be found. Hofmann says (though one must treat everything he says with enormous caution because he is a pathological liar) that he first got his taste for what he did from studying old documents for the above-stated purpose. He returned to Salt Lake City and, by his own account (but again, one must be skeptical), he read Fawn Brodie's *No Man Knows My History*, a rather critical biography of Joseph Smith, and not only lost his faith but also developed a violent distaste for it.

At any rate, he set to work to forge documents—manuscript documents at first—which fell into two distinct classes: those that triumphantly proved hitherto undocumented but essential tenets of the Mormon faith, and those which, more embarrassingly, failed to substantiate, or contradicted, the same type of tenet. One might think this would have been a counter-productive policy, and I can explain its efficacy only by a rather crude analogy which appeared in an excellent summary of the Hofmann affair in the *Los Angeles Times*. Documents, ran the argument, mean a lot to the Mormons because their divine revelation is of such very recent date: it is as if the resurrection of Jesus Christ could be disproved by the existence of motel receipts showing he was elsewhere on Easter Saturday night. This explains the attitude of the Mormon Church. They behaved in a completely Pavlovian way. They had to buy the *pro* documents and trumpet them to the world; they also had to buy the *anti* documents to suppress them, and they did.

Through these highly lucrative excursions into the gullibility of the Mormon Church, Hofmann was able to test out the gullibility of others. He got into the local trade in books, currency, and what are all too apt to be called "memorabilia." In the West, as is known, this trade revolves around local history and, the goods being in relatively short supply, they fetch very high prices, particularly banknotes. Very primitive wood-engraved and typeset banknotes were issued in the early days of what is now the state of Utah. Notes with a face value of one, two, and five dollars for the Deseret Currency Association and the Western Boundary Bank were known to exist. Hofmann very quickly produced ten, twenty, and even fifty dollar denominations which nobody had ever seen before, and the dealers in currency swallowed them with avidity. From these, he moved into the book business; faking association copies of Mormon or Western interest became a growing part of his business which brought him increasingly into the national, or East Coast, rare book business.

The Oath of a Freeman, perhaps the first piece of printed matter produced in North America, north of Mexico, is known to have existed by January 1639. Governor John Winthrop of Massachusetts noted its existence, along with an almanac, in his diary; neither of them is known to survive. The first surviving piece of printed matter in North America is the *Bay Psalm Book* (1640), of which there are eleven copies. The last to be sold brought $151,000 as long ago as 1951. So, when Hofmann decided to produce *The Oath of a Freeman*, he had gone a long way up market, and he set about it with characteristic ingenuity and thoroughness in March 1985.

First, he had to create a provenance, and he "planted" it on the Argosy Book Store at East 57th Street, New York City. The Argosy Book Store has a large stock of nineteenth century ephemera of every conceivable kind: ballads, election notices, and so on. Hofmann was not so injudicious as to put the *Oath* itself among these; indeed, it was not in existence then. What he did was to take a copy of a patriotic ballad written in honor of Abraham Lincoln's 1864 re-election and make a photograph of it. He removed its heading ("Give thanks, all ye people"), substituted a new heading reading "The Oath of a Freeman" set in slightly irregular Clarendon caps, re-photographed it, and printed it on a blank sheet of paper from 1860. Then he put it in a box in the Argosy Book Store, "found" it, and had it sold to him as *The Oath of a Freeman*, which was the title listed on the Argosy invoice. Thus, he had a genuine invoice which the Argosy Book Store was prepared to swear it issued.

Hofmann then set to work to create the *Oath* itself. He produced the original by photographing the pages of the *Bay Psalm Book* using the excellent 1956 Meriden facsimile. He enlarged these photographs and cut them up, letter by letter, sometimes using groups of conveniently adjacent letters, but very rarely whole words, creating the entire text of *The Oath of a Freeman*. He then reduced it down to the right size again and made a process line block. Hofmann knew that one can distinguish process block facsimiles from genuine type impressions because the height of the type is different, so he took a small industrial drill and ground down the height of letters individually on the block so that it would produce a slightly irregular impression. He made his own ink out of beeswax, carbon and linseed oil, making his carbon by burning seventeenth century paper because he was afraid that carbon dating might catch him out. Finally, he printed it by laying a sheet of genuine seventeenth century paper (a blank endleaf from a contemporary English book) on the surface of the inked block and pressed it down, using an ordinary clamp and a padded board and moving the clamp along to produce a convincingly irregular impression.

So far, it would be hardly possible to fault his technique. Hofmann actually created the *Oath* in March 1985 and it was offered to the Library of Congress in May of that year, with the Schiller-Wapner Gallery acting as intermediary. A long gap ensued while the Library of Congress examined it under magnification, ultra violet and infrared light, and with raked illumination, testing it in every conceivable way. Ultimately, after more than two months, the document was returned to Hofmann without establishing whether or not it was genuine. The Library of Congress simply said they were not satisfied as to title, in which they were absolutely right, but for not quite the reasons that they thought.

How all this led to murder is a now familiar story. I will only mention one fact here. Once again, it was chance and an unexpected concatenation of events that brought the forger and his deeds to light. There was Hofmann in the hospital, suffering from bomb blast injuries and unconscious, with detectives waiting at his bedside, all solicitude and anxiety. "What happened?" they asked, when he regained consciousness. "I opened the door of my car," he said, "something fell to the floor, and that's all I know." This simple but mendacious statement instantly converted him from third victim to first suspect, because the police could tell by the shape of the injuries on his legs that, in fact, he had been sitting in the car with the device on the seat beside him when it went off. So, rather as with Prokosch, the real case came to an end within seconds. There followed the long and cumbrous business of making a case that would stand up in court. Again, the outcome is known.

It was not until January 1987 that I was asked to look into the matter. I developed a number of arguments which proved, without reference to Hofmann's statements, that the *Oath* was a forgery. The first thing that strikes anyone familiar with seventeenth century printing is that the alignment of the lines is very bad, even by the standards of the worst typography of the period. What is not so immediately visible is the fact that the misalignment is not consistent with itself. If one looks at an example of distorted lines in the *Bay Psalm Book*, it will be seen that they make an even bowed shape, starting from the foot of the page and working up about eight to ten lines. The lines all are bowed the same way. Obviously, the furniture with which the forme was locked up was green and warped under pressure, thus creating the bowed shape. Here, however, the misalignment is all over the place; there are a number of places where the letters actually overlap between lines. Metal types can be made to do strange things, but—in the seventeenth century, at least—they may not be made to overlap each other.

There is also the rather interesting business of the border. The *Bay Psalm Book* is divided into five books, and a set of border strips appears as the head piece of each of these five divisions. It is clear that the compositor has arranged the first of these little arabesque ornaments in pairs and, in the first case, has treated them very simply: just a straightforward back to back line. In book two he has got a little more adventurous and inverted every second pair, giving a rather more varied pattern. He has repeated the same in the third line, though inverting the pattern of book two. He apparently embarks on the same pattern for book four and, inevitably, the case has become somewhat confused by now and in two places he puts not a pair but the same ornament repeated twice. When he reaches book five, he decides to revert to the easier pattern of book one, which he achieves with the odd duplication at the end.

Mark Hofmann's eye told him that there was something abnormal and different about book four. Having an uncertain grasp of the realities of seventeenth century printing, he instantly seized on this as an authenticating factor. People would be the more likely to believe that the *Oath* was the work of the same printers as the *Bay Psalm Book* if it had the same odd border. Thus, he converted what was clearly an error in the *Bay Psalm Book* into what could only be a deliberate act in the border of *The Oath of a Freeman*. That was another error in judgment.

The same problems affected the typographic arrangement as befell *Siena*. There are two-line initials for each psalm in the *Bay Psalm Book*. They obviously were meant to align with the top of the x-height of one line and the bottom of the x-height of the line below. The compositor, being ignorant as well as clumsy, did not grasp this and set the first word in caps and the misalignment of the drop-initials follows automatically. There is also misalignment in *The Oath of a Freeman*, but the "I" is in an impossible position, aligning at the top of the cap height, not at the x-height. Even if the character were turned upside down it would not fit any better. This is yet another error.

There are some further details. It is an odd fact that there is only one "ssi" ligature in the *Bay Psalm Book*, towards the end, on leaf Dd2. Normally, the letters "ssi" were made up either by having "s" followed by an "si" ligature, or an "ss" ligature followed by an "i." Hofmann, however, created a false "ssi," using an "ss" ligature followed by an "i" with no point (line 9). One can tell the difference because the "i" is much further from the "ss" than in the genuine "ssi."

The parentheses are another example. Like many a seventeenth century printer, Stephen Daye only had one parenthesis which he used one way up at the beginning and inverted at the end, so there is always a slight lack of alignment; the parentheses in the *Oath* align. Finally, there is the very interesting case of the suspension marks. These bars over the missing letters "m" and "n" as used in the *Bay Psalm Book* can be seen only when there is a desperate need to save space and justification. Here, the shape of the "o" is very conspicuous; it is too big and markedly out of line with the rest of the font, whereas the suspended "o" is appreciably smaller. In the forged *Oath*, the "o" with its suspension mark is an ordinary "o" with a suspension mark drawn in. Also, the justification is spectacularly wide; there was absolutely no need to suspend the "n." Again, it is a piece of *kitsch* authentication.

The last, and most decisive, point is the text. There are three texts of *The Oath of a Freeman*, dating from 1634 to 1647. In none of them is "Everliving-God" hyphenated, which poses the question as to why Hofmann's text is

THE OATH OF A FREEMAN.

I·A B· being (by Gods providence) an Inhabitant, and Freeman, within the iurifdictiō of this Common-wealth, doe freely acknowledge my felfe to bee fubject to the governement thereof; and therefore doe heere fweare, by the great & dreadfull name of the Everliving-God, that I will be true & faithfull to the fame, & will accordingly yield affiftance & fupport therunto, with my perfon & eftate, as in equity I am bound: and will alfo truely indeavour to maintaine and preferve all the libertyes & privilidges thereof; fubmitting my felfe to the wholefome lawes, & ordres made & ftablifhed by the fame; and further, that I will not plot, nor practice any evill againft it, nor confent to any that fhall foe do, butt will timely difcover, & reveall the fame to lawefull authoritee nowe here ftablifhed, for the fpeedie preventing thereof. Moreover, I doe folemnly binde my felfe, in the fight of God, that when I fhalbe called, to give my voyce touching any fuch matter of this ftate, (in which freemen are to deale) I will give my vote & fuffrage as I fhall judge in myne owne confcience may beft conduce & tend to the publick weale of the body, without refpect of perfonnes, or favour of any man. Soe help mee God in the Lord Iefus Chrift.

Figure 3 'The Oath of a Freeman,' from a contact negative

hyphenated. The answer lies with the translators. They must have had strong reasons, not yet explained, for rejecting the old Sternhold and Hopkins version, which would have been familiar and acceptable even to the early Massachusetts settlers. Some of their views are made clear in the preface, and one is that they were determined to represent the Hebrew text literally: where one word was used in Hebrew they wanted to have one word in English. There are some words in Hebrew which cannot be translated literally into English word for word, such as words with a reduplicative or strengthening sense or verbs which require an added preposition in English. Thus, when they had a strengthened word like "strong God" instead of just "God," they hyphenated it to indicate that it was one word in Hebrew. Obviously, "lift-up" and "Glorious-King" are examples of this desire to indicate that there was only one word in Hebrew. This is a need, or practice, peculiar to the *Bay Psalm Book*, but it was seized on by Hofmann as another peculiarity which he could, with advantage, adapt to his needs. Thus, he hyphenated "Everliving-God" on the analogy of "strong-God" and "Glorious-King" without understanding the textual absurdity.

I said that Hofmann very rarely used complete words, but he did on one or two occasions. The word "libertyes" in line 12 of the *Oath* can be proved to have been taken in its entirety from the *Bay Psalm Book* (leaf Cc2, recto, line 29). There is a unique thickening of ink in the counter of "y" and the relative alignment of the characters is identical. The same word in the *Bay Psalm Book* close by (leaf Cc1, verso, line 20) is quite different.

I will close with two facts about all this which put this impressive demonstration of typographic analysis in a rather humbler place than I may have seemed to suggest. The first is a fact which, in my view, made it all superfluous. There is, in line 19 of the *Oath*, a tiny speck of white on the "M" in "Moreover." It was George Throckmorton, the Utah state documents examiner, who noticed that this was not due to a printing fault, nor to a defect in the printing surface. It was caused by a tiny chip of photographic emulsion which had attached itself to the negative used for the line block while in the process house; it was still there when the police discovered the negative. As proof that the cunning forgery of *The Oath of a Freeman* stemmed from this negative, this was incontrovertible.

The other fact relates again to the border of the *Oath*. My own first suspicions were aroused not by any of the appearances I have tried to demonstrate, but by the simple fact that the border was too close to the text. Having handled, and indeed dropped, formes myself, I could not see how the printers could have put so little furniture between the text and the border, risking a pie with their makeshift equipment.

Perhaps there are one or two moral lessons to be drawn from this. The first is that all the equipment in the world will not reveal a fake if one does not know what to look for. Secondly, if anyone thinks that Mr. Hofmann is the last word, he or she is sadly mistaken. Owing to the increase in the price of artifacts of all sorts at the moment, with Van Gogh paintings going up to $54 million, forgers are springing up everywhere. No doubt more will be heard concerning what has been going on in Texas. From what I have seen, the forger or forgers, were not in the Wise-Forman class, let alone in the Hofmann class. Forger or forgers? Why were some produced, like Hofmann's, by photographic reproduction, while others, like Wise and Forman's, are typographic facsimiles? Who actually did it? None of those mentioned in Calvin Trillin's article in the October 30, 1989 issue of *The New Yorker* nor in Gregory Curtis' March 1989 *Texas Monthly* article suggest competence in either field. I am waiting to be enlightened. One last word: greed, whether collectors' or booksellers' greed, or the altruistic greed of churches, is the manure on which forgery grows like mushrooms. Greed springs eternal in the human breast, but honesty is the best policy. *Magna est veritas,* and let us hope that it will prevail.

Floor Discussion I: Forgery Detection

Duane Runnels: What was the approximate time the first Texas forgeries were made?

Tom Taylor: The earliest one I know of was an 1836 Bartholomé Pagés wanted poster [Streeter 1635], made in 1964. Progressively more forgeries were made through the 1970s and 1980s.

William B. Todd: Are you willing to divulge who the officials were [at the University of Texas at Austin] who have been so reluctant to take action in this matter of the Texas forgeries?

Tom Taylor: As I understand it, the word came from on high. I really do not know.

Don Carleton: Tom, I think you know what happened, and I am disappointed that you are not sharing it with the audience.

Tom Taylor: I will be glad to tell it as I understand it. When I first talked to you about this matter, it was your desire to do something about it. You told me there would be something done and asked me specifically not to talk to anybody about the fact that there were forgeries in the University of Texas collection or where they came from. I was silent for a number of months and then I was politely told that nothing was going to be done. It was indicated by various people that the word had come down from the University of Texas system's legal office that restitution was to be made by exchange of forged documents for bona fide rare documents rather than by demanding a cash refund, and that was that. Everybody was satisfied. Is that accurate?

Don Carleton: Yes, but that does not completely explain the situation. You came to me and reported the Barker Texas History Center had forgeries in its collections. We were very concerned and determined to do something about it. You suggested that perhaps the district attorney's office should be contacted and my response was, wait a minute, while I respected your judgment—and I still do—that it was still just your opinion that these documents were forgeries. I could do nothing until we informed the appropriate administrative officers and the general counsel of the university. There were a lot of other questions involved, and I stated I would appreciate your not doing anything until we had fully explored the matter with counsel. As anyone dealing with a large bureaucracy knows, it takes a long time to get the process moving on anything like this. The Office of General Counsel's response was that this matter was of major concern. After a thorough consideration of possible responses, counsel suggested that we take the documents to Mr. John Jenkins, present to him our evidence regarding forgery, and hear his response. Counsel felt that we really had no legal case unless we could prove intent. We returned the Travis "Victory or Death" letter [Streeter 185] and a document from the Eberstadt collection [Streeter 1082] which the university had purchased from Mr. Jenkins. He said he personally did not believe they were forgeries, but since we were displeased with the situation he was ready to refund our money because it certainly was not his intention to sell the university bad goods. He was wide open about us advising him what to do and he claimed that he certainly did not mean to cause the university any problem. Our problem was, how do you prove intent? Our subsequent action was based on the advice of the attorney at the University of Texas, which I think was good advice. I stand by it completely.

We told Mr. Jenkins we would like to have our money returned—$11,000 for the two documents in question, which were worth $5,500 each. John said the money was not available, that he was close to bankruptcy. I had good reason to suspect that Mr. Jenkins was probably close to being bankrupt. We were faced with the choice of forcing the man into bankruptcy and getting nothing back or going ahead and taking other material out of his inventory in exchange. The latter is what we decided to do. Once this was accomplished, we had no legal recourse because Mr. Jenkins' position was that, as far as he was aware, he had sold us authentic documents.

Tom Taylor: That is all well and good, but you and I both know that the document you said was in the Eberstadt collection [Streeter 1082] was not in that collection when it came down from New Jersey to Texas.

Don Carleton: No, I don't know that.

Tom Taylor: I know that I told people on your staff, if not you personally, that Streeter 1082 was never in the Eberstadt collection, but no one would listen. There are people who saw the Eberstadt inventory when it left New Jersey and there are those who saw that inventory after it came to Texas. Streeter 1082 had been added to the inventory when the collection was offered to the University of Texas.

Don Carleton: No, you never told me that.

Tom Taylor: The other point concerns the Travis letter [Streeter 185]. I could have told your general counsel, had I ever been asked, that in 1986 John Jenkins had to know about the forgery. At that time, a copy was offered by Little Rock, Arkansas dealer Gary Hendershott to H. Ross Perot. It was returned after Don Etherington [then Head of Conservation at the Humanities Research Center, University of Texas at Austin] took it to Yale for examination because that copy, which Hendershott had purchased from John Jenkins, had a deformed lower case "a" in the word "flag." That was exactly how I determined the Barker Texas History Center's copy was a forgery.

Don Carleton: I understand. But it is one thing to make remarks about what an institution can, or should, do with its resources and it is quite another what decisions and priorities have to be taken into account. Ours was a

Floor Discussion I

very problematic situation with regard to intent in proving in court whether or not John Jenkins intentionally sold us documents, knowing they were forgeries.

Tom Taylor: Do you have good reason to believe that he did?

Don Carleton: Absolutely.

Tom Taylor: You could have proven it by taking Mr. Jenkins to court and opening up his records. I do not think he could have shown where any of those forged documents came from, including those he sold to you. The reason there is no proof is that no one has asked for it.

Don Carleton: There is another problem involved here. The problem is the $11,000.

Tom Taylor: We are talking about a quarter million dollars, overall.

Don Carleton: I am referring to the University of Texas at Austin, its every day legal problems, and other pressing concerns generally.

Tom Taylor: What about the University of Texas at Arlington and at San Antonio, and the University of Houston? The general counsel for the University of Texas *system* made the decision.

Don Carleton: They spoke in this instance for the University of Texas at Austin. I do not know what Arlington's role was. I cannot speak for them, for the University of Houston, or for anyone else. I just want to point out that the Barker Texas History Center did try to do something, but in our counsel's opinion we really had no legal leg to stand on. The implication in your remarks was that someone at the University was involved in a cover-up. I am sure that was unintended, but I want to make certain that everyone understands that we hid nothing. I gave interviews to several reporters and made it clear that we had possible forgeries. We also cooperated fully with your research. We were concerned and wanted to do something about the forgeries, but we felt we had no legal case, which is different than a cover-up because we had nothing to cover up. At the time when I asked you not to say anything about the forgeries the matter was at a very sensitive point when we had no other information except your allegations, and we could do nothing with that information until all persons who needed to be involved were notified. That took time.

Pat Bozeman: Perhaps we can continue with this particular train of thought during the legal session on Friday afternoon.

Marcus McCorison: I want to congratulate Nicolas Barker on a brilliant exposition of arcane knowledge and how he demonstrated, without a doubt, the falsity of *The Oath of a Freeman*. I want to ask Tom Taylor if there have been a number of Revolutionary War broadside forgeries circulating throughout the trade. The first time we were aware of this was in a John Jenkins catalogue in 1976. Was there a Texas involvement with those broadsides? There are several of them—different varieties—all copied from a unique 1777 Lancaster, Pennsylvania broadside [Evans 15529] at the Library of Congress.

Tom Taylor: I have no idea about those.

Stuart Frank: I am disturbed by the implication that the University of Texas was unable, or unwilling, to do anything about this charge of forgery because they might not get their $11,000 back. On the other hand, the institution was unable, or unwilling, to do anything because is was only $11,000. If the University of Texas isn't going to stand for the principle, particularly when there is not a great deal of money involved, how can we expect smaller institutions, or individuals, to stand on principle? No court has decided on this issue because no one has seen fit to take those believed responsible to court. It may be true that Mr. Jenkins was not implicated, and maybe he had nothing to do with the forgeries, but this is not known because no one has done anything about it.

The Mark Hofmann case has been connected with documents outside Utah. In Massachusetts we are a little nervous as we have a long history and many forgeable materials. Has there been any connection as yet between the perpetrators of the Texana forgeries and documents pertaining to other regions of the country?

Tom Taylor: There is a possibility, but I know of nothing outside of the immediate interest to the Texas region. Printed documents are the easy part. I believe there are a lot of forged manuscripts in Texas which no one has looked into and I would be surprised if anyone does. In my opinion, the person who forged the printed documents may have been even better at forging manuscripts. I base this statement on various and sundry eye-witness accounts of Dorman David practicing people's handwriting, including that of Stephen F. Austin, William Barret Travis, and Davy Crockett.

Just today I saw a Texas Declaration of Independence [Streeter 165] with a forged signature written on the document. It came from Dorman David, and did not have an uninteresting provenance. It was signed by one of the San Jacinto heroes. I think there are probably a lot of manuscript forgeries, but I know nothing about manuscripts.

James L. Hayes: If individuals who may be involved in fraudulently producing documents are never held accountable in the courts they are going to get very good at producing forgeries, and even more will be produced than what there are right now.

Nicolas Barker: The British Library contains a number of forgeries, many of them dating back to the seventh and eighth centuries B.C. It regards itself as an institution of learning and as having a duty to expose the falsity of documents which are in our custody. This overrides any consideration of the title by which we came by these documents. As evidence of this, in 1990 the British Museum and the British Library jointly will mount an exhibition of fakes and forgeries, artifacts, manuscripts and books of every conceivable description. By doing this you might say we are exposing ourselves to every conceivable kind of attack from the criticism of the learned that we are fools, and to the legal onslaughts of those who conceive themselves to be judicially damaged by the assertion that objects connected with them are forgeries. In such circumstances we see our duty clear. I cannot see why the authorities at the University of Texas do not see their duty clear.

Session II:
Institutional Factors

RON TYLER, Chair
Texas State Historical Association

ELLEN S. DUNLAP, Rosenbach Museum and Library
Administrative Concerns

SCOTT CHAFIN, University of Houston System
Legal Considerations

WILLIAM L. JOYCE, Princeton University Library
Scholarly Implications

MARCUS A. McCORISON, American Antiquarian Society
Routine Handling of Forgeries

Discussion from the Floor

Administrative Concerns

ELLEN S. DUNLAP

I have been asked to speak about the administrative concerns facing an institution which finds itself involved in a case of forgery. Specifically, I have been asked to address the following questions:

- How do you deal with your board of trustees and with donors to your institution?
- What are the best ways to deal forthrightly with the problem in ways which will do the least damage to the institution?
- How do you manage the public relations aspects?

The Rosenbach Museum & Library has not yet had to face directly the thorny problem of forgery, but for more than two years we have been entangled in another kind of misery which has afflicted an alarming number of libraries in recent years: an apparent case of "inside theft" at the hands of a trusted former employee. In many ways, forgery and inside theft pose similar problems for library administration. Confronted with either, an administrator may ask the same questions:

- How is this going to reflect on our library and staff and all the good things we have been trying to do?
- How much of our limited resources—manpower, time, and operating funds—can be devoted to the investigation, analysis, and sorting out of so much dirty linen?
- Should one's dirty linen instead just be shoved under the bed?
- How can I face the prospect of spending so much time in the presence of lawyers?
- Why will the lawyers profit no matter what happens in the case?
- Why did I not take my father's advice and become a lawyer myself?
- How can I deal with the public's and the profession's right-to-know when we are in the midst of unraveling the facts and trying to comprehend them ourselves?
- In our litigious society, how can I pursue what I see as the rocky course of truth without putting myself, my family, and my institution in undue jeopardy?
- How can I, with the painful acuity of hindsight, deal with my own institution's apparent "need-not-to-know" that something might have been wrong before now?

Administration is a balancing act, and an administrator must be something of a tight-rope performer. A successful administration balances needs and resources, opportunities and constraints, personal necessities and institutional responsibilities, dreams and realities, action and contemplation. In our own particular world of special collections, we also try to balance the inter-related roles that booksellers, private collectors, researchers, and institutional custodians play: often supportive, sometimes conflicting, always strangely synergistic. These balancing acts are made all the more interesting because they have as their fulcra, or pivot points, the relationships among people—quirky, complex human beings. We cannot analyze administrative concerns without looking at people and trying to understand how or why they contribute to the "out-of-balance" state in which we may find ourselves at a particular time.

In cases of forgery and inside theft, we confront the misdeeds of those whom we accepted as colleagues in the community of books. When we recognize them at last as false friends, we also must cope with the realization that their crimes were driven as much by contempt as by greed. They have ridiculed the institution that we hold dear. Disdaining the rules, they thought themselves too clever to be caught or, to put it more directly, they thought you and I too witless to catch them. As an administrator, it is your duty to struggle back into your tight-rope walker costume and put the personal pain and animosity aside as best you can.

As soon as the basic facts of the misdeed are known, it is your responsibility (and a natural act of self-preservation) to inform your administration or board of trustees. Discovery of covert acts such as forgery and misappropriation of collection items is not always a straightforward process, however. It usually begins with a vague awareness that things are not quite right, that something is out of balance. Life is full of vagaries, and the world of rare books and manuscripts is littered with them. We are so used to things that do not add up on first glance that it often takes some time and a lot of evidence before that "something-is-not-right" feeling in the back of your brain or in the pit of your stomach grows sufficiently large to be uttered as an "Aha!" or an "Oh, my God!" of discovery.

Each of us must make, on a case-by-case basis, the judgment call about when it is proper to head for the administration building or the chairman's office with our concern over possible trouble. I would err in the direction of sooner rather than later. In the Rosenbach affair, the "Oh, my God!" moment came to me so forcefully and clearly that I had only to pick myself up off the ground before I bolted for my list of trustees' phone numbers. Here, in brief, is what happened:

> We received a call late on Thursday, February 26, 1987, from Mary Jo Kline at Sotheby's concerning a 1790 John Adams letter to John Trumbull that had come on the market and was about to be consigned to auction. Ms. Kline had checked with the Adams Papers project in researching the letter and had found it listed as being held by the Rosenbach. Her question was simple enough—"Is the letter yours?"—but pursuit of the answer consumed most of Friday for Rosenbach curator Leslie Morris. Leslie was frustrated by the fact that the number of letters from Adams to Trumbull in the slipcase on the shelf did not match the number as recorded (and then inexplicably emended) in the Rosenbach inventory book.

Administrative Concerns

Our card catalogue offered only further conflicting information as some of the cards in the numbered set had apparently been removed from the drawers. We asked ourselves, "Could this letter have been deaccessioned at some point?" There had been a series of sales from the Rosenbach over the years—most from the art collections—and complete records on deaccessions had never been assembled in one location. Ms. Kline faced a deadline for her catalogue and required an immediate answer from the Rosenbach. I did not want to block the Sotheby's sale on mere suspicion, but incontrovertible facts seemed in short supply at that moment. Even the old stand-by "institutional memory" was hard to come by at this point. Pat Willis was then our senior staff member, but her experience had been chiefly limited to the Marianne Moore archives. Leslie had been at the Rosenbach only three years and I only a few months more. If ever there was need for access to former staff, this was it, and I thought right away of Clive Driver. Mr. Driver served as curator (later director) of the Rosenbach from 1965 to 1978 when he had moved to Truro, Massachusetts, but he had continued on part-time assignment and on special projects ever since. He knew the collections well, had always been demonstrably proud of his ability to recall details about them, and had been director during the major period of previous deaccessions, so I placed a call to him late in the day on Friday.

I explained our predicament and described the Adams-to-Trumbull letter in considerable detail. "Could this letter," I asked Mr. Driver, "have been deaccessioned at some time after 1959, when it was reported to the Adams Papers?" He gave no indication whatsoever that he was familiar with the letter. We talked at length about it and the possibilities of deaccession, and he reported that he had been surprised himself to discover that items of significance had been sold off by the Rosenbach Trustees even before his arrival. He sympathized with our frustration over the state of the deaccession records but suggested—several times—that the matter was not worth pursuing further. I thanked him for his time and, before hanging up, we chatted about the then threatened sale of the *Dial* archives at Yale.

By Monday, even with a weekend's distance on the problem, Leslie and I were still unwilling to dismiss the matter as Mr. Driver had advised. We continued to balance our doubts and the ambiguous evidence at hand. It did not seem logical to us that the set of letters from Adams to Trumbull, of which the 1790 letter was part, would have been broken for cash alone; the Rosenbach had operated well in the black every year until 1965, the first year of Mr. Driver's tenure. Perhaps the Trustees had sold the letter or made a gift of it for some special reason. Perhaps it had been among the large amount of stock from the Rosenbach Company which they conveyed to John Fleming in 1955, although that transaction seemed well documented.

In search of the missing piece to our puzzle, Leslie and I decided to contact directly the dealer identified by Mary Jo Kline as the current holder of the letter and to ask if he felt at liberty to disclose his source of it. On Monday afternoon, Leslie called the dealer, Paul Richards in Templeton, Massachusetts. She explained the circumstances and, without a moment's hesitation, Mr. Richards told her that he had bought the letter just three months earlier from a retired librarian—a man living on Cape Cod from whom he had been purchasing quite regularly over the previous two or three years—a fellow named Clive Driver.

As Leslie relayed this information, those last two words hit me like a wall. I remember having to take a step back to stay upright. As we stood there in shock and read the fear as it grew in each other's eyes, that wall looked more and more like just the tip of an iceberg.

Forged Documents

My point in re-telling my war story—this much of which and more has appeared in newspaper accounts—is simply to provide a context for my basic thoughts on "administrative concerns." To date, we have identified as missing from the Rosenbach 115 items valued at almost $800,000. Of these, fifty-eight were sold or offered by Clive Driver to Paul Richards and other dealers; another ten were in Mr. Driver's possession. For most of these, we found that official records had been altered to make it appear that these items had been formally deaccessioned years ago from the Rosenbach collections. Of the forty-seven items as yet untraced, eighteen have records bearing emendations similar to those traced to Mr. Driver. The discovery, investigation, and recovery process has been tedious and gruelling. While Leslie and I personally had to suffer through days of legal deposition, Mr. Driver's own interrogation was cut short by his decision to plead Fifth Amendment privilege to almost every question. Who said these crimes are victimless?

Having set the Rosenbach stage, let me turn again to the first of my assigned topics: dealing with your board of trustees. My recommendation is not only that you tell them early when trouble develops, but also that as the case progresses you present the facts to them—over and over again, if necessary—in such a way that each personally can come to terms with inevitable conclusions. These are vexing matters, and each trustee will need your patience while he or she weighs the evidence. My own board has been wonderfully supportive in this ordeal, sharing with me and the staff in the range of emotions we have all felt, from shocked outrage to bone-tired frustration. One of your jobs is somewhat like that of a shepherd, keeping the group more or less together so that when action from them is required—such as the filing of a lawsuit—they are adequately prepared.

In the Rosenbach case, we thought it important to bring legal action as quickly as possible, even before the full extent of the problem could be known. While we have cooperated fully with the U.S. Attorney in Philadelphia and with the FBI and IRS agents assigned to the investigation, Rosenbach also filed a civil suit for the recovery of its property. In doing so, we retained the opportunity to investigate the case ourselves through the legal process known as "discovery," obtaining evidence via subpoena and deposition. Had we left the case to the federal authorities, we would not have had the same opportunity to examine and analyze the evidence, in all its complexities. (Since U. S. Attorneys and assorted agents will be unfamiliar with your institution's records and with rare books and manuscripts, examining the evidence yourself can be important.) In addition, had we left the matter solely to the criminal justice system and the prosecution had been unable to prove its case—as does happen—the Rosenbach may have been left vulnerable to a suit alleging malicious prosecution. I have learned that in a civil suit one can say through one's lawyer all kinds of things about one's opponent without such fear. (Of course, your opponents say things about you through their lawyers, too.)

Our chief objective has always been the recovery of our property. Given the lack of attention to the case to date by the U.S. Attorney, I think we made the correct decision in taking the case to the civil court. It has taken a very long time and more than $130,000 in legal and investigative expenses, but the case has at last been settled to our satisfaction, and the majority of the items should be returned to us shortly.

Administrative Concerns

The legal expenses are but a part of the costs to an institution in the investigation and pursuit of forgers and thieves, for there is also the drain on one's time, staff resources, and—most ephemeral of all these days—peace of mind. Having come face to face with the tip of the iceberg, as an administrator it is your job to start worrying immediately about how big the rest of that iceberg might be. Be it forgery or theft, the question is likely to be the same: "How hard have we been hit?" The detective work entailed can consume an entire staff if you let it and bring the forward momentum of an institution to a grinding halt. At the Rosenbach, we were faced with verifying the inventory records from the bottom up and collating vast amounts of detailed evidence as to when we could last account for the documents in question. While everyone helped with the initial task of inputting records into the special data base we created, I thought it best to limit the number of staff devoted to the time-consuming skullduggery of the affair. Our physical inventory of the collection might have been completed more rapidly with more staff resources, but all other activities at the Rosenbach would have been sacrificed.

With full knowledge of the evidence being vested in so few, however, it seemed wise to back up the institutional memory banks periodically onto paper during the investigation. From the earliest days of the case, Leslie and I have been admonished by our board chairman to "write it all down for the file," and there are times when we have wished we had had the time to do that more faithfully. The memoranda which we do have, however, are addressed not "to the file" but to our lawyers. During discovery, each litigant can obtain copies of relevant records from his or her opponents, and in this case we were required to duplicate massive amounts of possible evidence for Clive Driver and Paul Richards. Correspondence between client and counsel, however, is considered privileged. But if Hollywood ever calls, we have the rough notes for the screenplay already in hand. (That reminds me of another point under "administrative concerns"—keep a sense of humor!)

Turning to the last of my assignments, I have been asked to comment on the "public relations" aspects of dealing with institutional adversity. It is clearly a sensitive area. I distinctly remember thinking to myself, "We have tried to build visibility for the Rosenbach by all orthodox means; it is too bad that we will end up being most notorious as the little library that got ripped off." I am happy to report that my worst fear has not been realized. Those who supported the Rosenbach in the past continue to do so. Publicity about the case piqued the interest of some, and they visited the Rosenbach sooner rather than later as a result. But the bulk of the general public goes right on as before, oblivious these days to all but the most heinous crimes. Certainly the Texas forgeries case has garnered more headlines and feature stories, but with such an extensive roster of victims no one institution or collector needs to feel singled out.

My dealings with the press were influenced more by geography than anything else. The Rosenbach suit was filed in Boston, and of course there is a stringer at every federal court house just waiting to put anything with even a hint of juiciness on the wire as soon as it hits the filing clerk's in-basket. I could think of at least one investigative reporter in Philadelphia who, not happy at being scooped on a local story by the national wire, might have wanted to make more of it on her own. I must tell you, one could start digging for dirt at the

Rosenbach and find any number of sordid things: fraying carpets, unfiled memoranda, poorly paid staff, and more than a few uncatalogued books. Quite seriously, I wanted most to avoid having to say "no comment" to the reporter's questions. It sounded sheepish to me, as if the Rosenbach had something in this case of purloined letters about which to feel guilty or embarrassed. We did not.

As a tactical manoeuver, therefore, I delivered to the local reporter her own copy of the motion we had filed in Boston before the wire copy could reach her. I explained that, while I could not make any comments on the case at that time, our attorney would be happy to answer any questions. Relying on the precisely worded legal document instead of an interview with a then-rattled director, the reporter produced a fairly accurate piece for *The Philadelphia Inquirer*. *The New York Times*, on the other hand, picked up the story from the wire. I have always heard that you should not care what is said about you in the papers as long as your name is spelled correctly, so you can imagine my chagrin at appearing in the *Times* as "Dunlop" instead of "Dunlap." Would that this mis-spelling had been the least of my administrative concerns over these past two and a half years, and that such a triviality should be the least of yours.

Institutional Legal Considerations*

SCOTT CHAFIN

In the beginning—which seems an appropriate way to open a paper relating, at least in part, to history—I thought of my presentation at the Houston Conference on Forged Documents as something that might be dryly educational. That is, I assumed that since I am a lawyer and most of the audience was not, I should talk about the law—most specifically, remedies to the problem of forged historical documents when an institution is a victim. As a result of what happened during my presentation and my reflection upon it since, I decided this is not what I should address in this paper, except in the briefest form. Rather, I will discuss, generally without form, why I believe institutional legal considerations ought to be, if not the least, certainly not the most important, of our worries if we expect to do something about the nasty problem of forged historical documents. If this disappoints, I apologize. But it was clear to me that the interest of the audience, in response to my presentation, was not so much on remedies and liabilities and forms of action, but on "Why isn't somebody doing something?" It was also clear, to my utter amazement, that the audience meant that "somebody" to be lawyers, judges, and others associated with the administration of justice.

Looking back, which is what history does, after all, I suppose I should not have been so surprised. For it is justice, in its broadest meaning, that is at the root of the outrage over forged historical documents. We associate "justice" with "right" (as opposed to wrong) and "truth" and with the triumph of right and truth over malevolent wrong and falsity ("injustice"). To state that a forged document, viewed abstractly, is wrong is to state a principle that, if lacking in elaboration, is at least one which generally may be accepted by those who believe that historians, tellers of history other than historians, and the purveyors of historical documents ought to tell and display history as it really was, that is, in truth.

The institutions which acquire, hold, use, and display historical documents are, therefore, intensely interested in the truthfulness of those documents as documents or, to use the term most common to this subject, in their "authenticity." I attribute this interest in authenticity to two motivations: first, to the notion that truth is a good thing, and second, to money. The order in which I express these motivations does not necessarily relate—and I state this without any cynicism whatever—to any particular hierarchy of importance. The first

---

*The views expressed in this paper are solely those of the author and do not reflect those of the University of Houston System, its regents, officers, faculty, students, or staff.

requires no further elaboration; the second merely states the truth. When one pays money for, otherwise acquires, or holds a thing of purported value and that thing turns out not to have the value it was thought to have, one feels wronged.

The case studies discussed at the conference were all variations on this theme. They all elicited the same response from the community of people who value truth and authenticity in historical documents: outrage. As that most famous French tourist in nineteenth century America, Alexis de Tocqueville, observed, the common American (and we also might say Englishman, since the English pointedly remind us that most of what we are is derived from England) form of this outrage is to shout, "Sue the bastards!"

If it is an institution—an archive, library, museum, or university—which shouts this Anglo-American rallying cry of outrage, we face squarely institutional legal considerations. (This is what I talked about for the bulk of my oral presentation, but where I will skimp on the hard information here. It is not very exciting, with the exception of triple damages; the audience's response proved that, and any lawyer will tell you the same thing.) When confronted with alleged wrongs against our institutions, we institutional lawyers generally are concerned with only two things: liabilities and remedies.

I thought that the legal concern with liabilities might come as a surprise; some of the comments from the audience confirmed my suspicions. With universal acclaim, I heard the view expressed that professionals in this business have a duty to insure authenticity. "Duty" is a word one ought to use very carefully in a litigious society. Since I am normally on the defense side of the bar, if I hear a plaintiff's lawyer start sermonizing on the "duty" of my institution, I rarely view it as gratuitous advice; I frantically start warning people to hang on to their pocketbooks.

As I stated at the conference, my research failed to turn up a single published case in which a plaintiff has asserted that he or she relied upon documents thought to be authentic but which, in fact, were not, and that this reliance caused damage that could be measured with monetary certainty. Such a case, if there ever has been one, would start from the theory that the institution has a legal duty to guarantee authenticity. I emphasize the word "published" at the beginning of this paragraph because, in my fifteen years as a lawyer in this final quarter of the twentieth century, I have seen de Tocqueville's observation proved over and over: people will—and do—sue for anything. We may take some comfort in statistics. If such a case has ever succeeded, it has never been reported. Still, I would caution against promiscuously, and not a little pompously, holding forth on what one's "duty" is, unless one is willing to accept the idea that the legal system is not the only (and certainly not the best) forum for advancing solutions to the problem of forged historical documents, which I argue more directly below.

Whatever the nature of a problem, most institutional lawyers, for obvious reasons, tend to focus their attention first on potential liabilities. Liabilities can result in the involuntary diminishing of institutional assets. I confess that concern with institutional liability in this matter is closely related to the paranoid ravings of an institutional lawyer whose employer has been sued for almost everything and by almost everybody. The "layman" (a word I find fascinating, meaning "someone who does not know as much as I do about something important") is no doubt outraged with the very notion that an institution might be held liable for buying, receiving, possessing, and making available for important uses, a forged historical document. I shrug and answer that such is an institutional lawyer's concern with "liability."

I turn next to that side of the topic which was of more interest to the conference audience: that of remedies or, to put it more accurately in reflecting the audience's collective mood, "Suing the bastards." Truly, more often than not, institutional legal considerations will involve remedies: how do we get our money back, or, if no money was spent in acquiring a forged document, how do we minimize the damage to our reputation and, in the process, seek retribution against whoever was responsible for the despicable deed?

The legal theories behind such remedies are numerous and well known. There are remedies in tort and in contract. Most states have adopted consumer protection laws that confer statutory remedies upon wounded parties. Many of these, such as the Texas Deceptive Trade Practices Act, hold the possibility that the damaged institution might recover triple damages. (At the conference, Nicolas Barker labeled such laws as holdovers from the eighteenth century, evidence that Americans still live in a "frontier society.") In truth, all of these consumer protection laws are recent statutory phenomena, designed to discourage some of the more pernicious practices of free-wheeling free enterprise.

Thus, a wide variety of laws and legal theories exists to remedy the damage wrought by the manufacturers and purveyors of forged documents. It does not necessarily follow, however, that these remedies offer practical solutions from an institutional perspective. In the first place, the pursuit of legal remedies is not an abstract endeavor. The institutional victim holding forged documents does not merely round up a volunteer posse and charge off after the perpetrator. It must hire a lawyer, pay filing fees, employ experts and consultants, and foot the bill for the costs of what lawyers call "discovery." Institutional emotions run high, but—and I have seen this all too often—the battle flags are run down quickly when the invoices begin to arrive.

The University of Houston recently was involved in litigation over a $2,000 contract. There was no question but that truth and justice were on our side. When the attorney's fees in the case reached $3,000 (which they did very quickly), institutional passion for fighting the case began to wane. The lawyer we engaged to represent us in the litigation assured me that we would win the case, without doubt. But when the decision devolved upon me to litigate a principle or make a business judgment, I had no choice: we settled. A $2,000 contract ended up costing us $6,000, and all the time we were "right."

My point is this: being "right" does not always dictate institutional legal considerations. Aside from costs, there were stories told at the conference of political and public relations considerations, which often are viewed by curators and archivists as being more important than anything else. What are the practical ramifications from having publicly admitted, by pursuing legal remedies, that one has purchased forged documents? What are the damages to reputations, or to future purchases or the possibility of future gifts, or to fund-raising? In the case described by Ellen Dunlap, there was the fear of retaliatory litigation, especially if criminal charges were instituted against the perpetrator; her library chose instead to pursue civil action.

At the conference, I summarized my view of institutional legal considerations by observing that law and ethics ("right") are not necessarily the same thing, and for this observation I was roundly—and not without some justification—excoriated. The justification lay in my failure to preface that remark with the warning that my tongue was in my cheek, if not very firmly planted. I mean no disrespect, but I have no doubt that many of those who harrumphed in response would be the first to balk upon the presentation of an invoice.

Returning to our famous French tourist, de Tocqueville also observed:

> I know of no country, indeed, where the love of money has taken stronger hold on the affections of men and where a profounder contempt is expressed for the theory of the permanent equality of property.[1]

Is this a cynical view of what is, or should be? Perhaps. Still, one can scarcely argue with the reality of it.

Even though I am a lawyer, my law license is not a license to determine what is "right," based upon how much something costs. While institutional legal considerations might have a place in an overall review of the problem of forged documents, I hardly think they are paramount. Indeed, these considerations should come last.

In making such an observation—and the following statement—it is I who am the layman. Still I believe I am right in saying that, reduced to its essence, the study of history is the quest for the truth of what happened and why. Whether the results of that quest have relevance for present behavior or for predicting the future (noting briefly the debate over the reunification of Germany), I leave for wiser minds—for the history professionals, not the laymen. What I do know is that if the quest for truth is not the lodestar, the study of history is a fraud. That, of course, is why those who perpetrate false history in the form of forged documents—whether as makers or as distributors—are also frauds.

Since the Houston conference I have wondered whether I should apologize to the gentleman who asked a heated and impatient question at the conclusion of the floor discussion on institutional factors. He pointed out that a particular episode concerning forged documents had been discussed freely in the press and that reputations had been impugned. There were other facts, he argued, which had not been aired. How were those facts to be aired, he asked, and why, he implied, had not legal processes been instituted to give those with impugned reputations a forum for disclosing the truth? My response, also impatient, was that if those with impugned reputations felt wronged to a degree of pecuniary certainty, they should make their way to the courthouse and institute such proceeding as they believed necessary to afford them redress. In other words, I said, "Sue the bastards!"

Since that exchange, I have decided that I should not apologize, not because I do not sympathize with the gentleman's dilemma, but because I believe my response was instructive on the question of institutional legal considerations and on the responsibility of "doing something" about forged documents. Because de Tocqueville's observation about the litigiousness of American society was correct does not mean his observation was—or is—"right." To Ellen Dunlap, who expressed frustration with the refusal of the United States Attorney in Philadelphia to prosecute the perpetrator of stolen documents which resulted in harm to the Rosenbach Museum and Library, I offered the speculation that the U. S. Attorney was not necessarily insensitive to her institution's problem. Rather, I speculated, since his office undoubtedly is one of limited resources, he might have concerns which he considers more pressing: securities fraud in downtown financial institutions or cocaine smuggling at the Port of Philadelphia.

I suggested that the legal community and the public-at-large might view the problem of forged documents as one that concerns a very small community of overly-educated persons whose sole purpose in life seems to be spouting high-sounding principles of little interest to anyone else. I do not believe this, but the U. S. Attorney in Philadelphia may. That was little comfort, I am sure, to the library director, but it offers a realistic assessment of institutional legal considerations.

The problems of forged documents are genuine and serious. Legal considerations are important, liabilities are possible (if mostly inchoate), and remedies truly are available. But to the community of persons who believe the problems are genuine and serious, legal considerations must be viewed realistically. Legal remedies are not the panacea; they are merely an alternative. I would argue such remedies should be a last resort, for unless this community adversely affected by document forgeries takes a strong stand and discovers or invents its own remedies, it forfeits credibility and not a little dignity. I am not qualified, nor is it my task, to offer concrete forms for such remedies. I only trust that the community mentioned directly above will take a more dignified—and effective—approach than shouting, "Sue the bastards!"

References

1. Alexis de Tocqueville, *Democracy in America* (New York: Alfred A. Knopf, 1945), 51. Quoted from the Henry Reeve text, as revised by Francis Bowen, corrected and edited by Phillips Bradley.

The Scholarly Implications of Documentary Forgeries

WILLIAM L. JOYCE

In July 1946, in a review of *The Horn Papers* that appeared in the pages of the venerable *American Historical Review*, Princeton University Librarian Julian P. Boyd startled the American historical profession. He concluded that, after careful examination of the three volumes that constituted *The Horn Papers*:[1]

> I think the conclusion is inescapable that large parts of the documentary materials in the first two volumes, including diaries, maps, court records, memorandums, even lead plates and hieroglyphs, are sheer fabrications. I do not know of any similar publication of fabricated documents among the thousands of documentary publications issued by American historical societies.[2]

Actually, the Horn Papers had been very much a part of the lives of residents of Washington and Greene counties in western Pennsylvania, as well as in adjacent parts of western Maryland and northern West Virginia, for a good many years. Following a letter from William Franklin Horn of Topeka, Kansas, to some local newspapers in the early 1930s describing historical materials in his possession, portions of the Horn Papers began to appear in print in the Waynesburg, Pennsylvania *Democrat-Messenger*. Mr. Horn also made periodic trips back to his families' ancestral area and enthralled audiences with remarkable details of their forebears and provided comprehensive accounts of events that confounded the traditional histories of the region, especially Boyd Crumrine's well-regarded *History of Washington County, Pennsylvania, with biographical sketches of many of its pioneers and prominent men*.[3]

Collectively, the Horn Papers, which consisted of correspondence, diaries, court records, memoranda, land plats, and other documents and artifacts, made a strong appeal to the local pride and patriotism of residents of western Pennsylvania. As the account of the investigating committee, organized under the sponsorship of the Institute of Early American History and Culture at Williamsburg, Virginia, put it:

> Add all these elements together—the abundance of genealogical detail, the new information on well-known frontier figures, the artifacts and maps which the diaries indicated had been made or used by the pioneers themselves, the colorful dramatization of the section's role in American history—and it can readily be seen why the Horn documents and Mr. Horn himself were assured of an eager and enthusiastic audience.[4]

Despite the enthusiasm of local residents, however, difficulty and controversy dogged the effort to publish the papers. Critics frequently could not find corroborating evidence, though there was just enough complementary support in other sources to keep critics at bay. However, it soon became clear to the investigating committee that internal evidence supported Julian Boyd's charges. Not only were the papers ineptly transcribed, but there were anachronistic and doubtful words and phrases in many of the documents. Moreover, there were what the committee referred to as "biographical anomalies," historically incorrect or implausible statements, and stylistic similarities in documents purported to be by different authors.[5]

Closer examination of the documents and artifacts associated with the Horn Papers generated even grimmer results. A court docket and manuscript maps were subjected to careful examination of the paper and ink, and were judged to have been produced no earlier than 1930. Two lead plates said to have been buried by settlers in 1795 and found in Greene County were determined to have come from a lead source in Missouri which could not have been accessible to Americans at that time.[6]

Boyd's charges focused the attention of the professional community of historians on the volumes and, though there were defenders of the volumes and the authenticity of the documents printed in them, the committee to investigate the publication concluded that the documents were, in the end, found to contain "convincing evidence of their spuriousness. . .and therefore that historians and genealogists ought not to rely on any data."[7]

There was never any suggestion that the Horn Papers were printed with intent to defraud, or to make money for anyone, or that they were intended as a hoax or a mischievous prank. It is likely that the perpetrator wanted to dramatize the lives of the pioneers and settlers of western Pennsylvania, some of whom may well have been ancestors of the perpetrator or perpetrators. Whatever the motive, "the fantastic counterfeiter," as he was dubbed by colonial historians Arthur P. Middleton and Douglass Adair, was "the *only* American deserving to be mentioned with. . . [the] celebrated European forgers Charles Julius Bertram, Thomas Chatterton, or John Payne Collier," whose forgeries also entailed the creation of entire collections.[8]

If the uncovering of the forgery of the Horn Papers created a stir in 1946 because it was unprecedented in American historical and literary scholarship, one suspects that might not be so today among those of us already jaded, if not exhausted, by the dreary succession of forgeries, thefts, and other abuses plaguing contemporary scholarship. It is the purpose of this paper to consider documentary forgeries and forged imprints (but not art forgeries) from a historical perspective, to explore the scholarly role and responsibility in the detection and publicity of such forgeries, and to note how the persistence of forgeries have themselves affected the evolution of the scholarly process and research methodology. The *OED* definition of forgery, "the making of a thing in fraudulent imitation of something; also, especially the forging, counterfeiting, or falsifying of a document," provides not only the definitional context, but also records the first appearance of the word "forgery" in English, in Shakespeare's *The Rape of Lucrece*: "Guilty of treason, forgerie, and shift." (line 920). The appearance of the word in Blackstone's *Commentaries* (1769) as the "fraudulent making or alteration of a writing to the prejudice of another man's right," clarifies still more sharply the central issue surrounding forgery.

Scholarly Implications

If we view scholarship as the pursuit of learning, especially learning of languages, literary or historical science acquired through systematic study, and if we view such knowledge as an acquaintance with ascertained truths, facts, and principles, the fraudulence of forgery may be seen to strike at the very purpose of scholarship.

Among the recent events that have attracted notice, certainly the discovery of what have become known as the "Texas forgeries" takes center stage. The occasion of this very conference, these forgeries have been perpetrated on institutions and collectors interested in the period of the Texas Republic and early statehood. The forgeries appear to have been derived from copies of early printed documents stolen in the late 1960s from repositories, including the Texas State Library.[9]

Austin bookseller W. Thomas Taylor studied one document, copies of which have proliferated lately; that document, the Texas Declaration of Independence, was approved by settlers at Washington-on-the-Brazos in 1836. Thomas W. Streeter's *Bibliography of Texas* listed five copies in 1955, though Taylor has been able now to examine twenty copies.[10] At least eight are forgeries, and they all share several characteristics: they have no provenance before 1970; they are poorly printed; and the measurements of their type areas differ substantially from those of the originals. All together, Taylor has identified fifteen documents that are fabrications or forgeries, existing in approximately sixty copies. Five additional documents may yet prove to be forgeries.[11]

Another recent episode that has attracted even greater media attention was that of the Mormon document forgeries of Mark Hofmann. The story of Hofmann's machinations and murderous deceptions is indeed a tangled web, though his forgeries related to Mormonism appeared to be a near-perfect scam. He contrived to produce documents that his principal client was eager to acquire and then sought to suppress by consigning most of them to a vault accessible only to the Mormon church's highest officials. Had Hofmann's ambition and tangled finances not required him to keep producing documents on a wider scale, he may have continued to induce church officials to acquire his clever artifacts.

From the Anthon Transcript "discovery" Hofmann made in 1980, to the Joseph Smith, Jr. blessing, to "valley notes" (the earliest printed money used in Utah), and on and on, Mark Hofmann's extraordinary run of "discovered documents" continued. Hofmann also produced in 1985 the sensational "White Salamander" letter of Martin Harris, said to be written in 1830, which appeared to connect Joseph Smith more to folk magic and money digging than angelic revelation about gold tablets, the Book of Mormon, and the origins of the Church of Latter-Day Saints. The "discovery" soon thereafter of the "Oath of a Freeman" (the first piece of printing in British North America, of which there are no known surviving copies) and Hofmann's reports that he had located the fabled McLellin Collection raised enormously the consequences of his misdeeds, though the unravelling of his incredible enterprise was all but at hand.[12]

Yet another contemporary episode achieved even wider media scrutiny when the German news magazine *Stern* announced it had acquired the rights to publish the diaries of Adolf Hitler. *Stern* photographer Gerd Heidemann, who was an eager collector of Nazi memorabilia, purchased the diaries from Konrad

Kujau, an East German drifter and petty criminal, who had also become a forger. The gullible Heidemann, eager to believe in the diaries, offered Kujau on behalf of *Stern*'s parent company, Gruner and Jahr, two million deutsche marks for the diaries in early 1981. With *Stern*'s money flowing in, Kujau busily set about supplying the diaries.

As *Stern* considered the appropriate form of publication of the diaries, the issue of authentication arose. The editors sought out two internationally known experts who were, as it turned out, unsuited to the task. One specialized in biological evidence, not handwriting, while the other was a forensic specialist in documents, but did not know German. As the project entered the stage of syndication of rights in late 1982 and early 1983, *The Times* of London arranged for historian Hugh Trevor-Roper to review the diaries, while *Newsweek* secured the services of historian Gerhard Weinberg. After initially authenticating the diaries, both Trevor-Roper and Weinberg recanted their findings as *Stern* and *The Times* of London began publishing the diary. On May 6, 1983, Kenneth Rendell's judgment that the diaries were a forgery was eclipsed by the comprehensive—and conclusively damning—report orchestrated by Hans Booms at the West German *Bundesarchiv*.[13]

In the midst of these dramatic events, a map purporting to show that the Vikings charted North America long before the arrival of Columbus and which was branded a forgery in 1974, now could turn out to be genuine after all. A microscopic evaluation and X-ray analysis done in 1974 found significant amounts of titanium dioxide which was not invented until 1917. The use of a cyclotron, however, at the Crocker Nuclear Laboratory, University of California at Davis, has indicated that there are only trace amounts of titanium dioxide in the document, results that would be consistent with a genuine medieval document. While this test has not proven beyond a doubt that the document is genuine, it has renewed a vigorous debate and demonstrates the difficulty of warranting through scientific testing alone that a document is, in fact, genuine.[14]

As the events I have just reviewed suggest, forgery of books and manuscripts is a thriving enterprise of late. We should not presume, however, that such activity is unique or even any more active than has been true in the past. Since antiquity there has been a continuing struggle between forgers and scholars, and the malefactions of forgers have challenged scholars continually to review their research methods in an effort to detect forgeries and advance learning against the efforts of those who would turn it to their own nefarious purposes. Forgeries also have played a central role in religious and political history, as well as in literary history and, as a forthcoming and immensely important book, *Forgers and Critics: Creativity and Duplicity in Western Scholarship*, by the historian Anthony Grafton makes abundantly clear, the entanglement of forgers and scholars have enriched our sense of the past, sometimes in ways that we may not have altogether anticipated.[15]

The Roman scholar Varro judged that, of 130 plays by Plautus in circulation, some 109 were forgeries. The classical world developed, if out of necessity, the techniques of textual criticism—that of establishing correct texts and of collating manuscripts and emendations, and of quoting from original documents. They did so to evaluate texts and identify forgeries in a confusing

Scholarly Implications

world of competing religious and folkloric traditions and reevaluations of texts in inaccessible languages, as the forgeries of the plays of Plautus indicate. But the need of classical scholars to develop such textual criticism is no less real for scholars throughout history and to our own day, if the methods may have evolved and also embraced changing technological skills along the way.[16]

Serious forgery persisted throughout the early Christian era into the Middle Ages, when the emerging European nations enhanced their national identities by fabricating for themselves illustrious histories. The predominant form of forgery in the medieval period, however, became that of legal documents, with clerics and lawyers busily producing documents to buttress claims for possession of land or privileges. Perhaps the most elaborate of these productions was the *Donation* of Constantine, a document that emerged in the ninth century in which a grateful Emperor Constantine, before departing to Byzantium in the fourth century, was said to have conveyed the entire western empire to Pope Sylvester, who had allegedly cured the emperor of leprosy. The volume of faked documents was immense, with perhaps two-thirds of all documents issued to clerics before A.D. 1100 thought to be fakes. Gratian's *Decretum*, the underlying code of canon law, by itself contains some 500 forged legal texts. The sheer volume of such forgery further stimulated the detection of fakes as rules were developed by church and court officials to specify the form, appearance, and seals affixed to such documents.[17]

The advent of the Renaissance and the accompanying recovery and recopying of texts gave new life to forgeries from earlier periods, though the developing philological skills of the humanists were key to the identification of many contemporary and ancient forgeries. For example, the *Donation* of Constantine was shown to "contain profuse errors of fact and phrasing that proved its medieval origin beyond a doubt." Nonetheless, the use of scholarly skills to detect such forgeries also seemed to create an occasion for the creation of still others. Hapsburg court historian Wolfgang Lazius used his learning to show that Hebrew documents found in the Vienna suburb of Gumpendorf really proved that the Hapsburgs were directly descended from the Hebrew leaders who settled in Austria after the Flood![18]

From the Renaissance to our own day, scholars and forgers have been locked in an ambiguous tangle, whether for personal gain or other reasons. A more modern motivation for forgery was the need for national histories to be validated by the discovery of coherent sets of documents in the languages related to the vernacular languages of national cultures. It was such a situation that inspired Thomas Chatterton and James Macpherson in the eighteenth century to claim they had discovered ancient poems and epics. In the nineteenth century, A. C. Buell enriched his biography of John Paul Jones by forging documentation that represented Jones to be an even greater hero than he was, while forgeries also played no small part in the framing of the notorious nineteenth century pamphlet, *Protocols of the Elders of Zion*. The sophistication and innovations of forgers continue to elicit refinement and technical changes in the methods of scholarly criticism.[19]

Having primarily considered until now manuscript forgeries, we also should take note of the remarkable vitality exhibited by forgers of printed works, especially in the area of literature. From the standpoint of bibliographical notoriety, the forgeries and deceptions of Thomas J. Wise and Harry Buxton Forman have achieved a certain infamy that has led to, and been extended by, an intense scholarly scrutiny. From early suspicions about a certain copy of Elizabeth Barrett Browning's *Sonnets from the Portuguese*, English booksellers John Carter and Graham Pollard undertook their now famous investigation which led to publication of *An Enquiry into the Nature of Certain Nineteenth Century Pamphlets* (London: Constable and Co., Ltd., 1934). By studying the pamphlet (and a great many others of nineteenth century authors) in respect to its paper, typography, collation, negative evidence about the author, publisher, or printer, and the provenance and condition of surviving copies, Carter and Pollard concluded and phrased indirectly (to avoid being sued for libel) but unmistakably that Thomas J. Wise was responsible for these forgeries. Close analysis of the typefaces used in the forgeries and chemical analysis of the composition of the paper was central to the conclusions presented by Carter and Pollard. The more recent extension of their work by Nicolas Barker and John Collins in *A Sequel to an Enquiry into the Nature of Certain Nineteenth Century Pamphlets... The Forgeries of H. Buxton Forman and T. J. Wise Re-examined*, demonstrated that the charges of forgery against Wise needed to be expanded to become a conspiracy of fraud and deceit (aimed principally at the American collecting market) against both Wise and Forman, and that Forman in fact was something of a mentor to Wise.[20] More recently, Barker has undertaken an investigation of a group of twentieth century poetry pamphlets of Frederic Prokosch, extending further the methods of detection.[21]

It is clear that from the days of classical antiquity forgeries have played a central role in the maturation of the critical methods essential to the work of scholars in the humanities and social sciences. The reasons why forgeries have been so numerous are many and complex, and owe their vitality to the high stakes to which forgeries have been dedicated. Some forgers have been inspired by prospects of fame and fortune, not only the anticipation of literally creating a fortune but of achieving notoriety and recognition through discovery and association with something significant. Other forgers created their artifacts in support of a particular claim, or for ideological reasons, or to strengthen elements of a tradition. Still other forgers might have been amused or have taken sadistic pleasure, while yet others might have been motivated by hatred and vengeance, sheer contrariness or simple mendaciousness. The desire, or even the compulsion, to forge could and did affect many, and there are numerous cases of scholars exposing forgeries in one area, only to turn around and create them in yet others.[22]

Having read about "The Mystery of the Horn Papers," the estimable medievalist Theodor Mommsen, writing to the editor of the *William and Mary Quarterly* and citing the German scholar H. Breslau, noted that most "learned forgeries" owed their origins to one or more of three motives: first, the desire to furnish powerful families with a suitable genealogy back to some legitimizing source; second, the desire to put the history or literature of the forger's country or region in the best possible light; and third, the desire to boast of important historical discoveries or to produce documentary evidence for a new hypothesis. There are, of course, variations on these themes, especially the peculations of forgers who, in addition to boasting of their discoveries, seemed at least as gratified by filching large sums of money from the gullible.[23]

Whatever inspires the forger, all forgeries require several common characteristics if they are to be warranted as genuine. They must appear genuine not only in their creation, but also relative to where and how they were "found"; they must have a plausible provenance to explain their fate between their putative creation and their discovery; and, they must strive for authenticity when the physical artifact is tested for age and physical composition: color of ink, forms of script or type, or other components such as seals, writing instrument used, and the like. It is the inventiveness, the creative imagination, and the skills and knowledge of the forger that are locked in a continuing battle of wits with scholars and, increasingly, their technological allies, where the fate of forgeries is joined.[24]

The evolution of scholarly criticism of sources has been cumulative, built on the proven methods and inventive insights of learned predecessors. This relation is true of contemporary scholars whose research methods can be linked to the scholars of antiquity. While the German university professors of the late eighteenth and early nineteenth centuries may be credited with initiating the systematic and critical survey of sources, their methods were equally derivative of their predecessors, if applied with a new industry and to a wider extent. Indeed, the purpose and even the basic methods of scholarship have changed relatively little over the centuries, featuring systematic comparison in form and structure (with whatever technological tools might facilitate the comparisons) and a due regard to provenance. We can all agree with the first part of Mark Twain's advice to Rudyard Kipling: "Get your facts first," if not with the second, "and then you can distort 'em as much as you please." [25]

The evolution of scholarly criticism of sources also has led to the elaboration of two basic elements: those of internal and external criticism. In the latter, the scholar is enjoined to ascertain by whom a document was written, where, and under what circumstances. While one may depend upon an author's signature, or a printed attribution of authorship, or title, other instances may require identifying handwriting, initials, or organizational symbols, or studying clues (such as endorsements, or dockets, watermarks in paper, the type, the color of the paper, the ink, notations, and the like) in the document itself that either may reveal the author or some other identifying characteristic. The other element, that of internal criticism, entails analysis of the credibility of the statement or text. By systematically cumulating detail from all other relevant sources, the scholar is equipped to evaluate all facts within statements to insure their validity. It is the accretion of such detail, and the capacity to organize it in various ways, that is the essence not only of scholarship but of source criticism, as well. It is what equips a scholar to identify a forgery.[26]

There are innumerable means of identifying forgeries, ranging from a simple observation to sophisticated testing. Such means of identification include, but are not limited to:

- comparing the handwriting (including signatures) of the document with a genuine example of the purported author's handwriting or typewriting;

- recording as fully as possible the origins and ownership of the document in question;
- paying particularly careful heed to whose custody the document was in, and how generally reliable the authority of provenance information seems to be;
- making sure that any address leaves, wax seals, dockets, or endorsements line up properly when the document in question is refolded;
- checking carefully the size and format (including the presence of "chain lines") in the paper, and the chemical composition and any watermarks in the paper;
- examining carefully the ink used in the document;
- being intrinsically skeptical of any item of unusual content or rarity;
- reading the document for inconsistencies, information that the author of the document was not likely to have known, or any anachronisms;
- undertaking especially close examination of any document with shaky handwriting, or any evidence of erasure or alteration;
- identifying and dating the typeface(s) that might have been used;
- measuring the area of type of the document in question and comparing it to printing of an example known to be genuine;
- analyzing the binding and other components of the document in question, including the chemical composition of adhesives;
- observing whether the type of printing or illustration technique was appropriate for the item that it purported to be (to ensure, for example, that the *Bay Psalm Book* was not produced by a photoengraved plate);
- and, studying compositorial details of a printed forgery for additional evidence.[27]

The continuing increasing sophistication of forgers makes it likely that technological innovations will play a larger role in the future detection of forgeries. Technological tests have been much in vogue in attempting to resolve various documentary disputes, and these tests, especially on paper and inks, were essential in condemning the Hitler diaries, the Wise-Forman forgeries, and the Hofmann documents, if not the Vinland map. The increasing technology brought to bear on evaluating primary source materials includes such technically daunting hardware as the atomic particle accelerator, electron microscopes, optical microscopes, beta-radiography, energy dispersive X-ray fluorescence, Hinman collators, and ultraviolet lamps. Despite all this, there is remarkable continuity in critical methods, and the application of high technology remains a means dedicated to serving critical ends that have evolved over a very long period of time indeed. No one test could ever authenticate conclusively a document as genuine, though it might very well condemn a document as a forgery. But a careful and balanced review and consideration of a variety of tests of questioned books and documents undertaken in a skeptical, if neutral, spirit should establish the authenticity of many questioned documents and imprints.[28]

The growing sophistication and incidence of forgeries represents a serious challenge to scholarship, though their incidence is not unprecedented, as I have tried to suggest. A closely related problem to that of forgeries is that of plagiarism, which the *OED* defines as the "wrongful appropriation or purloining, and publication as one's own, of the ideas or the expression of the ideas...of another." As Tony Grafton notes in his splendid monograph, "plagiarism and forgery share a sense of literary property and individuality, and both are practiced, more or less successfully, through careful attention to textual details." It also might be said that both constitute intellectual theft and defraud those to whom the work has been represented as genuine. Charges of plagiarism recently have been made against a professor of biological sciences, whose work on the physiology of pigments that play a role in vision appeared in *Science* magazine. In another case, the head of Harvard's McLean Hospital was relieved of his duties after he was accused by a graduate student at the University of Rochester of plagiarizing for an article he had written years earlier. The scientific community has faced repeated episodes of forged experimental results in recent years that have further complicated the incidents of plagiarism. And, noting that it had been asked to address plagiarism in several recent cases, the American Historical Association felt the need to recast and publicize its policy statement on plagiarism.[29]

In the midst of negotiations between *Stern* and *The Times* of London for the publication rights to Hitler's diaries, reporter Phillip Knightley recalled the fiasco of the Mussolini diaries some fifteen years earlier, in 1968. At that time, the Thomson Organisation, then owner of the *Sunday Times*, paid a £100,000 down-payment to a Polish arms dealer who was acting as middleman, and £3,500 in cash in a brown paper bag to Vittorio Mussolini, the former dictator's son, to induce him to renounce his claims to the diary and allow him to purchase a sports car. As it turned out, the diaries were the creation of an Italian woman named Amalia Panvini and her eighty-four year old mother, Rosa. The affair cost the Thomson Organisation a great deal of money and made the *Sunday Times* the temporary laughing-stock of Fleet Street.

Recalling the episode, reporter Knightley drafted a memo containing advice for his bosses, especially the impetuous Rupert Murdoch, that we would do well to recall: Knightley warned Murdoch not to rely on the experts as all five in the Mussolini case authenticated the diaries as genuine; not to rely on the testimony of those who claim to be close to the suppliers of the originals; and to beware of secrecy and the need to decide quickly, which prevents appropriate examination and investigation of the sellers. In the event, Knightley's memo was prescient in its caution.[30]

For two millennia the battle lines between forgers and scholars have been drawn. With the one intent on defrauding the public, whether because of desire for pecuniary gain, vengeance, contriving a claim, filling an ideological void, or some other purpose or combination of purposes, and the other intent on preserving, as the *OED* would have it in its definition of knowledge, "ascertained truths, facts, and principles," the struggle persists. There can be little doubt that scholars have a responsibility to the community of learning to pursue and disseminate knowledge acquired through systematic study, to publicize forgeries, and to condemn their perpetrators and their means. Scholars need to report such forgeries as they discover, not only to their colleagues and peers, but to others with a direct interest such as librarians, archivists, and journalists. Indeed, librarians and archivists depend on scholars both to supply additional information about primary sources and also to advise them of misattributions, other mis-information and, of course, forgeries.

In order to identify and report such forgeries, however, scholars must first develop the skills to detect them. This requires formal training in source criticism and research methodology, and such courses have been in short supply in American graduate schools for at least a generation. Why such courses should have all but disappeared from too many graduate programs may be open to speculation, but their disappearance seems to coincide more or less with the dramatic expansion of higher education in the 1960s when the feverish rush to publication offered mobility in new sub-fields of study where research methodology may have been underdeveloped and unappreciated by those in search of more immediate reward. It would seem that a renewed effort in developing techniques appropriate to a variety of academic disciplines is necessary, ranging from renewed philological training for classicists to the study of diplomatics and paleography for medievalists, to the study of administrative history for historians of the twentieth century. It would further appear that the study of documentary forensics might be a good idea, especially in conjunction with training in how the resources of technology can be brought to bear on questioned documents. While it is no doubt desirable for scholars to be knowledgeable in the application of atomic particle accelerators, facility in the use of ultraviolet lights and other more modest devices and techniques would seem to be even more in order.

The systematic and critical study of sources must become an essential component of the training of young scholars. Armed with knowledge of the sources and trained in the balanced and comprehensive application of critical techniques, something the scholarly disciplines must place priority on achieving, forgers would face dismal prospects indeed. No one forger could master all the attributes of a questioned document or imprint; systematic study of all attributes, then, should reveal forgery. And, if occasionally successful, it is unlikely that a forger could be successful always. How academics develop the curricular model to teach source criticism, documentary forensics, and technological testing will be a major challenge of the 1990s.[31]

With a properly skeptical approach to all documents and imprints, especially those with spectacular content, little or no provenance, or other unusual attributes, the vigilant scholar will have done much to stem forgeries and affirm the centrality of learning and integrity to the study of research materials.

References

1. *The Horn Papers: Early Westward Movement on the Monongahela and Upper Ohio, 1765-1795*, ed. by W. F. Horn. 3 vols. (Waynesburg, Penna.: Greene County Historical Society, 1945).
2. Julian P. Boyd, *American Historical Review* 51 (July, 1946): 772.

3. *History of Washington County, Pennsylvania, with biographical sketches of many of its pioneers and prominent men*, ed. by Boyd Crumrine. (Philadelphia: L. H. Everts and Co., 1882).

4. Arthur Pierce Middleton and Douglass Adair. "The Mystery of the Horn Papers." *William and Mary Quarterly*, 3rd ser., 4 (October, 1947): 409-45, esp. 416-21. The quotation is on p. 421.

5. Middleton and Adair, "The Mystery of the Horn Papers," 429-30, 443-44.

6. Middleton and Adair, "The Mystery of the Horn Papers," 434, 439.

7. Middleton and Adair, "The Mystery of the Horn Papers," 444. For an example of a review supporting the authenticity of the Horn Papers, see the review of Paul Gates and Julian P. Bretz in *Pennsylvania History* 13 (October, 1946): 309-10.

8. Middleton and Adair, "The Mystery of the Horn Papers," 439-40, 443.

9. W. Thomas Taylor. "The Texas Forgeries." (Typescript): 5.

10. Thomas W. Streeter, *Bibliography of Texas, 1795-1845*, Vol. I, Part I. Texas Imprints, 1817-1838. (Cambridge: Harvard University Press, 1955), 152-154.

11. Taylor, "The Texas Forgeries," 11-12, 26.

12. Two monographs that review the tangled events of Hofmann's audacious forging activities are: Steven Naifeh and Gregory White Smith, *The Mormon Murders: A True Story of Greed, Forgery, Deceit and Death* (New York: Weidenfeld and Nicolson, 1988), esp. 86-188, and Linda Sillitoe and Allen N. Roberts, *Salamander: The Story of the Mormon Forgery Murders* (Salt Lake City: Signature Books, 1988), esp. "A Forensic Analysis of Twenty-one Hofmann Documents," by George J. Throckmorton: 531-52.

13. Robert Harris, *Selling Hitler* (New York: Pantheon Books, 1986) is a well-balanced account of this remarkable deception.

14. Malcolm W. Browne. "Map May Be From Vikings After All." *The New York Times* 136 (May 10, 1987): 24.

15. Anthony Grafton, *Forgers and Critics: Creativity and Duplicity in Western Scholarship* (Princeton, N. J.: Princeton University Press, forthcoming): 3-4. All references in this essay refer to typescript pagination and not those in the forthcoming monograph.

16. Grafton, *Forgers and Critics*, 12, 16.

17. Grafton, *Forgers and Critics*, 18-23. See also Giles Constable, "Forgery and Plagiarism in the Middle Ages," *Archiv für Diplomatik, Schriftgeschichte, Siegel- und Wappenkunde* 29 (1983): 1-41, and Michael T. Clanchy, *From Memory to Written Record: England, 1066-1307* (London: Edward Arnold, 1979).

18. Grafton, *Forgers and Critics*, 24-26, 28.

19. Grafton, *Forgers and Critics*, 29-30. For information concerning the activities of John Paul Jones' biographer, see also Milton W. Hamilton. "Augustus C. Buell, Fraudulent Historian." *The Pennsylvania Magazine of History and Biography* 80 (1956): 478-92.

20. Nicolas Barker and John Collins, *A Sequel to an Enquiry into the Nature of Certain Nineteenth Century Pamphlets... The Forgeries of H. Buxton Forman and T. J. Wise Re-examined* (London and Berkeley, Calif.: Scolar Press, 1983), esp. 9-11, 122.

21. Nicolas Barker, *The Butterfly Books: An Enquiry into the Nature of Certain Twentieth Century Pamphlets* (London: Bertram Rota, 1987).

22. Grafton, *Forgers and Critics*, 43-52.

23. "Letters to the Editor," *William and Mary Quarterly*, 3rd ser., 5 (1948): 462-63.

24. Grafton, *Forgers and Critics*, 53-60.
25. Grafton, *Forgers and Critics*, 76, 80-81, 98-100. Mark Twain is quoted in Philip C. Brooks, *Research in Archives* (Chicago: University of Chicago Press, 1969), 83.
26. Phillip Coolidge Brooks, *Research in Archives; the use of unpublished primary sources* (Chicago: University of Chicago Press, [1969]): 83-92.
27. For one set of guidelines as perceived by a prominent autograph dealer, see Charles Hamilton, "Thirteen Rules for Spotting Forgeries," in *Great Forgers and Famous Fakes: The Manuscript Forgers of America and How They Duped the Experts*, (New York: Crown Publishers, Inc., 1980): 261-68. There are also several books on forensic document examination: these include Ordway Hilton, *Scientific Examination of Questioned Documents*, rev. ed., (New York: Elsevier, 1982); Wilson R. Harrison, *Suspect Documents: Their Scientific Examination* (Chicago: Nelson-Hall Publishers, 1980), and Julius Grant, *Books and Documents: Dating Permanence and Preservation* (London: Grafton and Co., 1937). Aimed principally at experts testifying in legal proceedings, the authors of these books nonetheless describe procedures for identifying handwriting, the instruments and materials used to prepare documents and paper, as well as procedures designed to detect alterations of documents, and determining the age of documents.
28. Grafton, *Forgers and Critics*, 30-31, 103; Harris, *Selling Hitler*, 249-50, 298-99, 352-56; John Carter and Graham Pollard, *An Enquiry into the Nature of Certain Nineteenth Century Pamphlets* (London: Constable and Co., Ltd., 1934), 42-55; Naifeh and Smith, *The Mormon Murders*, 335-44, 391-94; Paul S. Koda. "Scientific Equipment for the Examination of Rare Books, Manuscripts, and Documents." *Library Trends* 36 (Summer 1987): 39-51; Richard N. Schwab. "The History of the Book and the Proton Milliprobe: An Application of the PIXIE Technique of Analysis." *Library Trends* 36 (Summer 1987): 53-84; Jennifer S. Larson. "When the Authenticity of an Item Is in Doubt." *Antiquarian Bookman* 83 (March 27, 1989): 1397-1403.
29. Grafton, *Forgers and Critics*, 85; "Question of Scientific Fakery Is Raised in Inquiry," *The New York Times* 138 (July 12, 1989); "Allegations of Plagiarism of Scientific Manuscript Raise Concerns About 'Intellectual Theft,' " *The Chronicle of Higher Education* 35 (July 19, 1989): A4, A7; Morton Hunt. "Did the Penalty Fit the Crime?" *The New York Times Magazine* 138 (May 14, 1989); "Statement on Plagiarism." *Perspectives, Newsletter of the American Historical Association* (January, 1980): 20-21. The "intellectual theft" of forgery and plagiarism is accompanied, of course, by physical thefts from libraries and archives of genuine source material, by both scholar and staff member alike. The case of writer and artist Charles Merrill Mount, for example, is but one of too many others like it. In response to such events, the Rare Books and Manuscripts Section of the American Library Association has been actively involved for the past decade in drafting guidelines for reporting procedures before and after thefts, and for promoting passage in the states of model legislation regarding theft and mutilation of library materials. See Lawrence W. Towner. "An End to Innocence." *American Libraries* 19 (March, 1988): 210-13, and the "Guidelines Regarding Thefts in Libraries." *College and Research Libraries News* 49 (March, 1988): 159-62.
30. Harris, *Selling Hitler*, 288-91.
31. Larson, "When the Authenticity...Is in Doubt,": 1398.

The Routine Handling of Forgeries in Research Libraries: or, Can Dishonesty Ever Be Routine?

MARCUS A. McCORISON

Thirty-five or forty years ago, sometime after World War II, the librarians of the American Antiquarian Society and the John Carter Brown Library were stirred with excitement. A book scout from Maine had located a copy of *The Oath of a Freeman*. Clarence Brigham and Lawrence Wroth were ecstatic. Was it possible, after three hundred years, that a legitimate example of the first printed document issued from a press north of Mexico (Evans 1) had actually turned up? Yes, it was possible; but no, it had not! On inspection, the ascenders and descenders were found to impinge upon one another, proving that the text had been pasted up from types from a facsimile of *The Whole Booke of Psalms* and printed from a line cut. (Two solid objects, such as two characters of printing type, cannot be in the same place at the same time.) In the early spring of 1985, when the Americanists' world was electrified by the news that a copy of the *Oath* had surfaced, the recollection of that earlier event made the staff of the American Antiquarian Society cautious but, as events unfolded, not sufficiently suspicious.

On March 28, 1985, I received a telephone call from the firm of Justin Schiller, Ltd. telling me that a customer of the firm (not identified) had brought to their establishment an impression of *The Oath of a Freeman* which, against all odds, appeared to be genuine. Schiller, Ltd., acting for the owner, offered the document first to the Library of Congress, the staff of which scrutinized it exhaustively. After concluding that they could not "contravene a mid-seventeenth century date for the broadside," LC decided to pass. The *Oath* then came to AAS, where our staff attempted to establish reasons for printing a seditious document, *The Oath of a Freeman*, in 1639 and to verify the authenticity of its text, with the same result as that of the Library of Congress. An offer to purchase at a figure greatly reduced from the asking price—subject to satisfactory results of precise scientific tests of ink, paper, analysis of the text, etc., all to be conducted at the expense of the owner—was refused by the owner's agents. We returned the document to New York City on September 11, 1985, little more than a month before October 15th, the day of the annual meeting of the AAS Council (at which we were allegedly considering the purchase) and the day that the bombs went off in Salt Lake City, killing two people. Thus was exposed a false life, as well as the numerous documents fabricated by a sick master craftsman, Mark Hofmann. It marked the end of innocence at the American Antiquarian Society, at least when it comes to vetting printed documents.

I suppose, years ago, we should have become more sensitive to the possibility, if the stakes are high enough, of fraud in the dealing of early printed Americana. However, we were loathe to abandon our illusions of the community of scholars and its mores. Because AAS rarely purchases manuscripts, thereby eliminating that source of trouble from our normal rounds and, until recently, the prices commanded by all but the most arcane of printed documents did not provide false dealers with profits worth the trouble of making reproductions accurate enough to pass in the trade, we at AAS just did not consider the possibilities for fraud to be significant. Furthermore, Hofmann being an exception, fabricators of false printed documents usually do not possess a knowledge of printing sufficient to produce a convincing product. Perhaps AAS staff had become blasé, having been exposed to so many copies of *The Ulster County Gazette* and to versions of one or another newspaper, most of them so poorly executed that only the most inexperienced possibly could have been taken in. No doubt, we should have tumbled to the arrival of changing times in 1976 when the late, lamented John Jenkins offered, in a bicentennial listing of American Revolutionary materials (in one of those enormous, unreadable catalogues of his), a broadside printed in 1777 in Lancaster, Pennsylvania pertaining to the sequestration of Loyalist property (Evans 15529), known only by a copy at the Library of Congress. When it arrived in Worcester we saw at once that it had been printed from a line cut and returned it, reporting to Mr. Jenkins that it was a reproduction. Imagine our surprise when, over the next several years it, or its illegitimate siblings, turned up and we, unwittingly or witlessly, re-ordered it on two different occasions, only to return the orphan to the seller. The fraud was publicly proved a year or two ago when James Green of the Library Company of Philadelphia compared a copy offered at auction by Norman Kane with the Library of Congress copy, learning that the copy in question was slightly smaller than the original. But who was the perpetrator of the crime? Was it the same person (or gang) who issued the Texas fabrications or two other unique Revolutionary War broadsides—one, issued in 1774 restricting trade with Great Britain (Evans 13702) and another of 1786 pertaining to Shays' Rebellion (Evans 19789)? A year ago, when not one but two copies of the latter appeared at AAS almost simultaneously, Georgia Barnhill of our staff compared them with the original Shays broadside at the Massachusetts State Library, confirming their status as copies.

Then there is our Texas connection! Those of you who read the annual reports of AAS may recall that we were given a copy of the infamous Thomas Rusk broadside of 1836, headed *Glorious News!*, announcing the Texans' victory at the Battle of San Jacinto. When we received it, it was laminated in plastic for no good reason that I could see, so I asked our conservator to remove the lamination, which he did. To his chagrin, the solvent used to free the adhesive caused the ink on the broadside to run. I was not informed of this circumstance until, after a chance remark about W. Thomas Taylor's investigations during a telephone conversation with William S. Reese, I was alerted to the inglorious troubles of this particular item. After a cursory examination and a few heated words with our conservation staff for failing to show me the now de-laminated broadside, I immediately saw that the item was merely an electrostatic copy. We then informed our donor and returned it to him. He, I understand, returned Mr. Rusk's little piece of paper to his bookseller for a refund of a few thousand dollars. Not long afterwards, the same generous donor gave us a broadside pertaining to James Lane, territorial governor of Kansas in the 1850s, which also was an obvious electrostatic copy of an original (it exhibited the fold lines in the original paper, the folds not being present in the paper of the copy). It, too, was sent back to its source.

My use of the terms copy, reproduction, or fabrication of a printed object bothers me, and it might be well if I define what I am talking about. Is there a difference between them? By reproduction I mean an object that is intended by its maker to be as close an approximation of its original as can be achieved. The 1777 Lancaster, Pennsylvania broadside is a reproduction. A copy is merely a mechanical duplication of an original, perhaps done on different paper or in a different medium from its original. I am reading from a copy at this moment. A fabrication is an object made without exact reference to an original but, in this context, bears characteristics that lead one to assume that it wears the stamp of authenticity, both in text and physical attributes. The Thomas Rusk broadside on the victory over Santa Anna and *The Oath of a Freeman* are examples of fabrications because they follow no known extant document. We should observe that, in each of these cases, the questioned object is a simple one; that is to say, it is not large, it does not bear an illustration, and the image is contained on one side of a single sheet of paper. To go beyond these parameters may well raise technical difficulties with which the perpetrator cannot effectively deal. So, we ought to be alert to the dangers inherent in broadsides that are both rare and costly.

While reproductions, copies, or fabrications can and will be misused, we ought not fall into the trap of condemning all as being produced for devious purposes. I cannot help but think of the marvelous examples produced for scholarly purposes or pleasure by the Meriden Gravure Company. (They invariably bore a notice of reprint in an area of the image that could not be masked.) Libraries regularly reproduce their rarities as keepsakes of special events. There is nothing wrong in making reproductions if they are clearly indicated as such; it is the deliberate selling of them as originals that is wrong. This, as a relatively frequent common practice, appears to be a recent phenomenon.

In recent years, it has been my experience that unrecorded and scarce eighteenth and early nineteenth century materials are no longer as common in the market as they once were. When unique items are offered now, usually they are ephemeral—small pamphlets or broadsides. And, their prices have escalated dramatically so that the wary institutional buyer, more than ever before, must weigh the research value of the piece against the cost of its uniquity. Private collectors, perhaps, do not have to make decisions on such bases. Furthermore, could it be that inexperienced dealers eager for stock, the number of whom seems to have increased markedly in the past few years, are unable to detect fraudulent items and have been gulled by their disreputable brethren, thereby misleading their customers?

Did the American Antiquarian Society err when handling the questionable *Oath*? Should we have done some things differently in handling the reproductions of the Revolutionary War broadsides? Did we act correctly in dealing with the electrostatic copies of the Texas and Kansas fakes? What should we do in the future when faced with such questions? We shall take each question, seriatim; an exercise in case studies.

The Oath of a Freeman! Yes, we did err. AAS did not prove that it was not what it was purported to be. On the other hand, I assert that we dealt with it responsibly, making judgments on its authenticity through the visual and intellectual means available to us. AAS is not equipped to conduct scientific tests on inks, paper, and the like. Few libraries are so equipped, either with scientific facilities or expertise of their staff members. We could not prove that the *Oath* was not what the sellers said it was. Its characteristics were such that we thought, logically, it had to be of a seventeenth century origin. In fact, the tests conducted by experts for the owner, following our return of the document to New York City, elicited diametrically opposed opinions as to ink and text. An argument has been advanced that the provenance of the *Oath* was so suspect that its authenticity was disqualified on that criterion alone. To come to that conclusion one must accept the notion that no true document can come to light unless it owns an unexceptionable provenance. That is, of course, absurd. Important printed and manuscript documents are found frequently in improbable places or from unpromising sources. The recent discoveries of a copy of Edgar Allan Poe's *Tamerlane* at a New Hampshire junk shop and a copy of the Proclamation Emancipation, signed by Abraham Lincoln, which had been thrown into a box in the cellar of a small, rural library, are cases in point. However, we made a serious mistake in not realizing that a fabricator might know as much (or more) about printing, paper, and ink as do we curators. Thus, we fatally underestimated the prescience of the perpetrator in anticipating the evidences for which we look. This is the important lesson to be learned from this case. Hubris is a terrible thing! In the end, however, believing that the research value of the document did not merit the exorbitant price that had been placed on it, I offered to purchase the *Oath* at a greatly reduced price, provided that the owner himself provide irrefutable evidence of its authenticity and provenance. My offer was declined and the document was withdrawn.

How did AAS do on the next question? Should we have done some things differently in handling the reproductions of the Revolutionary War broadsides? One might accuse us of failing memory if, within a period of ten years, the same faulty document crossed our path more than once, and we should have tumbled to the fact that something was awry in the rare book trade and done something about it. I plead *nolo contendre*. In defense, I can only excuse my negligence by stating that a great many interesting materials cross our path—some 5,000 acquisitions a year. These reproductions appeared to be so obviously false that it was assumed they would not mislead our colleagues. We returned the questioned broadsides, with reports of their faults, to the purveyors of them. As informed members of the trade, perhaps it was incumbent upon them also to warn their colleagues, through their well established channels, of the presence of bad apples in their communal barrel. Now, fortunately, under the unquakeable leadership of Jennifer Larson and Michael Hackenberg, the Antiquarian Booksellers Association of America has assumed a responsibility that the organization should have taken on long since; namely, the reporting of not only stolen goods but also of fraudulent items that are circulating in the trade. The next step should be to deal publicly with the dealers who abuse the trust of their colleagues and their customers.

Next, did we act correctly in dealing with the xerographic copies of the Texas and Kansas fakes? Without public knowledge that there was a significant body of questionable documents circulating in the Old Southwest, neither the purchaser of those fakes nor AAS were warned in a timely manner of such problems by anyone in the trade. On the other hand, when we at AAS examined them even cursorily, we saw at once that the documents were phony. Who was the culprit or the dupe: the seller, the buyer, or the recipient? On our part, the fakes were returned immediately to the donor and taken off our acquisition rolls, for we were certain that the purchaser had been taken for a good deal of money by a dealer who was either ignorant or unscrupulous, or both. In short, the relationship between dealers and their customers, either private or institutional, rests upon mutual trust and candor. If dealers know that something unethical is going on and the rest of us do not, then they do the world of book collecting and scholarship great harm. In the end, dealers are damaged most severely because they lose their personal integrity and damage the profession at large. If, as John Jenkins (a.k.a. Austin Squatty), past president of the Antiquarian Booksellers Association of America, claimed there was a cultural shift from the Northeast to Texas when he obtained the Eberstadt stock, it might be worthwhile considering just what kind of a shift actually occurred.

Finally, what should AAS do in the future when faced with such situations? As we always have done, we shall attempt to exercise our best judgment when we examine new material for authenticity as well as for pertinence to our collections. If the item is intended to defraud the purchaser, or if the nature of its difficulty is merely problematical, we shall return it to the seller with our opinion of the situation. We shall attempt to take time to report such incidents to the ABAA Committee on Questioned Imprints, just as we assume the seller will do likewise. On the other hand, if a librarian detects a problem, why did not the dealer before him or her? Whose responsibility is it to exclude such materials from the market? Ought not the trade police itself? If all else fails, there is yet another option: AAS can report such episodes to the police for investigation.

A week ago, I spoke in Philadelphia on the uses of computer technology for bibliography and humanistic scholarship. One of the points I tried to make was the ways in which the motivations and goals of a new generation of scholars, coupled to their methods of research, have affected the manners and ethics of their profession. Former informal protocols of acknowledgment and exchange of scholarship have given way to copyright and proprietorship—copyright, in fact, having been made totally ineffective by the intrusion of the computer. Just as scholarship no longer rests on mutual respect and good will between its practitioners, each having become grantspersons grabbing for a slice of the Mellon fellowship and tenure, that safe haven for the mediocre, so within our smaller community of rare bookmanship, ambitions outrun supplies of significant materials, and it becomes a matter of devil-take-the-unwary. It is a sorry commentary upon our present situation that we are even meeting on a topic such as this!

Floor Discussion II:
Inter-related Institutional Factors

Nicolas Barker: I listened with fascination and absolute horror to the presentations of Ellen Dunlap and Scott Chafin—horror which has been hardly diminished by facts and events in subsequent presentations of William Joyce and Marcus McCorison, which are more familiar. The overriding factor in this horror is the difference between American and British law. The roots of this can be traced to an extraordinarily interesting paper by Patrick Devlin in the *Columbia Law Review* in which he reviewed the effects of the canonization of the English Common Law by the 7th Amendment of the United States Constitution. [See Patrick Devlin. "Jury Trial of Complex Cases: English Practice at the Time of the Seventh Amendment." *Columbia Law Review* 80 (January 1980): 44-107.] In fact, these amendments crystallized a great deal of legal practice, including the doctrine of triple damages, which has long since been abandoned in Britain by the legal reforms of 1875-6. In America, you are living in an eighteenth century world. Yours is a frontier society of a quite terrifying absence of constraint.

I want to contrast Ellen Dunlap's story with an almost exactly similar event that overtook the British Library. Two German scholars arrived with a letter of introduction addressed to me, requesting that they should consult a very large collection of single sheet material which we keep in plan chests on the spot—it is very difficult to consult this collection in any other way. The letter of introduction was a forgery, and they removed some 300 of the more expensive, valuable and negotiable items. By English law we had no alternatives to consider. We called the police and they took the case right out of our hands. Thanks to their own very considerable skill in dealing with thefts of works of art and historic documents, we got the lot back through the action of Interpol. It took about three years, but it worked. During that time, we did our best to supply any information that was required of us, but we were specifically excluded from participation in what was a criminal investigation. This leads me back to the presentations of Ms. Dunlap and Mr. Chafin, and it leaves me with the wonderful word "buck" that keeps circling around. I use the word in both senses. I'd like to know where it stops in this country?

Scott Chafin: Let me first comment on the refutation that law has nothing to do with ethics and morality. That is an idea that I myself refute, and when I engaged in that playful little debate with our Executive Vice Chancellor, Hugh Walker, who is a physicist by training, my tongue was firmly planted in my cheek. I frequently see situations in which the law does not reflect my definitions of what is ethical or moral, and therein lies the problem. My definitions might not agree with yours, or anyone else's, for that matter. Whether the law should reflect ethics and morality is a question which I leave to those schooled in jurisprudence and legal philosophy. I will cite two examples showing that law often does not reflect ethics and morality. Recently, I attended a hearing in which a judge, although very directly stating that he did not think such an outcome was right, nevertheless signed an order because, as the assistant Attorneys General from Texas and from Arkansas pointed out, the doctrines of sovereign immunity are very much alive in both states and the judge simply had no choice, no matter what his view of "right" was.

Secondly, Marcus McCorison himself established the point when he said he feels he is under a duty to authenticate. When I say an academic library is not under that duty, I am speaking purely from a legal standpoint—that duty which would give rise to a cause of action, if there were such a duty. Then the scholars using those materials could sue the library, based on the outcome of their research, for some incalculable measure of damage to reputation and, perhaps, loss of book sales—who knows what? In fact, I was not able to find a single case, or other legal theory, which supported the notion that there is a legal duty on the part of academic libraries to authenticate these types of documents. That does not mean that an ethical obligation does not exist. Mr. McCorison believes very strongly that it does exist, and I agree. He also spoke about having to explain his negligence. As a lawyer, I do not read the word "negligence" the way he used it. If he means negligence the way I read it, then he better grab his wallet. If, on the other hand, he means he had a strong feeling of what was, or was not, done in a particular situation, then I do not disagree with that at all.

With respect to the doctrine of treble damages, I am not sure where it arose in the common law or how it was disposed of, but in Texas, this doctrine is a fairly recent phenomenon, embodied in statutory law for the purpose of serving both as a reward and as a deterrent to those who are the victims of particularly pernicious consumer fraud. The doctrine is very much alive in all the states' laws, as well as in federal law. I know of a particular plaintiff who now suffers from the results of two broken wrists because of a badly manufactured ladder. This person is very glad that the doctrine of treble damages is alive and well in this country.

Ellen Dunlap: The issues of morality and the law are troublesome ones to reconcile, but the justice system is not working very efficiently in our case. First, I hope that, by explaining how the matter of missing letters at the Rosenbach came about, you will see why we did not immediately call the police. In addition, we obviously were dealing with a federal case, because interstate commerce and the U. S. mails were involved. I have understood from the U. S. Attorney that he always takes the strategic view: what is the most efficient way to adequately handle this case? Sometimes I think that, by taking actions into our own hands at the Rosenbach, we gave the U. S. Attorney an "excuse" not to move more aggressively. I also learned that this case was of great interest to the local authorities in Philadelphia, although they quickly realized it did not fall within local jurisdiction.

Administration of justice in this country is in an acute situation. Funding is so scarce for our local district attorney that his staff must raise outside funds in order to work on special projects.

There is a danger speaking without notes on such a sensitive issue as the Rosenbach theft. I mentioned Paul Richards by name, and it would be unfair of me to omit saying that we know of at least two other book dealers who bought materials in question directly from Clive Driver, the former director of the Rosenbach Museum and Library: George Allen of Philadelphia and Jonathan Hill in New York. Both are seeking to return materials directly to us.

Richard Landon: I would like to return to the question of disclaimers and the expectation of expertise. This disturbs me, and others as well. It intimately involves issues of curatorial responsibility for collections, for relationships between the institution and scholars, as well as between the institution and the general public, and it comes back to the question of who gets consulted about what.

The word "connoisseurship" originally defined the ability to recognize the difference not only between the good and the bad, but also between the real and the fake. Thus, in the area of curatorial responsibility, there is a long tradition of the notion of connoisseurship as used in its real sense. As the director of a publicly funded institution, where we expect to be used not only by specialized scholars but also by the public, I feel a responsibility to be as informative as possible concerning authenticity and to use my experience to determine provenance. This question of provenance needs to be emphasized, as Marcus McCorison has done. Of course, documents lacking provenance turn up and are perfectly genuine. It is also true—and we have heard a good deal of testimony on this point—that scientific testing alone is not able to establish authenticity positively. I will cite an example of the importance of provenance. Last year, the University of Toronto purchased General James Wolfe's copy of Gray's *Elegy*, annotated by Wolfe. This is a ninth edition, so the value of the book itself is small. The value, as a cultural icon and from a scholarly sense, rests entirely on Wolfe's annotations. He actually had the book with him in Quebec and so it has come back to Canada for the first time since 1759.

We tried to establish the provenance absolutely from the moment that Wolfe's fiancée presented Gray's *Elegy* to him until it came into our hands. It took a great deal of trouble, time, and money, but we were able to establish and complete provenance. We did not resort to the kinds of scientific testing described by Mr. Cantu, yet we feel confident that the item is, in fact, genuine. Its scholarly significance rests entirely with the question of how General Wolfe acted in the battle on the Plains of Abraham in 1759, the British conquest of North America being of some significance in our history. It is worth emphasizing repeatedly that often provenance is more important than any kind of scientific test currently at our disposal.

I would be interested in further legal commentary on the question of disclaimers. One may say it is only a legal matter of liability and remedy, but, of course, it could be carried over by an individual curator to cover up incompetence. I think it worth making the point that many of the problems institutions get involved in are the result of curators—those responsible for making decisions and giving information—not, in fact, being competent to do their job. Perhaps some cover-ups occur not only because of institutional legal decisions in an attempt to deal with their institutional responsibility, but also may occur when individuals try to cover up their own incompetence.

Marcus McCorison: The contemporary application of the law in any generation reflects the ethics and morality of that generation.

Scott Chafin: There have been a number of lawsuits brought in this country that are generally couched in terms of academic malpractice, and some of this sounds similar to me. In such a case, a plaintiff says the institution owes me damages because it didn't educate me as it asserted it would. In general terms, that theory has never gotten anywhere, though there have been some specific, very limited cases. Again, I would draw the distinction between what is a duty in terms of the curator's profession and the duty which institutional lawyers are concerned about, which leads to just one more hand thrust into the institution's pocket.

Bill Joyce: I believe that it is a professional responsibility, and an element of accountability, for us to be able to warrant our resources, to know what they are, and to be able to tell the public, or our constituency of scholars, that what we have is genuine and that we, as curators, know what we have. Marcus McCorison is right. I do not think any of us would confess to anything less than that, and I think it goes further and becomes our responsibility.

Tom Taylor: I have a question for Scott Chafin. When the American Antiquarian Society got the 1836 Thomas Rusk broadside, "Glorious News," which turned out to be a forgery and which Marcus McCorison returned to the collector, is it, at that point, the collector's responsibility to deal with the Internal Revenue Service and with the dealer from whom he bought the document?

And, in the University of Houston's case, a Texas Declaration of Independence was given as a gift in 1984 and presumably was appraised for a lot of money. That document is still in the library's collection. If the document is not returned to the donor, and if it is retained in the library's collection, then the collector who gave it keeps a tax deduction which is not legitimate because the document is a forgery. The dealer who sold it to the collector keeps that person's money because the collector is not going to go back to him since he wants to keep his tax deduction. Thus, by retaining this document, you basically perfect a series of essentially fraudulent transactions. Do you have legal or ethical problems with that?

Scott Chafin: I have to plead total ignorance to the tax law. My basic understanding is that what the donor claims as a tax deduction is between him and the IRS, with respect to the value of the deduction claimed. I do not know whether the return, or failure to return, a document has anything to do with the legitimacy of that deduction. I would suggest posing that question this afternoon to Mr. Malouf, who is an expert on tax law.

Tom Taylor: As a university counsel, why don't you find out whether or not you should, in fact, return the forged Texas Declaration of Independence to the collector who gave it to the library?

Scott Chafin: If it is going to affect the collector's tax standing, and the collector asks for it back in order to solve that particular problem, then I would certainly advise the university to give it back.

Tom Taylor: But what about the use of your tax exempt status to create this transaction—that is not a problem?

Scott Chafin: It is a problem if the university is actively involved in a scheme to enrich someone else at the hands of the American taxpayer. If I investigated it and the university was, in fact, involved in such a scheme, then I would want something done about it.

Tom Taylor: But you already are involved in it.

Scott Chafin: With respect to the donor's problem with the IRS, I simply do not know, nor do I know whether we have been asked to return the document. I do not know what documents are in the library's collections, to tell the truth.

I should clarify that the University of Houston received its forged documents as gifts. With respect to the problem Texas documents, other institutions bought them, which leads to the whole analysis of remedies. Still, I am not aware of an available legal remedy that corrects the embarrassment of accepting a bum steer.

Nicolas Barker: The stationery at the British Library and the British Museum used to carry a message that said the curators accepted no responsibility for the monetary value or authenticity of the materials submitted for their examination. This statement has recently come off the writing paper because we were advised by the treasury solicitor that the liability did exist and that we could not, in fact, disclaim it. Obviously this is a civil question, and although our failure to detect the value or authenticity of an object might not be deemed criminal, the liability still exists.

Kevin MacDonnell: As a rare book dealer, I can look at this issue from different perspectives because I began as a collector and later received a master's degree in library science and worked as a rare book librarian. I have dealt with William Simpson and Dorman David, and for six years I worked for John Jenkins. I am acquainted with the people involved in the Texas forgery allegations, as well as with their personalities and their ways of operating.

In the absence of facts, all that is left is supposition and rumor. The only evidence present is the documents themselves and their provenance. This has been frustrating for a number of people, most of whom are former employees of The Jenkins Company, and other people who are in possession of certain facts. These people could provide direct testimony regarding things they saw which certainly would settle a lot of the questions everybody wants answered. But after awhile, I have begun to doubt their sincerity in really wanting to know the answers because nobody has brought this matter into a court of law.

Someone in my position would be an idiot to make statements outside of a courtroom. We have no forum, here or otherwise, in which to come forward and make known the things that we know. I could give names and dates, and I could tell who did what and when they did it, as well as who knew about it and when they knew it. I could not provide every piece of the puzzle, but I know twenty more people who could supply many more pieces of the puzzle. I think when a court of law got through examining the testimony and comparing it, and seeing who was credible and who was not, the answers would be clear.

No one seems to be motivated to bring a civil suit because [all parties] have been made whole, either through a "deal," a trade, or an apology. Or they have chosen not to take any action for their own reasons, and that goes for the collectors as well as for the libraries. It is astonishing to me that no one has been motivated to bring a suit when the Texas State fire marshall, the Travis County district attorney, and several former [Jenkins Company] employees are holding an enormous wealth of information and factual data. But these individuals are not acting on this information because no one has made a request for them to do so, or has applied pressure.

What does someone like me, or Tom Taylor, do? How do we settle the legal issues and get the facts out on the table? How do we discuss the issues in an intelligent and scholarly way and resolve them? It cannot be done through rumor. This issue is going to continue to do damage to librarians, to collectors, and to the book trade until it is resolved. A forum like this is good, because it encourages discussion, but it may be premature because all the facts are not available. Those with forged documents can talk only about their pieces of the puzzle. What is your answer, Mr. Chafin? How do you get to the facts and where do you proceed from there?

Scott Chafin: I will go back to my opening comment. It is amazing how everything becomes a legal problem. Let me play the cynic for a minute. Forums other than the courts are available for discussing all kinds of issues that bother society. I do not know this for a fact, but it may be that the United States Attorney in Philadelphia is more concerned with securities fraud and cocaine dealers than he is with what seems to be a petty little problem among a bunch of highly educated people. If a wrong has been committed for which there is a legal redress, then I suggest you get to the courthouse if you believe there is some legal cause of action, but I would like to know who the defendant is going to be. The University of Houston has limited resources and more important things to do than file lawsuits when, so far at least, the pecuniary damage seems to be pretty small. I can guarantee you that is the case in the state Attorney General's office, because in all of the University of Houston's cases with them, we have to do all the work, even though they get all the glory. Everything is not a legal problem, and I would put this whole problem in perspective from a legal standpoint. There are lots of forums in which to address issues other than courtrooms, where overworked judges and clerks are trying to keep defense attorneys and plaintiffs' attorneys at bay and are trying to make a workable system of justice.

Session III:
Tax and Legal Implications

DAVID FARMER, Chair
DeGolyer Library, Southern Methodist University

TOM M. DAVIS, Jr., Davis and Shank
Liabilities in Criminal/Civil Law

DONALD J. MALOUF, Malouf,
Lynch, Jackson, Kessler & Collins
Tax Donations/Appraisals

MARIE C. MALARO, George Washington University
Legal/Ethical Levels of Responsibility

Discussion from the Floor

Authenticity: The Duty to Investigate

TOM M. DAVIS, JR.

There have been several recent developments concerning the authenticity of art objects, forged documents, and rare books. This paper will explore a recent decision of a United States District Court in Indiana concerning the theft of an art object; in addition, it will explore, in general terms, the law in Texas and the civil liability of a proclaimed expert.

Recent Case Law

The most recent case to discuss ownership of stolen art objects was *Autocephalous Greek-Orthodox Church of Cyprus and the Republic of Cyprus v. Goldberg & Feldman Fine Arts, Inc.*[1] In this case, the plaintiff-church brought suit seeking possession of four early sixth century mosaics. These mosaics originally were made for and affixed to a church in Cyprus in the sixth century A.D. In 1974, Turkish military forces invaded Cyprus, taking control of the region in which the church was located. During the occupation of the territory, the military removed the mosaics from the church. The plaintiffs contended they never intended to give up ownership, that the mosaics were taken improperly without permission of the church or the republic and they should be returned. The defendant claimed the export was authorized by Turkish Cypriot officials and that, in any event, the defendant, Goldberg and Feldman Fine Arts, Inc., should be awarded the mosaics because it purchased them in good faith and without information or reasonable notice that the mosaics were stolen.

The court concluded that possession of the mosaics must go to the plaintiffs. This decision was made because the place where the mosaics were purchased—Switzerland—had an insignificant relationship to the suit. Because Indiana had greater contacts and a more significant relationship to this suit, the court ruled that substantive law of Indiana should apply. Under that state's law, a thief can *never* obtain title to stolen items and, therefore, can never pass right of ownership of said items to subsequent purchasers. Because the mosaics were stolen from their rightful owners, the defendant never obtained title or right to possession of the mosaics. The court also considered the case under Swiss law and reached the same conclusion; however, under Swiss law it is possible for a thief to pass good title. In order to transfer good title, the buyer must qualify as a good faith purchaser for value. The factors used to determine whether good faith status is reached are:

(a) whether the purchaser knew that the seller lacked title;
(b) whether an honest and careful purchaser would have had doubts with respect to the seller's capacity to transfer property rights, and if so;

(c) whether the purchaser reasonably inquired about the seller's ability to pass good title.

Examining these factors, the court decided that the defendant was not a good faith purchaser for value, because suspicious circumstances surrounded the sale of the mosaics which should have caused an honest and prudent purchaser in the defendant's position to doubt whether the seller had the capacity to convey property rights. Also, the defendant failed to conduct a reasonable inquiry to resolve that doubt.

The mosaics in question are unique, the paramount significance of their existence being considered as part of the religious, artistic, and cultural heritage of the church and the government of Cyprus, as well as being considered part of the national unity of the Republic of Cyprus. Therefore, the court awarded possession of the mosaics to the plaintiffs. Before trial, the issue of money damages was separated from the case. Thus, the only issue present before the court was the entitlement of possession to the mosaics.

A brief history is helpful in understanding the importance of this decision. A British colony from 1878 to 1960, the Mediterranean island of Cyprus has approximately 696,000 inhabitants. In the latter year, it became an independent republic. Turkish military forces invaded Cyprus on July 20, 1974, taking over the northern 37 percent of the island, the region which includes the village of Lythrankomi. To this day it remains under Turkish military occupation. Turkey is the only legitimate government in the world which recognizes this state. The United States recognizes only the plaintiff, the Republic of Cyprus, as the legitimate government of all Cypriot people.

In July 1976, the pastor of the Church of the Panagia Kanakari'a was forced to flee to non-occupied southern Cyprus in fear of his life, and by the end of that year all Greek Cypriots in Lythrankomi had relocated involuntarily to the southern part of the island, controlled by the Republic of Cyprus. When the pastor fled in 1976 the original mosaic was intact, but some time between August of that year and October 1979 the church was vandalized and the mosaic was removed forcibly and divided into four sections.

This original work of religious art was affixed to the apse of the church in the village of Lythrankomi in A.D. 530; its four portions are invaluable because it is one of only six or seven Byzantine mosaics to survive destruction over one thousand years ago during a period when religious articles were destroyed to prevent the worship of images. The original mosaic—made up of small pieces of colored glass, referred to in the art world as "tesserae"—depicts the figure of the young boy Jesus seated in Mary's lap. At one time, it was bordered by archangels and a frieze containing the busts of the twelve apostles. Time had taken its toll, and by 1960 all that remained of the original was the figure of Jesus, one of the archangels, and nine of the twelve apostles. Between 1959 and 1967, the mosaic was cleaned and restored under the sponsorship of the Department of Antiquities of the Republic of Cyprus, the Church of Cyprus, and Harvard University's Dumbarton Oaks Center for Byzantine Studies.[2] Were it not for an unusual series of events, the original mosaic, now separated into four pieces, probably would have remained at the original site, undisturbed in its deteriorating, but readily recognizable, state. Neither the Republic of Cyprus nor the Church of Cyprus ever authorized the removal or sale of the mosaics.

The Turkish Federal Republic of Cyprus sought permission to intervene, but the court denied its request because that government is not recognized by the United States.

In fact, the Republic of Cyprus did not hear of the theft until November 1979 when a visitor who had entered the northern occupied territory reported the crime to the Cypriot Department of Antiquities. Immediately upon receiving this knowledge, the government of Cyprus contacted the United Nations Education, Scientific and Cultural Organization (UNESCO), informing it of the significance of the lost art and seeking its assistance. The Cypriot government also notified museums and auction houses throughout the United States and Europe and, through world-wide correspondence, sought assistance in recovering the mosaics. Through these efforts, Cyprus finally located the mosaics in question.

The defendant, Goldberg and Feldman Fine Arts, Inc., purchased the mosaics under conditions that were not free of suspicion, knowing that:

(a) the seller had been convicted in France for forging Marc Chagall's signature to prints; and
(b) the seller also had been sued by an art gallery for failure to pay.

Following negotiations in Amsterdam on July 3, 1988, the two parties agreed on a purchase price of $1,080,000 for the four mosaics.

It was through the defendant's attempt to resell the mosaics that the Director General of the Ministry of Foreign Affairs in Cyprus learned of the mosaics' existence in Indiana. The plaintiff then wrote to the defendant requesting the return of the mosaics, and when the defendant refused, the plaintiffs filed suit. The defendant's failure to properly research the origin of the mosaics was discussed at length in the court's decision. Whether or not the defendant was a bona fide purchaser was insignificant once the court decided the mosaics were stolen, because Indiana law does not allow a purchaser to acquire title to stolen property. The court concluded that, because Goldberg and Feldman Fine Arts, Inc. failed to properly research the origin of the mosaics, or to question the credibility of the seller, good title never was obtained. The court decided that return of the property, and not money damages, was the proper remedy. Further, it awarded damages for the loss of use of the mosaics, although the amount of such damages was not determined in this proceeding.

The court also concluded that the plaintiffs, the Autocephalous Greek-Orthodox Church of Cyprus and the Republic of Cyprus, did timely file this action. The church's claim was not barred by the statute of limitations because it did not learn where the mosaics were located until late in 1988, filing suit in March 1989. Generally, the statute of limitations begins to run when damage is ascertained or is ascertainable by due diligence (when a plaintiff knew by due diligence, or should have known). A plaintiff who seeks protection under this discovery rule has the duty to use reasonable diligence to locate stolen items.

Aside from the discovery rule, there was the issue of fraudulent concealment. A cause of action for replevin (recovery of the item) generally runs from the date of theft, but if a stolen item is fraudulently concealed, the statute is tolled. In order to claim fraudulent concealment, a plaintiff must show due diligence in locating stolen property.

Texas Analysis

Applying Texas law to this case, a court would have come to the same conclusion. In Texas, a purchaser of stolen property will not acquire title to that property.[3] This puts the duty on the purchaser to ascertain ownership prior to any purchase taking place. It would appear that a Texas court would have decided the Cypriot mosaic case as did the U.S. District Court in Indiana, considering the lack of reasonable steps taken by the defendant to establish true ownership of the mosaics. Such reasonable steps to be taken by a potential buyer should include:

(a) contacting the country from which an item in question originates to inquire into the authority and condition of its title;

(b) contacting Interpol to determine whether an item in question has been reported stolen; and

(c) seeking independent, expert advice.

Forgery—Criminal Liability

The forgery of historical documents is also a major problem and is cause for concern. When giving an opinion on forgeries the seller, as well as the buyer, is at risk. The general forgery statute in the Texas Penal Code[4] states:

Forgery

(a) For the purposes of this Section:

    (1) "Forge" means:

        (A) to alter, make, complete, execute or authenticate any writings so that it purports;

            (i) to be the act of another who did not authorize the act;

            (ii) to have been executed at a time or place or in a numbered sequence other than was in fact the case; or

            (iii) to be a copy of an original when no such original existed;

        (B) to issue, transfer, register the transfer of, pass, publish, or otherwise utter a writing that is forged within the meaning of Paragraph (A) of this subdivision; or

        (C) to possess a writing that is forged within the meaning of Paragraph (A) with the intent to utter it in a manner specified in Paragraph (B) of this subdivision.

    (2) "Writing" includes:

        (A) printing or other method of recording information;

        (B) money, coins, tokens, stamps, seals, credit cards, badges, and trademarks; and

        (C) symbols of value, right, privilege, or identification.

(b) A person commits an offense if he forges a writing with intent to defraud or harm another.

(c) Except as provided in Subsections (d) and (e) of this section an offense under this section is a class A misdemeanor.

(d) An offense under this Section is a felony of the third degree if the writing is or purports to be a will, codicil, deed, deed of trust, mortgage, security instrument, security agreement, credit card, check or similar sight order for payment of money, contract, release, or other commercial instrument.

(e) An offense under this Section is a felony of the second degree if the writing is or purports to be part of an issue of money, securities, postage or revenue stamps, or other instruments issued by a state or national government or by a subdivision of either, or part of an issue of stock, bonds, or other instruments representing interest in or claims against another person.

This Section combines several of the older penal code provisions regarding forgery, including counterfeiting, previously covered by separate provisions, and it adds intent to harm in addition to intent to defraud. This expands the offense of forgery to include non-monetary and non-property injuries in addition to pecuniary losses.

In Texas, the criminal liability associated with forgery of historical documents appears to stem from the criminal simulation statute,[5] stating that:

(a) The person commits an offense if, with intent to defraud or harm another;
  (1) he makes or alters an object, in whole or in part, so that it appears to have value because of age, antiquity, rarity, source, or authorship that it does not have;
  (2) he sells, passes, or otherwise utters an object so made or altered;
  (3) he possesses an object so made or altered with intent to sell, pass or otherwise utter it; or
  (4) he authenticates or certifies an object so made or altered as genuine or as different from what it is.
(b) An offense under this Section is a class A misdemeanor.

In *Tawfik v. State*,[6] the court held that where the defendant sold scarabs, claiming them to be genuine artifacts of ancient Egypt, he should have been convicted of criminal simulation under §32.22 of the Texas Penal Code and not convicted of theft. The court stated that §32.22 extends to the forgery of ancient and modern works of art or rarity and to persons who sell, possess with intent to sell, or authenticate such forgeries with intent to defraud or harm another. Based upon the result in *Tawfik v. State*, a person who forges historical documents must necessarily be tried under §32.22 and therefore is not indictable under the general theft statute. The maximum penalty for a violation under this Section is a fine of $2,000, one year in prison, or both. Under both §§32.21 and 32.22 intent is a required element. This apparently cannot be shown absent proof of knowledge that the object was forged.[7]

Forgery of archaeological objects and antiquities was made criminal by R.C.S. art. 6145-9, §§14 and 17 (antiquities code) though there was no specific criminal statute applicable to forgery of paintings, sculpture, and other art objects prior to the inclusion of §32.22 of the Texas Penal Code. Subsection (a)(4) of this Section reaches experts upon whose authentication major art works customarily are sold. Restorations and repairs are not covered by this Section due to the lack of fraudulent intent. If forgery is disclosed by the dealer or by one making the repairs, all such work will be protected.

Deceptive Trade Practices Act

The Deceptive Trade Practices Act (DTPA) in Texas also may apply to forgery of art objects. This would come in the form of civil liability to a dealer who sells an art object or historic document, were that dealer to make representations to a buyer regarding the authenticity of the object or document. If a dealer makes a "knowing representation," he or she also could be subject to treble damages. The DTPA has numerous procedural requirements; therefore, many transactions do not qualify as causes of action. Although this is an ever-expanding area of Texas law, as yet there have been no Texas cases that have applied the DTPA to the forgery of art objects or historic documents.

Civil Liability of an Expert

In order to be criminally prosecuted, the Texas Penal Code, §32.22 requires that intentional conduct be proved; however, an expert may be liable in tort due to his or her negligence in connection with an opinion regarding the authenticity of an art object. This was discussed at length in Judith A. Bresler's 1988 article, entitled "Experts' Opinions and Liability"[8] in which she states that liability could be based on several theories, including negligent misrepresentation, disparagement, and defamation. Only when an expert volunteers information is he or she generally open to a claim based on disparagement or defamation. The strongest of these is the first: negligent misrepresentation, which consists of making a false, material misrepresentation to another person without a reasonable belief that the representation is true, such that another person reasonably and detrimentally relies on the representation. Therefore, liability could arise from negligently approving a forged document as authentic, failing to recognize a forgery prior to the reliance, or by wrongfully classifying an authentic object as a forgery.

To avoid liability on a misrepresentation claim, not only must an expert be knowledgeable in the area where expertise is stated, but that knowledge also must be properly applied. As a general rule, if an expert represents that he or she has special skills, said expert will be held to a higher duty. There are several ways an expert might give an opinion which would qualify as negligent misrepresentation, including:

(a) lack of minimal necessary knowledge;
(b) presentation of outdated information;
(c) negligence in applying expert knowledge.

The principal means of limiting liability in this area is through careful drafting of a contract. This can be accomplished by explicitly pointing out the scope of the expert's responsibility, indicating in writing that only the party requesting the information is entitled to rely upon it and that the information is not for publication or for use by others. In this particular area, expert liability has not been developed in Texas, but several jurisdictions have held experts liable because of opinions related to the authenticity of art objects.

The liability of a dealer has expanded to include other causes of action such as lost business opportunity. In order to recover damages, the plaintiff is required to show that he or she lost a sale due to the wrongful opinion of an expert; this would come in the form of a disparagement claim. The elements of disparagement[9] require the plaintiff to prove that:

(a) a legal protected interest was affected by the comment;
(b) the comment had an injurious character;
(c) the comment was false;
(d) the comment was published;
(e) the circumstances of publication were such that the reliance on the comment by a third party was reasonably foreseeable;
(f) the third party recipient understood the comment in its injurious sense;
(g) the third party recipient understood the comment as applicable to the plaintiff's interest;
(h) pecuniary loss resulted from the publication; and
(i) the defendant knew his or her statement to be false or acted with reckless disregard for the truth or falsity.

In her article, Judith A. Bresler applies this tort to a variety of circumstances. One such example concerns an art appraiser who, at a cocktail party, gave a false opinion as to the soundness of an investment with regard to an expensive painting. This off-handed opinion exposed the appraiser to a disparagement claim because the potential seller possibly would be able to satisfy the elements of disparagement as cited above. Such a liability also would arise if the appraiser recklessly disregarded the truth and gave an opinion which he or she knew to be potentially incorrect. It should be noted that the liability of an expert in rendering an opinion on an object of art or historic document will vary from state to state, and this variation applies to civil as well as criminal areas.

Conclusion

A buyer should carefully research the origin and authenticity of the objects he or she wishes to purchase to avoid the possibility of being forced to return said object and paying damages as well. In addition, the Texas Deceptive Trade Practices Act and a host of potential claims should cause an expert in the field of art or historic documents to proceed with caution, executing a carefully drafted contract, especially when significant amounts of money are involved. Those persons with acknowledged expertise also should avoid unguarded comments which could render them liable to pay damages to a seller upon a disparagement claim.

References

1. *Autocephalous Greek-Orthodox Church of Cyprus and the Republic of Cyprus v. Goldberg & Feldman Fine Arts, Inc.*, 717 F. Supp. 1374 (S.D. Ind. 1989).
2. See A. H. S. Megaw and E. J. W. Hawkins, *The Church of the Panagia Kanakari'a at Lythrankomi in Cyprus: Its Mosaics and Frescoes* (Washington: Dumbarton Oaks Center for Byzantine Studies, Trustees for Harvard University, 1977).

3. See *Olin Corp. v. Cargo Carriers, Inc.*, 673 S.W. 2nd 211 (Tex. App. - Houston [14th Dist.] 1984, no writ).
4. Texas Penal Code Ann., §32.21 (Vernon 1989).
5. Texas Penal Code Ann., §32.22 (Vernon 1989).
6. See *Tawfik v. State*, 643 S.W. 2d 127 (Tex. Crim. App. 1983).
7. See *Stueben v. State*, 547 S.W. 2d 29 (Tex. Crim. App. 1977).
8. Judith A. Bresler. "Experts' Opinions and Liability." *Art Law* (New York: Practicing Law Institute, 1988): 269-299.
9. *Id.*

Tax Donations and Appraisals

DONALD J. MALOUF

General Background[1]

Charitable deductions date back to the Revenue Act of 1917, which permitted taxpayers to deduct up to 15 percent of taxable net income for gifts to charitable organizations. That was the start of a policy by Congress to allow individual taxpayers to deduct charitable contributions, a policy which has not always been followed consistently either by Congress or by the Internal Revenue Service. Section 170 of the Internal Revenue Code of 1986 [2] is the provision which now sets forth the requirements for deductions of contributions to charities.

An individual who itemizes his or her deductions is allowed to deduct from adjusted gross income the value of charitable contributions if the requirements of §170 and other code sections are met. These requirements include the types of recipient organizations, the types of property interests donated, percentage limitations, and other prerequisites.

Gifts to charities also may be deductible for purposes of federal estate,[3] gift,[4] and generation-skipping taxes.[5] This discussion will emphasize only the income tax deduction. Most of the general rules relating to deductions for the income tax also apply to the deductions for the other types of taxes.

Charitable Contributions Defined

For a transfer to be a charitable contribution under §170, it must be a voluntary transfer of money or money's worth without present or anticipated receipt by the donor of more than an incidental[6] economic consideration or benefit in return.[7] As stated by the Tax Court, "If a payment proceeds primarily from the incentive of anticipated benefit to the payor beyond the satisfaction which flows from the performance of generous act, it is not a gift."[8]

Cases come out almost weekly dealing with the question of whether or not there is sufficient donative intent to constitute a gift. This determination rests principally on the facts of each case, and there is a wide range of decisions by the courts and the Internal Revenue Service, reflecting a considerable variety of factual situations. The simple rule appears to be that if the donor receives more than a small economic benefit, the deduction will be disallowed, at least in part.

This rule also applies when an individual makes a payment, for example, to his or her library support group in connection with a fund-raising activity. This includes charity balls, bazaars, banquets, shows, and similar events. Typically, one may receive in return a material benefit. The burden is on the taxpayer to establish that the amount paid is not the purchase price of the benefit received and that all or part of the payment, in fact, qualifies as a gift.[9]

The Omnibus Budget Reconciliation Act of 1987 ("OBRA") added §6133 and §6710 to the Internal Revenue Code. These effectively impose a penalty of $1,000 (with a cap of $10,000 a year) on a §501(c)(3) organization for each day it fails to include a statement in any solicitation for nondeductible contributions, which statement must say that the payments are not tax deductible charitable contributions.

Permitted Donees

Section 170(c) lists the types of organizations to which charitable contributions may be deductible. The most relevant type, for purposes of this discussion, includes a corporation, trust, or community chest, fund or foundation organized and operated exclusively for "... charitable, scientific, literary, or educational purposes..."[10]

Contributions

Subject to certain percentage and other limitations, §170 allows a deduction for outright gifts of cash and other property to permissible charitable organizations. However, the taxpayer must not retain any interest with respect to use or financial benefits from such donation.[11]

Bargain Sales

A popular means for transferring a collection to a library or museum is a "bargain sale." This occurs when property is transferred to a charitable organization at a sales price less than the fair market value of the property. This transaction is treated for tax purposes as part sale of the property and part charitable contribution.[12] Taxable gain is recognized by the transferor on the sale portion. But the transferor may still take a charitable contribution under §170 equal to the excess of the fair market value of the property over its sales price.

For example, Taxpayer A sells a rare historical document from his collection to a library for $1,000. The document is worth $2,000. The document has an adjusted basis (cost) in Taxpayer A's hands of $1,000. Taxpayer A is required to allocate to the sales portion that part of his basis which bears the same ratio to his basis as the sales price bears to the fair market value of the document. Thus the basis allocable to the $2,000 sales price is $500 ($1,000 sales price/$2,000 value). Taxpayer A therefore must recognize a gain of $500 ($1,000 sales price, less $500 allocated basis). Taxpayer A would be eligible to deduct $1,000 as a charitable contribution ($2,000 fair market value, less $1,000 sales price).[13]

Timing

As a general rule the deduction under §170 is available only with respect to amounts for which "payment" is made within the year.[14] Except for accrual basis corporations,[15] the year in which the actual payment occurs controls.[16] This is true even though someone may make a pledge to contribute his or her collection in a transaction which is legally enforceable. On the other hand, since the deduction may be taken only in the year in which payment is made, the Internal Revenue Service has ruled that the use of appreciated or depreciated property to satisfy a prior pledge of a specific dollar amount does not result in the realization of a gain or loss by the donor.[17]

Because books and papers are tangible personal property, the rules relating to gifts of a future interest in tangible personal property are relevant to this discussion. A contribution of a future interest in tangible personal property is considered to be made only when all intervening interests in and right to the actual possession or enjoyment of the property have expired or are held by persons other than the taxpayer.[18] For this purpose, the term "future interest" includes situations in which a donor purports to make a gift of a present interest but has an oral understanding with the charity that "has the effect of reserving to, or retaining in, such donor a right to the use, possession, or enjoyment of the property."[19] For example, Taxpayer B makes a gift of her rare book collection to a library, but there is an "understanding" that the books will remain in Taxpayer B's home until her death. The gift is not regarded as occurring for tax purposes until Taxpayer B's death.

Contributions of Property—Evaluation

Where the charitable gift consists of property rather than money, the amount of the contribution is the fair market value of the property at the time of the contribution (reduced as provided under §170(e)(1) relating to appreciated property).[20]

Treasury Regulations state the general proposition that the "fair market value" is "the price at which property would change hands between a willing buyer and a willing seller, neither being under any compulsion to buy or sell and both having reasonable knowledge of relevant facts."[21]

The Internal Revenue Service takes the position that the fair market value of property purchased at a discount and contributed to a charity should be its purchase price and not its nondiscounted value, for purposes of determining the amount of the charitable contribution deductions. Thus, in Rev. Rul. 80-69,[22] the taxpayer (who was not a dealer) purchased an assortment of gems at wholesale prices from a promoter who engaged in similar wholesale transactions with other taxpayers. Relying upon the appraisal of the promoter as to the nondiscounted value of the gems, the taxpayer contributed the gems to a museum thirteen months after his purchase, claiming a charitable contribution equal to three times the purchase price. The IRS, however, concluded that the wholesale purchase price at which the promoter sold the gems to the taxpayer was, in fact, the fair market value of the gems. It thus ruled that the charitable contribution deduction was limited to the actual purchase price.

In Rev. Rul. 80-233[23] and Rev. Rul. 80-329[24] (each of which involved a valuation of Bibles donated to charities) the Internal Revenue Service ruled that the most probative evidence of fair market value is the range of prices at which similar quantities of Bibles actually sold in arms-length transactions. In the latter ruling the IRS went one step further, asserting that the price paid by the donor does not conclusively determine the fair market value if comparable lots were sold to others at a lower price.

There are enumerable cases and rulings involving valuation questions and the effect of various factors on value. Basically, one can be reasonably accurate if these are approached with common-sense analysis. For example, if restrictions are placed by the donor on the use of the property by the donee, they naturally will have an effect on the amount of the deduction. Thus, in *Transamerica Corp. v. U.S.*[25] the Claims Court held that the taxpayer was not entitled to a deduction for a charitable contribution of old films to the Library of Congress. In that case, the donor had retained the right to commercial exploitation of the films. The Court looked at the fact that the donee had no right to market the films and thus concluded that the gift had no fair market value.

When the property donated is associated with the donor's trade or business, charitable deductions for that property may be offset by the income that would go unrecognized at the time the donated property was acquired by the taxpayer. For example, in *Haberly v. U.S.*[26] a school principal received unsolicited sample textbooks. He donated them to the school library, claiming a charitable deduction. The court held that he received taxable gross income to the extent of the value of such books in the year of the donation. Likewise, in Rev. Rul. 70-498,[27] the value of books accepted by a book reviewer during his employment with a newspaper and donated to a charitable organization was found to be includible in the reviewer's gross income. The theory here is that the transfer of these items constitutes a taxable "accession to wealth" in the year of the contribution.[28] The act of the taxpayer in taking the deduction from the donated property indicates his clear intent to exercise complete dominion over the donated property.

Appreciated Property

Prior to the Tax Reform Act of 1969, a taxpayer who contributed appreciated property to a charitable organization was generally permitted a charitable deduction for the fair market value of the property at the time of contribution. He or she was not taxed on the appreciation in the value of the property at the time of the gift.[29] Under the rules as they existed at that time, it was possible for a taxpayer to realize a greater after tax benefit by making a gift of appreciated property than by making a cash gift. In fact, it could be even more beneficial for a taxpayer to give property to a charity than to sell it.

The Tax Reform Act of 1969 changed the treatment of charitable gifts of appreciated property through the enactment of §170(e). This provision requires reduction from fair market value in calculating the amount of the charitable contribution for certain gifts of appreciated property. It also enacted §1011, which set forth the method of calculating gain on bargain sales. Even so, there are still substantial benefits under many circumstances for making gifts of appreciated property rather than cash.

In general, no gain is recognized on the transfer of appreciated property to a qualified charity for less than adequate consideration; however there are two major exceptions to this rule. The first is the "bargain sale" discussed earlier. The second exception applies when a charity sells the property shortly after the transfer and it is determined that the sale was a part of an overall plan, requiring a reordering of the steps. In such circumstances the donor is treated as having sold the property for cash (thereupon realizing and recognizing gain) and contributing the cash proceeds to the charity.[30]

In the case of "ordinary income property," the charitable contribution is required to be reduced by the amount of ordinary income that would have resulted had the contributed property been sold at its fair market value at the time of contribution. "Ordinary income property" includes "property any portion of the gain on which would not have been long-term capital gain if the property had been sold by the donor at its fair market value at the time of the contribution to the charitable organization."[31] Examples of ordinary income property found in the regulations include inventory items,[32] works of art created by the donor,[33] a manuscript prepared by the donor,[34] letters and memoranda prepared by or for the donor,[35] a capital asset held by the donor less than one year,[36] certain stock,[37] and certain assets on which previous deductions are recaptured as ordinary income.

For example, an individual who is a rare book dealer contributes books out of his inventory to a library. The books have a fair market value of $20,000 and a cost of $5,000. Since inventory items are property previously held for sale to customers in the ordinary course of the dealer's business, had the property been sold, the dealer would have recognized ordinary income in the amount of $15,000. Under §170(e)(1)(A), the dealer's contribution of $20,000 is reduced by $15,000. Ironically, a forged document contributed by the forger would fall under the foregoing rule, he being either the creator of the art or the preparer of the manuscript.

This concept of ordinary income property has been used by the Internal Revenue Service to limit charitable contributions by nondealer individual donors. For example, in Rev. Rul. 79-256[38] a taxpayer raised ornamental plants as a hobby. After holding the plants for more than a year, he donated a large number of them to various charities. The taxpayer then claimed a charitable deduction equal to the fair market value of the plants. In another situation,[39] a taxpayer purchased a large number of limited edition lithographic prints by an established artist at a reduced price. After holding the prints for more than a year, the taxpayer donated the prints to various art museums, claiming a charitable contribution equal to the fair market value of the prints at the time of the contribution. In a third situation,[40] a taxpayer purchased a large number of books from a company located outside the United States at a volume discount and stored the books in a warehouse for twelve months. At the end of that time, the taxpayer donated the books to a charitable organization and claimed the deduction equal to the sum of the official retail list prices for the books.

In each of these instances the Internal Revenue Service took the position that the "frequency and continuity" of the charitable contributions and the absence of any period of accumulation and enjoyment of the property suggested that the activities of the donor were substantially equivalent to the activities of a dealer selling property in the ordinary course of trade or business. This was true even though none of the donors considered themselves to be actively engaged in the trade or business relating to the property. Thus, the IRS concluded that the contributed property in each case must be treated as ordinary income property and that the taxpayer's contribution must be reduced under §170(e) by the amount of gain that would not have been recognized as long-term capital gain had the property been sold by the donor at its fair market value at the time of the contribution.

There is a special rule, not discussed here, that permits regular corporations to take increased charitable deductions for contributions of inventory or depreciable property to a public charity or private operating foundation where the property will be used for the care of the ill, the needy or infants.[41]

Tangible Personal Property

When an individual makes a charitable contribution of tangible personal property, the general rule is that he or she can deduct the fair market value at the time of the gift.[42] However, this is dependent upon the use by the donee of such property in a way that is related to the purpose or function constituting the basis of the donee's exemption (or in the case of a governmental unit, to any purpose or function described in §170(c)). Otherwise, the amount of the deduction must be reduced by 100 percent of the amount of gain that would have been long-term capital gain had the property been sold by the individual taxpayer for its fair market value at the time of the contribution to charity.[43]

For example, if a rare book is contributed to an educational institution and that book is used for educational purposes by being placed in its library for study by researchers and for display, the use is a related use, not an unrelated use. But if the book were sold and the proceeds used by the organization for educational purposes, the use of the property is an unrelated one.[44]

For purposes of applying these rules, the donor may treat his or her gift of personal property as being put to a related use only if:

1) the donor establishes that the property is not, in fact, put to an unrelated use by the donee; or
2) at the time of the contribution it is reasonable to assume that the property will not be put to an unrelated use by the donee.[45]

Contributions to Private Foundations

Since the libraries to whom this paper may be of interest would seldom be private foundations, suffice it to say that the deductions for charitable contributions of any appreciated long-term gain property to or for the use of most private foundations by individual donors must be reduced by 100 percent of the long-term capital gain which would have been recognized on sale of the property.[46] This does not apply to contributions of publicly traded stock.[47]

Percentage Limitations

A donor of appreciated long-term capital gain property is limited to a deduction in the amount of 30 percent of his or her contribution base for the year.[48] The taxpayer may elect, however, to deduct such contributions under the 50 percent limitation, provided he or she elects to reduce the deduction by 100 percent of the amount that would have been long-term capital gain had the properties been sold.[49] If a contribution of appreciated long-term capital-gain property is made to certain exempt organizations not described in §170(b)(1)(A) (such as a private non-operating foundation), the donor is limited to a deduction equal to only 20 percent of his or her contribution base for the year.[50]

Appreciated Property as a Tax Preference

The Tax Reform Act of 1986, §701, revised the alternative minimum tax for noncorporate taxpayers and extended the alternative minimums tax to corporations. Revised §57(a)(6) now treats as a preference "the amount by which the deduction allowable under §170 would be reduced if all capital-gain property were taken into account at an adjusted basis." This amount (the appreciation element of the charitable contribution) must be added to the taxpayer's alternative minimum taxable income.

Substantiation Requirements

The potential benefit of liberal valuation of property contributed to charities has been almost too tempting for taxpayers and has produced a serious enforcement problem for the Internal Revenue Service. Tax shelter programs based upon aggressively valued charitable contributions have flourished. For example, *Anselmo v. Comm'r* [51] involved bulk purchases of low quality gemstones from financial planners and subsequent contributions of those gemstones to the Smithsonian Institution. Because of this and other cases, the problem of overvalued charitable contributions became a major concern in the Tax Reform Act of 1984.

The 1984 Act attacked overvalued property with several weapons. Contributions of property worth more than $5,000 ($10,000 in the case of closely held stock) are subject to detailed appraisal requirements. Form 8283 must be completed and attached to the Federal income tax return if the claimed deduction for property contributed exceeds $500. (See Appendix I.)

The charity that receives a property contribution and sells or otherwise disposes of it within two years must report this disposition to the Internal Revenue Service on Form 8282 and send a copy of that report to the donor. (See Appendix II.)

Previously existing penalties were strengthened and expanded. These rules make it more difficult for a donor to justify an overly liberal valuation of property and make it very expensive for the donor who claims an excessive value.

Appraisal Requirements

In May 1988, proposed and final regulations were issued pursuant to the Tax Reform Act of 1984 requiring qualified appraisals for verification of most property contributions.[52]

Donors claiming deductions for contributions of appreciated property must now comply with a set of appraisal requirements. These donors include individuals, closely held corporations, personal service corporations, partnerships, and S corporations. Proposed regulations would impose the appraisal requirements on all taxpayers (including C corporations, estates, trusts, and pooled income funds).

The appraisal rules apply to all forms of property, other than publicly traded securities, where the claimed value of the property (plus all similar items of property contributed during the year) exceeds $5,000. All types of tangible property are affected, including, for example, art work, books, and rare documents. Certain modifications to these rules, not discussed here, apply in the case of non-publicly traded stock.[53]

Where the substantiation requirements are applicable, the donor must obtain a qualified appraisal for the contribution, attach an appraised summary to the return on which the deduction is first claimed for the contribution, and include on the return such additional information as the regulations require (including the cost basis and acquisition date of the contributed property). The appraisal must have been made not earlier than sixty days before the due date of the contribution.[54]

If the appraisal is made after the contribution, it can be made up until the date on which it must be received by the donee, which is the due date of the return on which the deduction is first claimed. The regulations require the taxpayer to retain any qualified appraisal, presumably to have it available for audit.

The Tax Reform Act of 1984 defined the term "qualified appraisal" as an appraisal prepared by a qualified appraiser that includes the following items:

(i) a description of the property appraised;

(ii) the fair market of the property on the date of contribution and specific basis for valuation;

(iii) a statement that such appraisal was prepared for income tax purposes (presumably to subject the appraiser to possible liability under §6701 for aiding and abetting the understatement of the donor's tax liability);

(iv) the qualifications of the qualified appraiser;

(v) the signature and tax identification number of the appraiser; and

(vi) such additional information as the Secretary chooses to include in the regulations.[55]

Only one qualified appraisal is required for a group of similar items of the property contributed in the same taxable year if the appraisal includes all the required information for each item. The appraiser, however, may select any items whose aggregate value is appraised at $100 or less for which a group description rather than a specific description of each item will suffice.

Although a critical element of the appraisal rules is the requirement that a "qualified appraiser" be used, the Act[56] emphasizes the independence of the appraiser rather than his or her professional qualifications. A qualified appraiser is one qualified to make appraisals of the types of property donated and one who is neither the taxpayer, nor a party to the transaction in which the taxpayer acquired the property (except in limited circumstances), nor the donee, nor any person employed by any of the foregoing persons or a relative or a spouse of any of the foregoing, nor an appraiser regularly used by the parties who does not perform a majority of his or her appraisals in the taxable year for other persons.[57]

Many accepted practices had to be changed radically in response to these rules. Previously, it was not uncommon for a donor to request the assistance of the donee in valuating contributed property. Indeed, sometimes the donee may be uniquely suited to estimate the value; however, the qualified appraisal rules eliminate participation by the donee in the valuation. Eliminating the person who sold the property to the donor helps to discourage tax shelter transactions in which an investor purchased a package deal and received as part of such a package a high appraisal for the subsequent contribution.

A special rule is provided for appraisal fees.[58] An appraisal will not be treated as a qualified appraisal if all or part of the appraisal fee is based on a percentage of the appraised value. There is a special exception, however, for fees based on a sliding scale that are paid to a generally recognized association regulating appraisers.

Art Advisory Panel

The Commissioner of Internal Revenue maintains an Art Advisory Panel of nationally prominent art museum directors, curators, and art dealers. The panel assists the Internal Revenue Service in the review of selected cases involving valuations of major art objects. These principally include American and European paintings and sculptures.[59]

A number of art publishing tax shelters with non-recourse financing were actively promoted in the last few years. An Art Print Advisory Panel was established in the National Office to aid the IRS in determining the fair market value of certain depreciable assets in these ventures. The panel includes publishers, distributors and retailers of prints, as well as museum curators.[60]

Neither of these groups, however, passes on literary, dramatic, musical or historical memorabilia,[61] which are excluded from the definition of a "work of art" for this purpose.

Reporting Requirements of Donee

A charitable donee who, within two years of the date of the gift, sells, exchanges, or otherwise transfers donated property for which the donor had claimed a deduction exceeding $5,000 must report the transfer to the Internal Revenue Service on Form 8282 (Donee Information Return).[62] This form requires that the donee attach a description of the property, the date contributed, the date of disposition, and the amount received upon disposal. Form 8282 must be filed within ninety days of the disposition, with a copy provided to the donor. Since the donee organization is required to sign the donor's Form 8283 for any contributed property with a value in excess of $5,000, the donee should have the information available to determine whether it is necessary to file a Form 8282 when the contributed property is disposed of.

The reporting requirements apply if the amount for which the deduction was claimed by the taxpayer on his or her return for the contribution (other than publicly traded securities) exceeds $5,000 for any single item of property or, in the aggregate, for similar items of such property. Unlike the appraisal requirements, there is no higher limitation applicable for closely held securities in this instance. In addition, §6721, which imposes penalties for failure to furnish various statements, was amended to apply penalties to a charity's failure to comply with these information reporting requirements.

An organization which fails to file the required report is subject to a penalty of $50 per incident, up to a total penalty of $100,000 per year. In addition, an organization that fails to supply a copy to the donor is subject to a penalty of $50 per incident, up to a total penalty of $100,000 per year. These penalties may be excused if the donee establishes that its failure was due to a reasonable cause and not to willful neglect.[63]

If the failure was due to *intentional* disregard of the filing requirement, then the penalty for each incident is $100 or 5 percent of the value of the property, whichever is greater, with no cap on the total penalty. Section 6723 imposes similar penalties for intentional failure to supply the correct information on Form 8282.

Donee reporting of sales of donated property is not required if the appraisal summary signed by the donee respecting the items sold contains a statement signed by the donor that the value of the donated item does not exceed $500.[64] The regulations state that for this purpose items that form a set, such as a collection of books by the same author, are considered as one item.

Reporting is not required for an item consumed or distributed for no consideration, provided that the disposition is furtherance of the donee's exempt purpose. For example, a library that collects books for distribution among the poor is not required to report such a distribution.[65]

Overvaluation Penalty

Before the Tax Reform Act of 1984, the Code[66] applied a penalty on a sliding scale from 10 to 30 percent upon any underpayment of tax attributable to an overstatement of value or adjusted basis for any property claimed on a return. The penalty was not applicable to any property which had been held by the taxpayer for more than five years.[67] The 1984 Act, §155(c), expanded and strengthened the existing penalty in several respects.

First, §6659(c) was revised to delete the requirement that property be acquired within the previous five years. Thus, the valuation overstatement exists whenever a value or adjusted basis of any property claimed on any return is 150 percent or more of the amount determined to be the correct valuation or basis.

The 1984 Act[68] also added §6659(f) to prescribe special rules for overvaluations of charitable contributions of property. Where the understatement of tax is attributable to an overvalued charitable contribution deduction, the penalty applies at a flat 30 percent rate. The charitable contribution penalty of §6659(f) thus continues the 150 percent threshold for application of §6659, but it applies the maximum penalty of 30 percent in the case of a charitable contribution.

The Internal Revenue Service's ability to waive the penalty was also limited by the 1984 Act. In the case of an overstatement deduction, the penalty may be waived if the IRS determines that: (a) the claimed value of the property was based on a "qualified appraisal" made by a "qualified appraiser," and (b) in addition to the appraisal, the taxpayer made a "good faith investigation" of the values of the contributed property. The legislative history provides no insight into the intended scope of the good faith investigation requirement. Presumably, this is intended to allow a penalty to be imposed on a taxpayer who uses an appraisal showing an inflated value that the taxpayer had reason to know (or should have reason to know) is improper. An example would be a taxpayer who conceals material facts from the appraiser, or fails to notify the appraiser of a misunderstanding of facts concerning the property.

In addition, §158 of the Act amended the statute to make the overvaluation penalty "time-sensitive." Thus, the penalty will bear interest from the due date of the return to the date of the eventual payment.[69] Section 6659 penalties will be imposed only if the tax underpayment for the year as a result of all overvaluations is at least $1,000.

Other Civil Penalties

In addition to the penalty for overvaluation a number of other very costly civil penalties can apply where a charitable gift has been overvalued. These include: (a) 5 percent negligence penalty plus increased interest;[70] and (b) a 75 percent fraud penalty plus increased interest.[71] In addition, the Internal

Revenue Service may impose a 25 percent penalty where there is a substantial understatement of tax (i.e., the greater of 10 percent of the required tax, or $5,000).[72]

Criminal Offenses

A gift of a forged document or other work may frequently come from a high profile donor. Just as these people are sought after as patrons of museums and libraries, the same notoriety makes them likely targets for criminal tax investigations. The government is fond of making examples of leading citizens (and, indeed, leading charitable organizations) to frighten others away from overly aggressive tax planning.

Criminal tax offenses are in addition to the civil penalties.[73] A discussion of these tax offenses is beyond the scope of this paper, except for the following summary presentation of the most serious and frequently encountered provisions.

1. *Evasion.* Section 7201 provides that:

   Any person who willfully attempts in any manner to evade or defeat any tax imposed by this title or the payment thereof shall, in addition to the other penalties provided by law, be guilty of a felony and, upon conviction thereof, shall be fined not more than $100,000 ($500,000 in the case of a corporation),[74] or imprisoned not more than five years, or both, together with the costs of prosecution.

The elements that the government must prove beyond a reasonable doubt are: (a) the existence of a tax deficiency; (b) an affirmative act of evasion or attempted evasion of tax or the payment of a tax; and (c) willfulness.[75] An important matter to note here is that the statute covers *any* tax. Therefore, one can be convicted under §7201 for attempted evasion of *another's* taxes.

2. *Willful Failure to File and Failure to Pay.* Section 7203, a misdemeanor provision, provides:

   Any person required under this title to pay any estimated tax or tax, or required by this title or by regulations made under authority thereof to make a return, keep any records, or supply any information, who willfully fails to pay such estimated tax or tax, make such return, keep such records, or supply such information, at any time or times required by law or regulations, shall, in addition to other penalties provided by law, be guilty of a misdemeanor and, upon conviction thereof, shall be fined not more than $25,000 ($100,000 in the case of a corporation), or imprisoned not more than one year, or both, together with the cost of prosecution.

3. *Subscribing to a False Return, and Aiding and Abetting.*

Section 7206, a felony provision, is violated by, among other things, any person who "[W]illfully makes and subscribes any return, statement or other document. . ., under the penalties of perjury. . ., which he does not believe to be true and correct as to every material matter."[76] It also includes any person who "[W]illfully aids or assists in, or procures, counsels, or advises the preparation or presentation under, or in connection with any matter arising under, the

Internal Revenue Laws, of a return, affidavit, claim, or other document, which is fraudulent or is false as to any material matter," notwithstanding whether the person actually required to file the document knows or consents to the fraud or falsehood.[77] The maximum fine is $250,000 ($500,000 in the case of a corporation), or three years' imprisonment, or both, plus costs.

4. *Submitting a False Document.*

A maximum fine of $10,000 ($50,000 for a corporation) and imprisonment for up to one year, or both, plus costs, is imposed under §7207. This is a misdemeanor provision and applies to any person "who willfully delivers or discloses to the Secretary [of the Treasury] of any list, return, account, statement, or other document...known by him to be fraudulent or to be false as to any material matter."

5. *Statute of Limitations.*

Section 6531 provides that an indictment must be brought within six years of the commission of the offense for most tax crimes, including those set forth above and conspiracy to evade or defeat any tax.

6. *Conspiracy.*

Title 18, U.S.C. §371 provides that if two or more persons conspire either to commit any offense against the United States, or to defraud the United States, or any agency thereof, in any manner or for any purpose, and one or more of such persons do any act to effect the object of the conspiracy, then each individual faces the maximum fine, or imprisonment, or both; however, if the effect of the conspiracy is a misdemeanor, then the punishment for the conspiracy cannot exceed that for the misdemeanor itself.

The elements of the offense that the government must prove beyond a reasonable doubt are: (a) an agreement between two or more persons to commit an offense or defraud the government, and (b) an overt act in furtherance of the agreement. The act in furtherance of the conspiracy need be commitment by only one of the conspirators, and the act need not be itself illegal.[78]

This conspiracy statute, along with the §7206(2) charge of aiding and assisting in the preparation of false returns, is among the government's most used tools in prosecuting attorneys, accountants, and other tax advisors who may have been involved in the activities of a targeted taxpayer.[79]

The government is clearly targeting tax professionals for prosecution much more than in the past. This targeting also seems to be spilling over to museums, and logically then to dealers, librarians, and libraries that assist the taxpayer in overvaluing false documents.

The general limitation for prosecution under Title 18, U.S.C., the federal criminal code, is five years after the commission of the offense; however, some cases apply the §6531(a) six-year limitation for conspiracy to evade or defeat any tax as applicable to any tax conspiracy charge.

7. *False Statement to Government Agent.*

Once a matter goes bad it seems to go terribly bad, and the librarian who finds that he or she has received false documents as a donation had better play it very straight with the examining IRS agent. Indeed, Title 18, U.S.C. §1001 provides for the maximum fines and imprisonment for a person who "knowingly and willfully falsifies, conceals, or covers up by any trick, scheme, or device a material fact or makes any false, fictitious or fraudulent statements or representations, or makes or uses any false writing or document knowing the same to contain any false, fictitious or fraudulent statement or entry." This provision is often used to prosecute persons who submit false information to IRS agents and officers in the course of their tax investigations. There is no question that a statement made to an IRS agent conducting a tax investigation constitutes a matter within the scope of this statute.[80]

8. *Perjury.*

Under Title 18, U.S.C. §1621, perjury occurs when one willfully states or subscribes to a material matter of fact not believed by him or her to be true, after having sworn under oath to be truthful. This also would be included in the filing of a false tax return subscribed under penalties of perjury, and hence can overlap the similar scope of §7206(1).

9. *Aiding and Abetting.*

Under Title 18, U.S.C. §2, whoever "aids, abets, counsels, commands, induces, or procures" the commission of a crime, or "causes" its commission by another is as guilty as the principal committer of the crime. This general statute is applied to tax crimes.[81]

Case Study

To illustrate how these rules might apply in the case of forged documents, let us look at the following hypothetical facts: Dealer D sells a rare document to Collector C for $5,000. Collector C, after enjoying the document in his collection for a number of years, decides to contribute it to Library L during 1987. He hires Appraiser A, a qualified appraiser, who determines that the document's fair market value is then $25,000. In April 1988 Collector C files his 1987 Federal income tax return, deducting $25,000 for the gift. He attaches the required Form 8283 and gives a copy to Library L. In late 1988, Bookseller B examines the document in the library and declares that it is a forgery. Much to everyone's consternation, the document is indeed a forgery.

To complicate the human element of this example, let us say Collector C is a major contributor of Library L, and is someone who has promised the library a huge endowment in the future. Collector C declares that he has confidence in the authenticity of the document and would greatly resent Library L's taking a contrary position.

Here are at least some of the alternatives for Library L:

a. Return the document. The disposition within two years will have to be reported to the service on Form 8282. This also will put Collector C's tax advisors in a quandary over whether or not to amend his return. Collector C can be expected not to be pleased.

b. Give the document to another institution. The disposition within two years will have to be reported on Form 8282. It will also raise the issue of whether the property is used for Library L's charitable purpose, thus at least knocking out Collector C's deduction for the $20,000 of purported appreciation in value.

c. Sell the document. Again, this would have to be reported. A low sales price would raise a red flag as to the value of Collector C's gift.

d. Keep the document and say nothing. This raises serious ethical questions, as well as possibly reflecting on the quality and authenticity of the remainder of Library L's collections.

None of these is a very comfortable choice. As an attorney, I would recommend to the librarian involved that all of the relevant facts be assembled promptly and that the matter be presented to the governing board. The board must then live up to its fiduciary duty and resist the temptation to accommodate Collector C. The attorney to the board might recommend immediately informing Collector C and Appraiser A, suggesting that Collector C might want to obtain and contribute the genuine document. Collector C's tax counsel will be faced with the dilemma of whether or not Collector C should file an amended return. The deductible amount is the fair market value of the gift. By definition, that assumes that both buyer and seller are aware of all relevant facts, including the genuineness of the document. Erroneously perceived facts at the time of the gift are not relevant. Notwithstanding a good faith appraisal at that time, subsequently disclosed facts which prove the true value affect the amount of the deduction.

The passive approach to the problem (i.e., not doing anything), is indeed tempting. One tends to believe that once swept under the rug the matter will stay there—at least until the IRS agent knocks on the door. At that time any prior hesitation can complicate the lives of the individuals involved.

For example, the Internal Revenue Service, reading the March 1989 issue of *Texas Monthly* and other periodicals, learns that there has been an epidemic of donations of forged documents to libraries, and an agent is sent out to investigate. He contacts the library and asks the rare books librarian, "Do you have any documents which have been given to you and which you reasonably believe may be forgeries?" At that point *any* effort to assist Collector C by lying or even being evasive may result in the librarian and Collector C becoming prison roommates! If the librarian lies to the agent, he or she could be criminally prosecuted for giving a false statement. If he or she lies under oath, the crime gets worse, involving huge fines and also imprisonment. If the library has been part of a scheme to encourage gifts through unrealistic valuations by big backer, Collector C, the library could lose its tax exemption. The IRS is not bashful about going after the organization where there are perceived abuses of the exempt status, e.g. the recent attack on the exemptions of those churches and schools sponsored by the more notorious television evangelists.

Once the agent and his supervisors become convinced that there is a pattern of abuses through cozy arrangements among the collector, the dealer, the appraiser and the recipient, everyone involved could be the subject of civil examinations and criminal investigations.

Very few people involved in the field of rare books and documents are the type who seek notoriety—especially not *this* type of notoriety.

Where an organization has established sound policies and procedures for dealing with potential problems, it will be able to act promptly and forthrightly when irregularities are perceived, and the horror story set forth immediately above can remain a fiction.

References

1. Much of this paper is based on the excellent work of Messrs. Elliott, Schneider, and Weizmann in 281-2d T.M., *Charitable Contributions-General Rules*.
2. Unless otherwise indicated, all section references are either to the Internal Revenue Code of 1986, as amended, or to U.S. Treasury Regulations.
3. §§2055 and 2106(a)(2).
4. §2522.
5. §2642(a)(2).
6. *Toole v. Tomlinson*, 63 U.S.T.C. ¶ 9267 (M.D. Fla. 1963).
7. *Commr. v. Duberstein*, 363 U.S. 278 (1960).
8. *DeJong v. Commr.*, 36 T.C. 896, 899 (1961), aff'd, 309 F.2d 373 (9th Cir. 1962).
9. Rev. Rul. 67-246, 1967-2 C.B. 104.
10. §170(c)(2)(B).
11. The Tax Reform Act of 1969 imposed limitations on deductions for partial interests in property not in trust, gifts of income interests from property in trust and gifts of remainder interests in property in trust. These are not usually applicable in a typical gift of books and documents and are therefore beyond the scope of this paper.
12. Reg. §1.170A-4(c)(2)(ii).
13. If the document is subject to indebtedness, the amount of the indebtedness is treated as an amount paid for the document, whether or not the library agrees to assume or pay the indebtedness.
14. §170(a)(1).
15. §170(a)(2).
16. Reg. §1.170A-1(a)(1).
17. Rev. Rul. 55-410, 1955-1 C.B. 297.
18. §170(a)(3).
19. Reg. §170A-5(a)(4).
20. Reg. §1.170A-1(c)(1).
21. Reg. §1.170A-1(c)(2).
22. 1980-1 C.B. 55.
23. 1980-2 C.B. 69.
24. 1980-2 C.B. 70.
25. 88-2 U.S.T.C. ¶ 9501 (Cl. Ct. 1988).
26. 513 F.2d 224 (7th Cir. 1975), cert. denied, 423 U.S. 912.
27. 1970-2 C.B. 6.
28. *Holcombe v. Commr.*, 73 T.C. 104 (1979).
29. *See* Rev. Rul. 55-138, 1955-1 C.B. 223.
30. *See* Rev. Rul. 60-370, 1960-2 C.B. 203.
31. Reg. §170A-4(b)(1).
32. *Id.*
33. *Id.*
34. Regs. §§1.170A-4(b) and 1211(3).
35. *Id.*
36. *Id.*

37. For example, §306 stock. *See* Reg. §170A-4(b)(1) and Rev. Rul. 80-33, 1980-1 C.B. 69.
38. 1979-2 C.B. 105.
39. *Id.*
40. Rev. Rul. 79-419, 1979-2 C.B. 107.
41. §170(e)(3).
42. Reg. §1.170A-(c)(1).
43. §170(e)(B)(i).
44. *See* Reg. §1.170A-4(b)(3)(i).
45. Reg. §1.170A-4(b)(3)(ii).
46. §170(e)(1)(B).
47. §170(e)(5).
48. §170(b)(1)(C).
49. §170(b)(1)(C)(iii).
50. §170(b)(1)(D).
51. 80 T.C. 872 (1983), aff'd, 85-1 U.S.T.C. ¶ 9331 (11th Cir. 1985).
52. T.D. 8199, 53 Fed. Reg. 16076 (May 5, 1988).
53. *See* Reg. §1.170A-13(c)(2)(ii).
54. Reg. §1.170A-13(c)(3)(i)(A).
55. Reg. §1.170A-13(c)(3).
56. 1984 Act §155(a)(5).
57. Reg. §1.170A-13(c)(5).
58. *See* Reg. §1.170A-13(c)(6).
59. IRS Valuation Guide, ¶ 42(16)4.1 (11-6-84).
60. IRS Valuation Guide, ¶ 42(16)5.2 (5-14-82).
61. IRS Valuation Guide, ¶ 42(16)4.2 (11-19-82).
62. §6050L.
63. §6721(a) and §6724.
64. Reg. §1.6050L-1(a)(2)(i).
65. Reg. §1.6050L-1(a)(3).
66. §6659.
67. *Id.*
68. §155(c)(1)(B).
69. §6601(e)(2).
70. §6653(a).
71. §6653(b).
72. §6661.
73. §§7201-7241. A very good detailed discussion of the substantive elements of tax-related crimes is contained in the Criminal Tax Manual, a looseleaf publication of the Tax Division of the Department of Justice.
74. The Criminal Fine Enforcement Act of 1984 set the maximum fines at $250,000 for individuals and $500,000 for corporations for all felonies, for offenses committed after December 31, 1984. The law increased the maximum fine for a misdemeanor committed after December 31, 1984, to $100,000 for both individuals and corporations. *See* 18 U.S.C. §3623. All of the penalties mentioned in this part of the discussion should be read in that context.

75. *Sansone v. U.S.*, 380 U.S. 343, 351 (1965).
76. §7206(1).
77. §7206(2).
78. *Yates vs. U.S.*, 354 U.S. 298 (1957).
79. *See* Sheldon M. Sisson. "The Sandman Cometh: Conspiracy Prosecutions and Tax Practitioners." *Tax Lawyer* 31 (1978): 805.
80. *See U.S. v. Rogers*, 466 U.S. 475 (1984).
81. *U.S. vs. Myrph*, 707 F.2d 895 (6th Cir. 1983), cert. denied (1983).

Appendix I

Department of the Treasury
Internal Revenue Service

Instructions for Form 8283
(Revised March 1990)
Noncash Charitable Contributions
(Section references are to the Internal Revenue Code, unless otherwise noted.)

General Instructions
Paperwork Reduction Act Notice
We ask for this information to carry out the Internal Revenue laws of the United States. We need it to ensure that taxpayers are complying with these laws and to allow us to figure and collect the right amount of tax. You are required to give us this information.

The time needed to complete and file this form will vary depending on individual circumstances. The estimated average time is:

Recordkeeping	20 min.
Learning about the law or the form	26 min.
Preparing the form	35 min.
Copying, assembling, and sending the form to IRS	35 min.

If you have comments concerning the accuracy of these time estimates or suggestions for making this form more simple, we would be happy to hear from you. You can write to either IRS or the Office of Management and Budget at the addresses listed in the instructions of the tax return with which this form is filed.

Purpose
Use Form 8283 to report certain required information about noncash charitable contributions. Do not report on Form 8283 out-of-pocket expenses for volunteer work or amounts you gave by check or credit card. Treat these items as cash contributions.

Additional Information
Do not use this form to figure your charitable contribution deduction. For information on computing the amount of the deduction, see your tax return instructions. You may also want to get **Pub. 526,** Charitable Contributions (for individuals), and **Pub. 561,** Determining the Value of Donated Property. If you contribute depreciable property, get **Pub. 544,** Sales and Other Dispositions of Assets.

Who Must File
You must file Form 8283 if the amount of your deduction for all noncash gifts is more than $500. (For this purpose, "amount of your deduction" means your deduction BEFORE applying any income limitations that could result in a carryover. The carryover rules are explained in Pub. 526.)

If you must complete Form 8283, you may need to complete Section A, Section B, or both, depending on the type of property and the amount claimed as a deduction. See **Which Sections To Complete.**

Form 8283 is filed only by:
- Individuals
- Partnerships
- S corporations
- Closely held corporations
- Personal service corporations
- Other C corporations

Note: *C corporations, other than personal service corporations and closely held corporations, must file Form 8283 only if the amount claimed as a deduction is over $5,000 and the property was donated after June 6, 1988.*

Reductions to Fair Market Value (FMV).—
Make any required reductions to FMV before you determine if you must file Form 8283. Attach a computation to your tax return showing the reduction. The amount of the reduction (if any) depends on whether the property is ordinary income property or capital gain property. See the FMV discussion below.

When To File
File Form 8283 with your tax return for the tax year you contribute the property and first claim a deduction.

Fair Market Value (FMV)
Although the **amount** of your deduction determines if you have to file Form 8283, you also need to have information about the **value** of your contribution to complete the form.

Fair market value (FMV) is the price a willing buyer would pay a willing seller when neither has to buy or sell, and both are aware of the sale conditions.

You may not always be able to deduct the FMV of your contribution. Depending on the type of property donated, you may have to reduce the FMV to get to the deductible amount, as explained below.

Ordinary income property is property that would result in ordinary income or short-term capital gain if it were sold on the date it was contributed. Examples of ordinary income property are inventory, works of art created by the donor, and capital assets held for 1 year or less (6 months or less if acquired before January 1, 1988). The deduction for a gift of ordinary income property is limited to the FMV less the amount that would be ordinary income or short-term capital gain if the property were sold at its FMV.

Capital gain property is property that would result in long-term capital gain if it were sold at its FMV on the date it was contributed. It includes certain real property and depreciable property used in your trade or business, and generally held for more than 1 year (more than 6 months if acquired before January 1, 1988). You usually may deduct gifts of capital gain property at their FMV. However, you must reduce the FMV by the amount of the appreciation if:
- the capital gain property is contributed to certain private nonoperating foundations;
- you choose the 50% limit instead of the special 30% limit; or
- the contributed property is tangible personal property that is put to an unrelated use by the charity.

Qualified Conservation Contribution.—If your donation qualifies as a "qualified conservation contribution" under section 170(h), attach a statement that shows the claimed FMV of the underlying property before and after the gift and the conservation purpose furthered by the gift.

Which Sections To Complete
Section A
Include in Section A only items (or groups of similar items as defined on page 2) for which you claimed a deduction of $5,000 or less per item

(or group of similar items). Also include certain publicly traded securities even if the deduction exceeds $5,000.

The publicly traded securities you should report in Section A even if the deduction claimed exceeds $5,000 are:

1. Securities listed on an exchange in which quotations are published daily;

2. Securities regularly traded in national or regional over-the-counter markets for which published quotations are available; or

3. Securities that are shares of a mutual fund for which quotations are published on a daily basis in a newspaper of general circulation throughout the United States.

Section B

Include in Section B only items (or groups of similar items) for which you claimed a deduction of more than $5,000 (except for certain publicly traded securities reportable in Section A).

Similar Items of Property

Similar items of property are items of the same generic category or type, such as stamp collections, coin collections, lithographs, paintings, books, nonpublicly traded stock, land, or buildings.

Example. *You claimed a deduction of $400 for clothing, $7,000 for publicly traded securities (quotations published daily), and $6,000 for a collection of 15 books ($400 for each book). Report the clothing and the securities in Section A and the books (a group of similar items) in Section B.*

With certain exceptions, items reported in Section B will require information based on a written appraisal by a qualified appraiser.

Special Rule for Contributions of Inventory and Scientific Equipment by Certain C Corporations

A special rule applies for deductions taken by C corporations under section 170(e)(3) or (4) for contributions of inventory or scientific equipment. To determine if you must file Form 8283, or which section to complete, take into account only the amount claimed as a deduction in excess of the amount you would have deducted as cost of goods sold (COGS) had you sold the property instead. This rule is **only** for purposes of Form 8283. It does not change the amount or method of computing your contribution deduction.

You must attach a statement to your tax return (similar to the one in the example below) if, because of this rule,

Page 2

you do not have to file Form 8283. Also attach a statement if, because of this rule, you must complete Section A instead of Section B.

Example. *You donated clothing from your inventory for the care of the needy. The clothing cost you $5,000 and your claimed charitable deduction is $8,000. Complete Section A instead of Section B since the excess of the deduction over what would have been your COGS deduction is $3,000 ($8,000 –$5,000). Attach a statement to Form 8283 similar to the following:*

Form 8283—Inventory

$8,000	contribution deduction
–$5,000	COGS (if sold, not donated)
=$3,000	for Form 8283 filing purposes.

Specific Instructions

Identification Number

Donors who are individuals must enter their social security number. All other donors should enter their employer identification number.

Partnerships and S Corporations

A partnership (S corporation) that claims a contribution deduction of over $500 must file Form 8283 with Form 1065 (1120S). If the total deduction of any item or group of similar items exceeds $5,000, the partnership (S corporation) must complete Section B of Form 8283 even if the amount allocated to each partner (shareholder) does not exceed $5,000.

The partnership (S corporation) must give a completed copy of Form 8283 to each partner (shareholder) who receives an allocation of the contribution deduction shown in Section B of the partnership's (S corporation's) Form 8283.

Partners and Shareholders

The partnership (S corporation) will provide information about your share of the contribution on your Schedule K-1 (Form 1065 or Form 1120S).

In some cases, the partnership (S corporation) must give you a copy of its Form 8283. In these cases, attach a copy of the Form 8283 you received to your tax return. Deduct the amount shown on your Schedule K-1, not the amount shown on the Form 8283.

If the partnership (S corporation) is not required to give you a copy of its Form 8283, combine the amount of noncash contributions shown on your Schedule K-1 with your noncash contributions to see if you must file Form 8283. If you need to file Form 8283, you do not have to complete all the information requested in Section A for your share of the partnership's (S corporation's) contributions. Do not complete line 1, columns (a)–(f) and (h). Instead, write "From Schedule K-1 (Form 1065 or 1120S)" across columns (c)–(f). Enter your share of the contribution on line 1, column (g).

Section A

Part I, Information on Donated Property

Line 1

Column (b).—Describe the property in sufficient detail. The greater the value, the more detail is needed. For example, a car should be described in more detail than pots and pans.

For securities, include the following:

• name of the issuer,

• kind of security,

• whether it is regularly traded on a stock exchange or in an over-the-counter market, and

• whether it is a share of a mutual fund.

Note: *Columns (d), (e), and (f) do not have to be completed if the amount you claimed as a deduction for the item is $500 or less.*

Column (d).—Enter the approximate date you acquired the property. If it was created, produced, or manufactured by or for you, enter the date it was substantially completed.

Column (e).—State how you acquired the property (i.e., by purchase, gift, inheritance, or exchange).

Column (f).—Do not complete for:

• Publicly traded securities; or

• Property held 12 months or more (6 months or more if donated in tax years beginning before June 7, 1988).

Keep records on cost or other basis.

Note: *If you have reasonable cause for not providing the acquisition date in column (d), or the cost basis when required in column (f), attach an explanation.*

Column (g).—Enter the fair market value (FMV) of the property on the date you gave it. If you were required to reduce the FMV of your deduction, or if you gave a qualified conservation contribution, you must attach a statement. FMV, reductions to FMV, and the type of statement you may have to attach are explained on page 1.

Column (h).—Enter the method(s) used to determine the FMV of your donation. FMV of used household goods and clothing is usually much lower than when new. For this reason, standard formulas or methods to value this kind of property are generally not appropriate.

A good measure of value might be the price that buyers of these used items actually pay in consignment or thrift shops.

Examples of entries to make include "Appraisal," "Thrift shop value" (for clothing or household goods), "Catalog" (for stamp or coin collections), or "Comparable sales" (for real estate and other kinds of assets). See Pub. 561.

Part II, Other Information

Attach a separate statement if Part II applies to more than one property. Give the required information for each property separately. Identify which property listed in Part I the information relates to.

Lines 2a–2e

Complete lines 2a–2e only if you contributed less than the entire interest in the donated property during the tax year. Enter on line 2b the amount claimed as a deduction for this year and in any earlier tax years for gifts of a partial interest in the same property. If the organization that received the prior interest in the property is the same as the one listed on line 1, column (a), do not complete line 2c.

Lines 3a–3c

Complete lines 3a–3c only if you attached restrictions to the right to the income, use, or disposition of the donated property. Attach a statement explaining:

- The terms of any agreement or understanding regarding the restriction; and
- Whether the property is designated for a particular use.

An example of a "restricted use" is furniture that you gave only to be used in the reading room of an organization's library.

Section B

Note: *Section B was revised after the 1989 Pub. 526 and Pub. 561 were printed. Therefore, the references in those publications to the various parts of Section B are incorrect. Also, the rules regarding the submission of photographs for art valued at $20,000 or more were changed after the 1989 Pub. 561 was printed. The new rules are discussed under* **Art Valued at $20,000 or More** *in the instructions for Part I below.*

Part I, Information on Donated Property

You must have a written appraisal from a qualified appraiser that supports the information in Part I. However, see the **Exception** below.

Use Part I to summarize your appraisal(s). Generally, you do not need to attach the appraisals, but you should keep them for your records. But, see **Art Valued at $20,000 or More** below.

Exception.—You do not need a written appraisal if the property is:

1. Nonpublicly traded stock of $10,000 or less;
2. Securities for which market quotations are readily available (see Regulations section 1.170A-13(c)(7)(xi));
3. Property donated by C corporations (other than closely held corporations or personal service corporations) after June 6, 1988; or
4. Inventory and other property donated by closely held corporations and personal service corporations after November 9, 1988, which are "qualified contributions" for the care of the ill, the needy, or infants within the meaning of section 170(e)(3)(A).

Although a written appraisal is not required for the types of property listed above, you must provide certain information in Part I of Section B (see Regulations section 1.170A-13(c)(4)(iv)) and have the donee organization complete Part IV.

Art Valued at $20,000 or More.—If your total deduction for art donated after 1987 is $20,000 or more, you must attach a complete copy of the signed appraisal. For individual objects valued at $20,000 or more, a photograph of a size and quality fully showing the object, preferably an 8 × 10 inch color photograph or a color transparency no smaller than 4 × 5 inches, must be provided upon request.

Appraisal Requirements

The appraisal must be made not earlier than 60 days before the date you contribute the property. You must receive it before the due date (including extensions) of the return on which you first claim a deduction for the property. For a deduction first claimed on an amended return, the appraisal must be received before the date the amended return was filed.

A separate qualified appraisal and a separate Form 8283 are required for each item of property except for an item which is part of a group of similar items. Only one appraisal is required for a group of similar items contributed in the same tax year, if it includes all the required information for each item.

The appraiser may select any items whose aggregate value is appraised at $100 or less for which a group description rather than a specific description of each item will suffice.

If you gave similar items to more than one donee for which you claimed a deduction of more than $5,000, you must attach a separate form for each donee.

Example. *You claimed a deduction of $2,000 for books given to College A, $2,500 for books given to College B,* and $900 for books given to a public library. You must attach a separate Form 8283 for each donee.

See Regulations section 1.170A-13(c)(3)(i)–(ii) for the definition of a "qualified appraisal" and information to be included in the appraisal.

Line 2

Note: *You* **must** *complete at least column (a) of line 2 (also column (b) if applicable) before submitting Form 8283 to the donee. You may then complete the remaining columns.*

Column (a).—Describe the property in enough detail so that a person not familiar with it could tell that the property appraised is the property that was contributed.

Column (c).—Include the FMV from the appraisal. If one was not required, include the FMV you determine to be correct.

Columns (d)–(f).—If you have reasonable cause for not providing the information asked for in any of these columns, attach an explanation so that your deduction won't be automatically disallowed.

Column (g).—A bargain sale is a transfer of property which is in part a sale or exchange, and in part a contribution. Enter the amount received ("consideration") for bargain sales after June 6, 1988.

Column (h).—Complete column (h) only if you were not required to get an appraisal, as explained earlier.

Column (i).—Complete column (i) only if you donated securities for which market quotations are considered to be readily available because the issue satisfies the 5 requirements described in Regulations section 1.170A-13(c)(7)(xi)(B).

Part II, Taxpayer (Donor) Statement

If you (the donor) complete Part II, the donee is relieved of filing Form 8282 for items valued at $500 or less. (See the **Note** in the Part IV instructions on page 4 for more information on the filing of Form 8282 by the donee.)

Complete Part II only for items included in Part I that have an appraised value of $500 or less per item. Be sure to clearly identify these items in Part II. This is necessary because the donee may not know the value of the donated property, since you are not required to show it in Part I on the donee's copy of Form 8283.

The amount of information you give in Part II depends on the description of the donated property you enter in Part I. If you separately show a single item as "Property A" in Part I, and that item

Page 3

is appraised at $500 or less, then the entry "Property A" in Part II is enough. However, if "Property A" consists of several items and the total appraised value is over $500, list in Part II any item(s) you gave that is (are) valued at $500 or less.

All shares of nonpublicly traded stock, or items in a set, are considered one item. For example, a book collection by the same author, components of a stereo system, or six place settings of a pattern of silverware are one item for the $500 test.

Example. *You donated books valued at $6,000. The appraisal states that one of the items, a collection of books by author "X" is worth $400. On the Form 8283 that you are required to give the donee, you decide not to show the appraised value of all of the books. But you also don't want the donee to have to file Form 8282 if the collection of books is sold. If on line 2 of Part I your description of Property A includes all the books, then specify in Part II the "collection of books by X included in Property A." But if in Part I your Property A description is "collection of books by X," the only required entry in Part II is "Property A."*

In the above example you may have instead chosen to give a completed copy of Form 8283 to the donee. The donee would then be aware of the value. If in Part I you include all the books as Property A, and thus enter $6,000 in column (c), you may still want to describe the specific collection in Part II so the donee can sell it without filing Form 8282.

Part III, Certification of Appraiser

If you had to get an appraisal, the appraiser MUST complete Part III to be considered qualified. See Regulations section 1.170A-13(c)(5) for a definition of a qualified appraiser.

Persons who cannot be qualified appraisers are listed in the Certification of Appraiser (Part III) of Form 8283. Usually, a party to the transaction will not qualify to sign the certification. But a person who sold, exchanged, or gave the property to the donor may sign the certification if the property is donated within 2 months of the date the donor acquired it and the property's appraised value does not exceed its acquisition price.

An appraiser may not be considered qualified if the donor had knowledge of facts that would cause a reasonable person to expect the appraiser to falsely overstate the value of the property. An example of this is an agreement between you and the appraiser about the property value when you know that the agreed amount exceeds the actual FMV.

Usually, appraisal fees cannot be based on a percentage of the appraised value unless the fees were paid to certain not-for-profit associations. See Regulations section 1.170A-13(c)(6)(ii).

Part IV, Donee Acknowledgment

The donee organization must complete Part IV. Before submitting page 2 of Form 8283 to the donee for acknowledgment, complete at least your name, identification number, and description of the donated property (line 2, column (a)). If tangible property is donated, also describe its physical condition (line 2, column (b)) at the time of the gift. Complete the Taxpayer (Donor) Statement in Part II, if applicable, before submitting the form to the donee. See the instructions for Part II.

The person acknowledging the gift must be an official authorized to sign the tax returns of the organization, or a person specifically designated to sign Form 8283. After completing Part IV, the organization must return Form 8283 to you, the donor. A copy of Section B of this form must be provided to the donee organization. You may then complete any remaining information required in Part I. Also, Part III may be completed at this time by the qualified appraiser.

In rare and unusual circumstances, it may be impossible to get the donee's signature on the appraisal summary. The deduction will not be disallowed for that reason if you attach a detailed explanation why it was impossible.

Note: *If the donee (or a successor donee) organization disposes of the property within 2 years after the date the original donee received it, the organization must file* **Form 8282**, *Donee Information Return, with IRS and send a copy to the donor. An exception applies to items having a value of $500 or less if the donor identified the items and signed the statement in Part II (Section B) of Form 8283. See the instructions for Part II.*

Failure To File Form 8283, Section B

If you donate property required to be reported in Section B and you fail to attach the form to your return, the deduction will be disallowed unless your failure was due to a good faith omission. If IRS asks you to submit the form, you have 90 days to send a completed Section B of Form 8283 before your deduction is disallowed.

☉ U.S. Government Printing Office: 1990-262-'51/00082

Form **8283**
(Rev. March 1990)
Department of the Treasury
Internal Revenue Service

Noncash Charitable Contributions

▶ Attach to your tax return if the total claimed deduction for all property contributed exceeds $500.
▶ See separate Instructions.

OMB No. 1545-0908
Expires 2-28-93

Attachment Sequence No. **55**

Name(s) shown on your income tax return | Identification number

Note: *Compute the amount of your contribution deduction before completing Form 8283. (See your tax return instructions.)*

Section A — Include in Section A **only** items (or groups of similar items) for which you claimed a deduction of $5,000 or less per item or group, and certain publicly traded securities (see Instructions)

Part I — Information on Donated Property

1	(a) Name and address of the donee organization	(b) Description of donated property (attach a separate sheet if more space is needed)
A		
B		
C		
D		
E		

Note: *If the amount you claimed as a deduction for the item is $500 or less, you do not have to complete columns (d), (e), and (f).*

	(c) Date of the contribution	(d) Date acquired by donor (mo., yr.)	(e) How acquired by donor	(f) Donor's cost or adjusted basis	(g) Fair market value	(h) Method used to determine the fair market value
A						
B						
C						
D						
E						

Part II — Other Information
If you gave less than an entire interest in property listed in Part I, complete lines 2a–2e.
If restrictions were attached to a contribution listed in Part I, complete lines 3a–3c.

2 If less than the entire interest in the property is contributed during the year, complete the following:

   a Enter letter from Part I that identifies the property _____ . (If Part II applies to more than one property, attach a separate statement.)

   b Total amount claimed as a deduction for the property listed in Part I for this tax year _____ ;
for any prior tax year(s) _____

   c Name and address of each organization to which any such contribution was made in a prior year (complete only if different than the donee organization above).

Name of charitable organization (donee)

Address (number and street)

City or town, state, and ZIP code

   d The place where any tangible property is located or kept _____
   e Name of any person, other than the donee organization, having actual possession of the property _____

3 If conditions were attached to any contribution listed in Part I, answer the following questions and attach the required statement (see Instructions): | Yes | No

   a Is there a restriction, either temporary or permanent, on the donee's right to use or dispose of the donated property?

   b Did you give to anyone (other than the donee organization or another organization participating with the donee organization in cooperative fundraising) the right to the income from the donated property or to the possession of the property, including the right to vote donated securities, to acquire the property by purchase or otherwise, or to designate the person having such income, possession, or right to acquire? . . . .

   c Is there a restriction limiting the donated property for a particular use? . . . .

For Paperwork Reduction Act Notice, see separate Instructions.   Form **8283** (Rev. 3-90)

Form 8283 (Rev. 3-90) Page 2

Name(s) shown on your income tax return	Identification number

Section B Appraisal Summary—Include in Section B only items (or groups of similar items) for which you claimed a deduction of more than $5,000 per item or group. *(Report contributions of certain publicly traded securities only in Section A.)*

If you donated art, you may have to attach the complete appraisal. See the **Note** in Part I below.

Part I Information on Donated Property *(To be completed by the taxpayer and/or appraiser.)*

1 Check type of property:
- ☐ Art* (contribution of $20,000 or more)
- ☐ Art* (contribution of less than $20,000)
- ☐ Real Estate
- ☐ Coin Collections
- ☐ Gems/Jewelry
- ☐ Books
- ☐ Stamp Collections
- ☐ Other

*Art includes paintings, sculptures, watercolors, prints, drawings, ceramics, antique furniture, decorative arts, textiles, carpets, silver, rare manuscripts, historical memorabilia, and other similar objects. **Note:** If you donated art after December 31, 1987, and your total art contribution deduction was $20,000 or more, you must attach a complete copy of the signed appraisal. See Instructions.

2

	(a) Description of donated property (attach a separate sheet if more space is needed)	(b) If tangible property was donated, give a brief summary of the overall physical condition at the time of the gift	(c) Appraised fair market value
A			
B			
C			
D			

	(d) Date acquired by donor (mo., yr.)	(e) How acquired by donor	(f) Donor's cost or adjusted basis	(g) For bargain sales after 6/6/88, enter amount received	See Instructions	
					(h) Amount claimed as a deduction	(i) Average trading price of securities
A						
B						
C						
D						

Part II Taxpayer (Donor) Statement—List any item(s) included in Part I above that is (are) separately identified in the appraisal as having a value of $500 or less. See Instructions.

I declare that the following item(s) included in Part I above has (have) to the best of my knowledge and belief an appraised value of not more than $500 (per item). *(Enter identifying letter from Part I and describe the specific item):* _____

Signature of taxpayer (donor) ▶ Date ▶

Part III Certification of Appraiser *(To be completed by the appraiser of the above donated property.)*

I declare that I am not the donor, the donee, a party to the transaction in which the donor acquired the property, employed by, married to, or related to any of the foregoing persons, or an appraiser regularly used by any of the foregoing persons and who does not perform a majority of appraisals during the taxable year for other persons.

Also, I declare that I hold myself out to the public as an appraiser or perform appraisals on a regular basis; and that because of my qualifications as described in the appraisal, I am qualified to make appraisals of the type of property being valued. I certify that the appraisal fees were not based upon a percentage of the appraised property value. Furthermore, I understand that a false or fraudulent overstatement of the property value as described in the qualified appraisal or this appraisal summary may subject me to the civil penalty under section 6701(c) (aiding and abetting the understatement of tax liability). I affirm that I have not been barred from presenting evidence or testimony by the Director of Practice.

Please Sign Here

Signature ▶	Title ▶	Date of appraisal ▶
Business address		Identification number
City or town, state, and ZIP code		

Part IV Donee Acknowledgment *(To be completed by the charitable organization.)*

This charitable organization acknowledges that it is a qualified organization under section 170(c) and that it received the donated property as described in Part I on _____ (Date).

Furthermore, this organization affirms that in the event it sells, exchanges, or otherwise disposes of the property (or any portion thereof) within 2 years after the date of receipt, it will file an information return (**Form 8282**, Donee Information Return) with the IRS and furnish the donor a copy of that return. This acknowledgment does not represent concurrence in the claimed fair market value.

Name of charitable organization (donee)	Employer identification number	
Address (number and street)	City or town, state, and ZIP code	
Authorized signature	Title	Date

☆U.S. Government Printing Office: 1990-262-151/00079

Appendix II

Form **8282** (Rev. March 1990) Department of the Treasury Internal Revenue Service	**Donee Information Return** (Sale, Exchange, or Other Disposition of Donated Property) ▶ See instructions on back.	OMB No. 1545-0908 Expires 2-28-93 **Give Copy to Donor**

Please Print or Type

Name of charitable organization (donee)	Employer identification number
Address (number and street)	
City or town, state, and ZIP code	

Note: *If you are the original donee, DO NOT complete Part II, or column (c) of Part III.*

Part I — Information on ORIGINAL DONOR and DONEE YOU GAVE THE PROPERTY TO

1a Name of the original donor of (first person to give) the property	1b Identification number

Note: *Complete lines 2a–2d only if you gave this property to another charitable organization (successor donee).*

2a Name of charitable organization	2b Identification number (EIN)
2c Address (number and street)	
2d City or town, state, and ZIP code	

Part II — Information on PREVIOUS DONEES—Complete this part only if you were not the first donee to receive the property.
If you were the second donee, leave lines 4a–4d blank. If you were a third or later donee, complete lines 3a–4d. On lines 4a–4d give information on the preceding donee (the one who gave you the gift).

3a Name of original donee	3b Identification number (EIN)
3c Address (number and street)	
3d City or town, state, and ZIP code	
4a Name of preceding donee	4b Identification number (EIN)
4c Address (number and street)	
4d City or town, state, and ZIP code	

Part III — Information on DONATED PROPERTY

(a) Description of donated property sold, exchanged, or otherwise disposed of (attach a separate sheet if more space is needed)	(b) Date you received the item(s)	(c) Date the first donee received the item(s) (if you weren't the first)	(d) Date item(s) sold, exchanged, or otherwise disposed of	(e) Amount received upon disposition

For Paperwork Reduction Act Notice, see instructions on back. Form **8282** (Rev. 3-90)

General Instructions

(Section references are to the Internal Revenue Code.)

Paperwork Reduction Act Notice

We ask for this information to carry out the Internal Revenue laws of the United States. We need it to ensure that taxpayers are complying with these laws and to allow us to figure and collect the right amount of tax.

The time needed to complete this form will vary depending on individual circumstances. The estimated average time is:

Recordkeeping . . . . 3 hrs., 7 min.
Learning about the law
or the form . . . . 30 min.
Preparing and sending
the form to IRS . . . . 34 min.

If you have comments concerning the accuracy of these time estimates or suggestions for making this form more simple, we would be happy to hear from you. You can write to the **Internal Revenue Service,** Washington, DC 20224, Attention: IRS Reports Clearance Officer, T:FP; or the **Office of Management and Budget,** Paperwork Reduction Project (1545-0908), Washington, DC 20503.

Purpose

Donee organizations use Form 8282 to report information to the Internal Revenue Service about dispositions of certain charitable deduction property made within 2 years after the donor contributed the property.

Definitions

Note: *For purposes of Form 8282 and instructions, the term "donee" includes all donees, unless specific reference is made to "original" or "successor" donees.*

Original Donee.—The first donee to or for which the donor gave the property. The original donee is required to sign an appraisal summary presented by the donor for charitable deduction property.

Appraisal Summary.—Section B of **Form 8283,** Noncash Charitable Contributions.

Successor Donee.—Any donee of property other than the original donee.

Charitable Deduction Property.—Property (other than money or certain publicly traded securities) contributed after 1984 for which the original donee signed, or was presented with for signature, an appraisal summary on Form 8283.

Generally, only items or groups of similar items for which the donor claimed a deduction of more than $5,000 are included on an appraisal summary. There is an exception if a donor gives similar items to more than one donee organization and the total deducted for these similar items exceeds $5,000. For example, if a donor deducts $2,000 for books given to a donee organization and $4,000 for books to another donee organization, the donor must present a separate appraisal summary to each organization. For more information, see the Instructions for Form 8283.

Who Must File

Form 8282 must be filed by original and successor donee organizations who sell, exchange, consume, or otherwise dispose of (with or without consideration) charitable deduction property within 2 years after the date the original donee received the property. For successor donees, the form must be filed only for property transferred by the original donee after July 5, 1988.

Exceptions.—There are two situations where Form 8282 does not have to be filed.

1. Items valued at $500 or less.—You do not have to file Form 8282 if, at the time the original donee signed the appraisal summary, the donor had signed a statement on Form 8283 that the appraised value of the specific item was not more than $500. If Form 8283 contains more than one similar item, this exception applies only to those items that are clearly identified as having a value of $500 or less. However, for purposes of the donor's determination of whether the appraised value of the item exceeds $500, all shares of nonpublicly traded stock, or items that form a set, are considered one item. For example, a collection of books written by the same author, components of a stereo system, or six place settings of a pattern of silverware, are considered one item.

2. Items consumed or distributed for charitable purpose.—You do not have to file Form 8282 if an item is consumed or distributed without consideration. The consumption or distribution must be in furtherance of your purpose or function as a tax-exempt organization. For example, no reporting is required for medical supplies consumed or distributed by a tax-exempt relief organization in aiding disaster victims.

When To File

If you dispose of charitable deduction property within 2 years of the date the original donee received it and you do not meet exception **1** or **2** above, you must file Form 8282 within 125 days after the date of disposition.

Exception: *If you did not file because you had no reason to believe the substantiation requirements applied to the donor, but you later became aware that they did apply, file Form 8282 within 60 days after the date you became aware you are liable.*

The above exception would apply if you were never given an appraisal summary, and it was reasonable to believe that the property you received was worth $5,000 or less.

Missing Information

If Form 8282 is filed by the due date, you must enter your organization's name, address, and EIN and complete at least Part III, column (a). You do not have to complete the remaining items if the information is not available. For example, you may not have the information necessary to complete all entries if the donor's appraisal summary is not available to you.

Where To File

Mail Form 8282 to the Internal Revenue Service Center, Cincinnati, OH 45944.

Penalties

You may be subject to a penalty if you fail to file this form by the due date, fail to include all of the information required to be shown on this form, or fail to include correct information on this form (see Missing Information above). For Forms 8282 required to be filed after 1989 (determined without regard to extensions), the penalty is generally $50 for each such failure. For more details, see sections 6721 and 6723.

Other Requirements

Information You Must Give a Successor Donee.—If the property is transferred to another charitable organization within the 2-year period discussed earlier, you must give your successor donee the following information:

1. The name, address, and EIN of your organization;

2. A copy of the appraisal summary (the Form 8283 that you received from the donor or a preceding donee); and

3. A copy of this Form 8282 within 15 days after you file it.

You must furnish items 1 and 2 within 15 days after the latest of:

• The date you transferred the property,
• The date the original donee signed the appraisal summary, or
• If you are also a successor donee, the date you received a copy of the appraisal summary from the preceding donee.

Note: *The successor donee organization to whom you transferred this property is required to give you their organization's name, address, and EIN within 15 days after the later of:*

• *The date you transferred the property, or*
• *The date they received a copy of the appraisal summary.*

Information You Must Give the Donor.—You must give a copy of your Form 8282 to the donor of the property.

Appraisal Summary.—You must keep a copy of the appraisal summary in your records.

☆U.S. Government Printing Office: 1990-262-151/00081

Legal and Ethical Levels of Responsibility

MARIE C. MALARO

Let me begin by telling a story. It is not pure fiction but is based on an actual situation.

A few years ago, the newspapers in a certain city published a series of articles which questioned the removal of numerous valuable objects from the collection of the state museum. The newspaper reports, which proved to be essentially correct, described the situation as follows.

The state in question is famous for the role it played in the early development and manufacture of firearms. The state museum had acquired an extensive collection of guns recording this history and the collection was nationally and internationally known. The director of the museum was not an expert on guns. Over the years, however, on the advice of an outside consultant, a noted gun dealer, this director arranged for the removal and exchange of several groups of guns from the museum's collection. Most of the disposals were handled by the consultant, who had ingratiated himself by serving in a volunteer capacity at the museum.

Under state law, no objects were to be deaccessioned from the state museum collection without the approval of the State Library Board, which was responsible for the governance of the museum. It appeared that the director was aware of this statute, but there were no established internal procedures for reaching the Board. The director made no secret of what he was doing and he appeared to have no self-serving motives. There were internal documents which described these trading activities. His immediate supervisors were not disturbed by the activity and no Library Board member ever raised a question. It was not until the newspaper stories began (stories prompted by the curiosity of dealers and gun collectors who wondered why certain rare guns were on the market) that state officials started to pay attention. There was an investigation[1] and the museum director was fired.

The director did not go away quietly; instead, as a state employee, he demanded a hearing on his dismissal. Under state procedure, the case was referred to an arbitrator. After a hearing the arbitrator ordered that the director be reinstated on the ground that, from the evidence presented, it must be inferred that the Library Board approved of what had been done.[2] In other words, it was found that the director acted with implied authority. The arbitrator based this conclusion on the following points:

(1) During the investigation of the director's conduct, no Library Board member or supervisor of the director came forward to testify personally on the merits of the case against the director. This failure to testify was interpreted to favor the director.

(2) There were no internal policies which made it clear what procedures were to be followed by museum staff when questions arose concerning the management of the collections. When such procedures are lacking, ordinarily blame cannot be placed on staff.

(3) There were opportunities for Library Board members and other officials to know what was going on and there was no evidence that they ever questioned the director. Only when their own reputations were on the line because of the subsequent publicity was attention paid to the matter.

Meanwhile, the state's Attorney General had been asked to determine whether the state could take any legal action to obtain the return of the guns to the museum or whether the state could obtain money damages to compensate for the loss of the prized objects from the collection.[3] The Attorney General concluded that there was no effective way for the state to seek redress.[4] Among the reasons given were the following:

(1) It would be difficult to prove in court the actual dollar loss to the state because the "value" of an historic object is open to many interpretations. In these particular transactions, no detailed records were created as to why the exchanges were made, how value was determined at the time of exchange, etc.

(2) The guns in question were now scattered all over the country and the cost of legal action to seek their return would be prohibitive.

(3) It would be difficult to prove in court that the director and the volunteer gun consultant acted without authority because no supervisor ever questioned the activity.

(4) It would be difficult to prove in court that the director and the volunteer gun consultant acted contrary to expected standards because there was no articulated code of conduct in place at the museum which addressed the activity in question.

I have taken the time to relate this story because it is a classic. One can point to many other recent incidents where collecting organizations have found themselves embarrassed and frustrated when irregularities come to the attention of the public.[5] Too often these organizations end up burying their heads in the sand, hoping the adverse publicity will die down. And why? Such organizations usually elect silence when they realize that their failure to manage collecting responsibilities aggressively has backed them into indefensible positions. Permit me to elaborate.

Any lawyer who has worked for any period of time with a collecting organization soon realizes that if that organization calls upon its legal advisor only after there is publicity about alleged irregularities, the battle is already all but lost. This is so because the law tells us that collecting organizations have an obligation to take affirmative steps to establish internal collecting policies. If a collecting organization has not done this, it is immediately on the defensive when problems arise. Let us look more closely at what the law appears to say.

Most libraries, universities, museums, and historical societies are classified as nonprofit, educational organizations. They are created in order to serve a public purpose, but typically they are not part of government. They are managed by independent boards of trustees and they make up part of what we sometimes refer to as the "third sector."[6] Historically, those who served on boards of nonprofit organizations were rarely challenged on their quality of governance, but this situation is changing as the public becomes more educated and more affluent and as organizations such as libraries, museums, and historical societies take on a greater importance for the average person. This, quite naturally, creates a greater interest in how well these organizations are run. As a result of this increased interest, we have seen over the last few decades more legal actions questioning the quality of board governance. These cases have been of particular interest to lawyers who advise nonprofits because they raised questions not yet answered by the courts. Our system of justice relies heavily on precedent (i.e. how was an earlier, similar case decided by the court?) but, if there is little or no precedent on a particular issue, a lawyer can make only educated guesses when advising a client on potential liability. Now that we have had a few cases bearing on board governance, it is prudent to analyze them carefully.

One issue of major importance to nonprofits is the rule of thumb courts will apply when judging the conduct of members of nonprofit boards. Will these individuals be judged by the same standard applied to the for-profit (i.e. business) world or will they be judged by a higher standard because of the nature of their quasi-public responsibilities? The standard the law applies to the for-profit world is quite low, as anyone reading the newspaper these days knows. Members of governing boards of for-profit organizations are not held personally liable unless it can be proven that they are guilty of gross negligence or fraud. Gross negligence amounts to all but willful neglect or misconduct so, in reality, board members of business organizations have considerable latitude before they are personally accountable. There are those who argue that the business standard is not appropriate for nonprofit organizations because nonprofit organizations are created to benefit the public, they must maintain high standards of integrity in order to serve the public effectively, and managers of nonprofits are subject to little oversight. For these reasons, many insist that a higher standard of accountability for nonprofit boards is essential in order to encourage faithful attention to duties.[7]

When one reads carefully the series of cases which concern the standard of care imposed on those charged with governing nonprofit organizations, one finds a discernable tendency on the part of both state attorneys general and judges to expect a bit more from board members of nonprofits. While cumulatively these cases do not provide definitive guidance, a cautious interpretation of them suggests the following conclusions:[8]

(1) Trustees of nonprofit organizations have an obligation to establish policy and to use diligence in overseeing the implementation of that policy by staff.

(2) Trustees must be conscious of conflict of interest situations and should establish policies and procedures which prevent instances of real or apparent abuse of power.

(3) Trustees must perform their duties honestly, in good faith, and with a reasonable amount of diligence and care.

If these legal warnings are taken seriously, the board of any collecting organization should have in place policies which govern the acquisition, utilization, care, and disposition of collection material, they should actively promulgate codes of conduct for themselves, staff members, and volunteers, and they should be diligent in exercising oversight. These are not terribly demanding standards. The law does not require that boards always be right; it merely expects that boards will honestly address policy questions and will act in a reasonably prudent manner when issues of consequence arise. If a board has neglected the policymaking role and/or its oversight role, the board itself is vulnerable when any activities of the organization are publicly questioned. As in the story which began this discussion, if there is public inquiry, the board, by virtue of its failure to exercise oversight, may be found to have given implied authority to staff to engage in questionable activity, or investigators could probe more deeply and charge the board itself with avoiding its responsibilities. Faced with these alternatives, a delinquent board usually does nothing of consequence, hoping to avoid at all costs an objective evaluation of the alleged wrongdoing.

Upon closer examination, one can see how careful governance within a collecting organization can inhibit the perpetuation of theft, fraud, or misuse of historic documents. The prudent governing board of a collecting organization has in place policies and procedures which provide guidance on at least the following points:[9]

(1) There is an articulated scope of collecting. No organization can collect everything, so the prudent board sets collecting limits which reflect staff expertise and the capability of the organization to manage the material in a reasonable manner.

(2) Criteria are established for judging the suitability of objects offered, for determining the quality of the provenance of the objects offered, and for judging the ability of the organization to acquire good title.[10]

(3) Standards are set regarding the documentation needed to support an acquisition and the documentation records which are to be maintained.

(4) There are rules regarding the deaccessioning of objects from the collections. These procedures require stringent internal review, outside opinions where appropriate, and complete record keeping.

(5) Guidance is also given on the process used to determine an appropriate method of disposal (by exchange, sale, gift) and appropriate transferees (to other educational organizations, commercial organizations, individuals, etc.).

(6) Standards are set concerning access to collection objects (balancing security and conservation concerns with legitimate public needs), the maintenance of inventory control, and the importance of prompt action when objects appear to be missing, or subject to abuse, or appear to be fakes, or forgeries.[11]

(7) Authority is clearly delegated with regard to who is to make certain decisions concerning collections management and what written records are to be made of their decisions.

(8) A code of conduct is articulated for officials, staff, and volunteers which resonates to current professional ethical codes.[12]

When such policies and procedures are in place, the organization is encouraged to handle matters of consequence in a timely manner. For example, even modest efforts to check the authenticity and adequacy of title of objects offered to the collections can uncover irregularities before the trail turns cold.[13] This was demonstrated in a recent case concerning four sixth century Byzantine mosaics which appeared on the European market and were purchased by an American dealer for resale. When the works were offered to the Getty Museum, a curator, suspecting the mosaics were from Cyprus, inquired of experts from that country. The mosaics were, in fact, national treasures which had been stolen from a Cypriot church. The Cypriot government successfully sued the American dealer in a U.S. court and obtained the return of the mosaics. If dealers and donors know that libraries, museums, and historical societies routinely ask searching questions, regardless of whether an item is a gift or a purchase, more caution will be encouraged all along the line.

The same salutary effects occur when a collecting organization is capable of spotting missing objects in a timely manner and it reports them promptly to the authorities.[14] Recently, the Baltimore Museum of Art recovered missing objects and helped solve a series of museum thefts because it promptly advertised its loss to authorities and dealers. Similarly, the National Archives and the Library of Congress were able to prosecute successfully a theft of historic documents from their collections because they were able to establish the losses and took timely action.[15] Also, advertising a loss of an original made it harder to market fakes drawn from the original. (I might add here that recent cases, described in footnote 11, indicate that collecting organizations which fail to report thefts in a timely manner and fail to keep searching for lost material may be unable to claim their losses after a period of time if the material eventually comes into the possession of good faith purchasers. In other words, the law is beginning to place a burden on those who lose property to search for it if they want to be able to reclaim the property.)

It is recognized that frequently, even after investigation, definitive answers on authenticity and title are not available at the time of acquisition. Assuming the donee organization makes a good faith judgment that it can accept an object of doubtful provenance, there is a continuing scholarly obligation to review periodically relevant evidence as it becomes available. When the organization's policies and procedures encourage such periodic review and establish what actions are to be taken if fraud is then suspected, the chances are infinitely better that constructive steps will be taken.

My message, then, is quite simple — it is that any collecting organization that seriously wants to check theft, forgery, and misuse of historic documents has to start with itself. It has to establish and follow sensible collection management policies and procedures which require the organization to make informed decisions regarding a broad range of collection issues. Collecting organizations are frequently an important link in illegal activity involving historic documents and, if they neglect to use that link consistently and aggressively to impede illegality, they are often powerless to take action when a case really strikes home.

I should caution that if one only takes steps that are required by the law when dealing with possible theft or fraud, not much will change. The law sets the lowest standard. The law is not designed to make us virtuous; its purpose is to prevent us from seriously wronging one another so that we can maintain a fairly stable society. The law also requires that one prove a charge. Accordingly, much questionable conduct escapes the arm of the law.[16]

What prompts us to strive for loftier goals is a personal moral code evidenced by our acceptance of relevant professional codes of ethics.[17] A professional code is rooted in such concepts as service to others and individual accountability. A professional code asks more of us than the law demands and, when an organization seriously promulgates a professional code of ethics, it creates an atmosphere where it is very difficult for theft, fraud, and misrepresentation to go undetected for long. When a collecting organization adopts such a code, and reminds board, staff, and volunteers to read the code at least once a year, instances of board inertia, staff confusion, and unresolved conflicts of interest should be rare.

In summary, if collecting organizations seriously want to do something about theft, fraud, and misrepresentation of valuable historic materials, they must:

(1) Establish in advance strict internal policies and procedures governing the acquisition, use, and disposal of collection objects;

(2) Delegate responsibility clearly and insist on complete and accurate record keeping;

(3) Promulgate for governing boards, staff, and volunteers standards of conduct which are consistent with relevant professional codes of ethics.

References

1. State of Connecticut, Department of Public Safety, Division of State Police: Investigation Report #H85-354514, dated 4/23/86.
2. In the Matter of Arbitration between the State of Connecticut & Administrative and Residual Employee Union (P-5). Bargaining Unit: Re David White; Office of Labor Relations File #16021730076/87 (State of Connecticut).
3. See 8/7/86 letter to Governor William O'Neill from Col. Lester Forst, Commissioner of the Department of Public Safety, and John Kelly, State's Attorney (State of Connecticut).
4. See letter of 2/24/88 from Attorney General Joseph Lieberman to Governor William O'Neill with attached investigative report dated 2/21/88 and titled "Colt Firearms Collection/Connecticut State Library."
5. See, for example, the series of articles appearing in the *New York Times* regarding the troubles of the New York Historical Society, 6/28/88, 6/30/88, 7/10/88, 7/13/88, 7/19/88, 7/25/88, 7/26/88, and 7/28/88. Also, in the late summer and fall of 1987, the *St. Louis Post Dispatch* carried numerous front page articles on trouble at the

Missouri Historical Society. The director of the Society was alleged to have taken valuable objects from the collection and to have been involved with the transfer of fakes.

6. The government and the commercial sectors are common to most societies. In the United States, "nonprofits" are so numerous and powerful that they are now referred to as the third sector of our society.

7. See, for example, J. Fishman. "Standards of Conduct for Directors of Nonprofit Corporations." *Pace Law Review* 7 (1987); S. Katz. "Museum Trusteeship: The Fiduciary Ethic Applied." *The Journal of Arts Management and Law* 16 (Winter 1987); M. Malaro. "Restricted Gifts and Museum Responsibilities." *The Journal of Arts Management and Law* 18 (Fall 1988). But, for a different point of view, see G. Marsh. "Governance of Non-Profit Organizations: An Appropriate Standard of Conduct for Trustees of Museums and Other Cultural Institutions." *Dickinson Law Review* 85 (1981).

8. *Stern v. Lucy Webb Hayes National Training School for Deaconesses and Missionaries*, 381 F. Supp. 1003, 1014 (D.D.C. 1974); *Lefkowitz v. Museum of the American Indian, Heye Foundation*, Index No. 41416/75 (N.Y. Sup. Ct., N.Y. County, June 27, 1975); *State of Washington v. Leppaluoto* (Sup. Ct., State of Washington, Klickitat County, No. 11781, April 5, 1977) (the two preceding cases were eventually settled when the collecting organization agreed to adhere to requirements set down by the Attorney General of the state in question); *Rowan v. Pasadena Art Museum*, Case. No. C 322817 (Cal. Sup. Ct., L.A. County, September 22, 1981). It is of interest to note also that, in 1988, the National Charities Information Bureau issued "Standards in Philanthropy" (nine standards by which to measure governance and management of philanthropic organizations). One segment of this document reads as follows: "The board should be an independent volunteer body. It is responsible for policy setting, fiscal guidance, and ongoing governance, and should regularly review the organization's policies, programs, and operations."

9. For a detailed discussion of collection management policies, see M. Malaro, *A Legal Primer on Managing Museum Collections* (Washington, D.C.: Smithsonian Institution Press, 1985).

10. On the issue of acquiring good title, in addition to material cited in notes 9 and 11, see also the recent court decision involving a claim from the country of Cyprus against a U.S. art dealer. At issue was the title to four Byzantine mosaics created in the early 6th century. The mosaics had found their way into the commercial market and were purchased by an American art dealer. Cyprus, claiming the mosaics were national treasures, sued to recover them. One issue was whether the American dealer could establish that she had purchased the mosaics in good faith. The court found that she was not a good faith purchaser. The court reasoned that, because of the nature of the items offered and the method of offer, a prudent person would have questions about the provenance and hence the burden fell on the dealer to prove she had taken reasonable steps to investigate title. In this case, the dealer could establish that she had made only a few superficial inquiries and even these could not be documented. Also, the dealer admitted that she was not an expert on Byzantine mosaics and yet she never consulted an independent expert regarding the offered items. *Autocephalous Greek-Orthodox Church of Cyprus and the Republic of Cyprus v. Goldberg & Feldman Fine Arts*, 717 F. Supp. 1374 (S.D. Ind. 1989).

11. Several recent cases make it imperative that collecting organizations recognize the importance of reporting thefts to the proper authorities. In *DeWeerth v. Baldinger v. Wildenstein & Co.*, 836 F.2d 103 (2d Cir. 1987), *cert. denied*, U.S. ,108 S. Ct. 2823 (1988), it was held that the owner of stolen artwork forfeited her right to claim the work when she eventually located it because she had not used diligence in reporting the work as stolen and searching for it. The decision is a dramatic change from what

had been the majority view — that an owner has a right to reclaim stolen property whenever he/she locates it. (See Malaro, *Legal Primer, supra*, for more background information. Note especially Section D(5) of Chapter IV of that text.) An even more recent decision, *The Solomon R. Guggenheim Foundation v. Mrs. Jules Lubell*, New York Law Journal, 2/15/89, p. 22, involved a museum. Here, the Guggenheim tried to retrieve from an innocent buyer a painting which the museum first suspected as missing in the mid-1960s. While it searched its own premises, it never reported the loss to the proper authorities nor did it take any steps to warn the art trade. The museum first learned of the whereabouts of the work in 1986. It was in the possession of the Lubell family, which had purchased the work in 1967 from a reputable dealer. The museum demanded the return of the work, Lubell refused, and the museum sued. The defendant asked the court to dismiss the case (motion for summary judgment) on the grounds that there was no way the museum could prove due diligence in searching for the work and hence the statute of limitations had run. The trial court dismissed the case. On appeal, the court held that there were issues that should have been tried and the case was sent back to the lower court for a full hearing (N.Y. App. Div., January 25, 1990). For a recent case in which an owner was allowed to recover lost work because the statute of limitations was deemed not to have run because the owner exercised due diligence in searching, see *Autocephalous Greek-Orthodox Church of Cyprus and the Republic of Cyprus v. Goldberg & Feldman Fine Arts*, as cited in note 10.

12. Professional codes of ethics which relate to museums, historical societies, etc., are listed below. These codes are also instructive for libraries with regard to their collections of rare books, historical documents, and important archival material. Museum Ethics: The report of the Committee on Ethics of the American Association of Museums. This code is considered to be the nationwide consensus of the profession on broad ethical issues (adopted 1978). (Copies available from the AAM, 1225 Eye Street, N.W., Suite 200, Washington, D.C. 20005.) Curators' Code: Code promulgated by the Curators' Committee of the American Association of Museums. It addresses more specifically ethical issues faced by curators (adopted 1983). (Printed in *Museum News*, February, 1983.) Registrars' Code: Code promulgated by the Registrars' Committee of the American Association of Museums. It addresses more specifically ethical issues faced by registrars (adopted 1985). (Printed in *Museum News*, February, 1985.) Art Museum Directors' Code: A Code of Ethics for Art Museum Directors as adopted by the Association of Art Museum Directors (1981 revision). (Copies available from the Association of Art Museum Directors and from the AAM [see address given above].) Professional Practices in Art Museums: The report of the Ethics and Standards Committee of the Association of Art Museum Directors (1981 revision). (Copies available from the Association of Art Museum Directors and from the AAM [see address given above].) ICOM Code of Professional Ethics: The statement of professional ethics of the International Council of Museums. ICOM is the international, non-governmental, and professional organization representing museums and the museum profession worldwide (adopted 1986). (Copies available from ICOM, Maison de L'Unesco, 1 rue Miollis, 75732 Paris Cedex 15, France.)

13. In the Cyprus case described in note 10, the challenge regarding validity of title was sparked by a museum's inquiry into provenance when the object was offered to that museum.

14. A recent article in *Museum News* (July/August, 1989, pp. 10-12) describes how prompt action by the Baltimore Museum of Art helped solve a series of art thefts. When the Baltimore Museum discovered that a group of gold pocket watches was missing from its collection, it promptly reported this to law enforcement officials and provided detailed information and photographs of the watches to dealers and auction houses throughout the world. A New York dealer spotted the watches and

law enforcement officials were able to apprehend two individuals who were responsible for a series of art robberies. When interviewed, museum officials stressed the importance of advanced planning and good communications if a museum hopes to act responsibly when a theft occurs.

15. In 1987, the Library of Congress and the National Archives brought charges against Charles Merrill Mount, an art historian, for stealing rare documents from their collections. Mount was convicted and sentenced to five years in federal prison (see report in *Aviso* (American Association of Museums publication) July, 1989, p.2).

16. A recent case which illustrates the difficulty of proving one's claim legally to historic artifacts is *Government of Peru v. Benjamin Johnson, et al.*, Case No. CV 88-6990-WPG, U.S.D.C. C.D. California (June 29, 1989). In this case, Peru tried to establish its ownership of 89 artifacts which it claimed were stolen from a Peruvian site. The defendant argued that he was a good faith purchaser. The court stated: "The plaintiff must overcome legal and factual burdens that are heavy indeed before the court can justly order the subject items to be removed from the defendant's possession and turned over to the plaintiff. The trial of this action has shown that the plaintiff simply cannot meet these burdens."

17. See list given under note 12.

Floor Discussion III:
Tax and Legal Implications

Marie Malaro: Let me pose a hypothetical case in which an organization realizes it has obtained a forgery as a gift. Normally, if one sues or brings a civil action, one must show damages. A collecting organization is unable to show damages when it has received something as a gift. It must then turn back to the donor and urge that he or she do something.

I also wish to add a few practical comments to Mr. Malouf's hypothetical case of the collecting organization which acquires something that has a highly inflated value. First of all, the [tax] changes were put into effect mainly because of abuses of collecting organizations, so certainly the message to those organizations is not to monkey around with values. The collecting organization must sign the summary form also, but it clearly states on that form that, in signing it, one does not support the valuation. In other words, the burden has been thrust upon the appraiser. Still, the appraisal has to be quite detailed: an appraiser cannot simply state that he is John Jones and a document is worth $25,000. An express list of questions must be answered.

If the collecting organization is aware that a highly inflated value has been assigned to an item, someone in that organization might speak privately to the donor, though nothing is necessarily put in writing. If the donor is on notice that an appraisal is wrong, he is in serious trouble. The collecting organization might indicate that it may pay to take another look at an appraisal, but the law clearly does not put the burden on the organization to police that. The collecting organization's burden is to determine if an item truly is suitable for its collection. If it is, and the intention is to keep it in the collection indefinitely, then the organization is in the clear. In the case of the IRS questioning an appraisal, the institution should be on solid ground if it can demonstrate that an item is suitable for the collection and that an appraisal is fair. I believe the donor is on solid ground if he honestly sought out an appraiser and honestly thought the appraisal was fair.

The person who is going to be on the hook is the appraiser. The IRS will have to prove that he was negligent, and that is sometimes difficult to prove if the appraiser has done his homework and has really tried to gather some facts.

Donald Malouf: I totally agree with you. In your hypothetical case, there is a cast of good guys, and what you state generally is the case. When things start to fall apart is later when, unbeknownst to anybody who was involved, problems arise concerning the authenticity of an item. The focus then shifts to the donor's tax deduction, and problems can arise when someone tries to fend off the Internal Revenue Service and tries to distract

Forged Documents

them by giving false statements or inadequate information.

Marie Malaro: I will agree that poorly informed staff and boards of trustees create problems where there need not be any, which is why it is important for them to understand why certain statutes have been passed and to act accordingly. If they do their job meticulously, usually things will work out. In the case of a collecting organization which acquires something as a gift and it turns out to be a forgery, that organization will have a difficult time trying to initiate any action. If it cannot interest the authorities in bringing a criminal action, it cannot prove damages in order to start a civil action if the item was a gift. Does anyone have any suggestions for such a case?

Donald Malouf: The donor would be in an interesting situation as well, because if his appraisal is a favorable one, it may cost him more to do right than it would to let the matter alone.

Marie Malaro: Do you think the IRS would penalize the donor if he had gotten an appraisal?

Donald Malouf: The IRS would penalize him in the sense that they would disallow his deduction, and that would be his concern.

Marie Malaro: But the IRS would have to prove an item is a forgery, which sometimes is difficult to do. They would have the burden of proof. It is one thing to raise a suspicion, which the collecting organization ethically might want to do, but to prove it . . .

Donald Malouf: Which goes back to valuation. What is an item worth, if all facts are known? If the facts disclose merely a doubt as to authenticity, then you have a reasonably good tax case on your hands. It depends upon the motive. If it is the donor's desire to make sure the library gets the authentic item, then he probably would want to go after whoever did the wrong thing.

David Szewczyk: I do appraisals every year for tax purposes. What would you advise if an item turns out to be a forgery and the appraisal has been paid for by the library? This is often the case with large donations and it changes things because the library is in the position of having gotten the appraisal expert, and then the donor says that the library's expert valued an item at, say, $25,000. Based on the information of the expert the library hired and paid for, the donor submits his IRS form.

Marie Malaro: Has the library paid for you to do the appraisal?

David Szewczyk: It is often the case that the library pays for the appraisal of a large donation.

Marie Malaro: If I am advising a museum, I would say absolutely not. First, the donee organization should point out the 1984 tax change to the donor's lawyer, if he or she is not already aware of it. An appraisal to be valid must be a disinterested one. The donee organization is an interested party and it is purchasing the appraisal, hence a suspicion is raised. Normally, the donor's lawyer agrees and does not want the fee paid. Even if the donor persists, it is still not good policy for the donee organization because it sets a standard and other donors may come to expect similar treatment. In the rare case where it might be argued that it could be done, I usually advise the donee organization to give the donor a list of appraisers, let the donor choose the appraiser, and request that the appraisal be sent to the donor. Only the bill goes to the donee organization; that is as far as I would go. The idea of a donee organization consistently using the same appraiser and sending its donors to that person is, I believe, very risky.

Donald Malouf: That practice raises substantial questions as to the independence of the appraiser. I, too, would regard it as risky.

David Szewczyk: But you do not see a problem with the organization actually paying for the appraisal?

Marie Malaro: If the organization consistently pays for the appraisal and consistently directs the donor to you, I think the donee organization has established a pattern. The test is, does this look as though there is a reasonable connection? A reasonable connection could be that the appraiser knows what his job is, which is to make that donor happy so the material will go to the donee organization. If a reasonable person could infer that, your appraisal is tainted.

Donald Malouf: There is a statement which must be signed by the appraiser, verifying that he or she is not the donor, the donee, a party to the transaction in which the donor acquired the property, is employed by, married to, or related to, and so forth, or, that the appraiser is not regularly used by any of the foregoing persons and does not perform the majority of appraisals during the taxable year for other persons. If you are doing too many appraisals for the same organization, you cease to be a qualified appraiser for that purpose.

Donald Farren: Is there a statute of limitations on any of these acts or crimes? I am thinking of a case where a forgery is discovered after the passage of a long period of time, or everybody keeps mum for a long period of time.

Donald Malouf: Generally, six years from the event will cover it for criminal law purposes. The question, though, comes up if there is a series of forged documents. Is this all one crime, is this a conspiracy that continues, and is the last act in this series the measuring point for that six years? In the case of an isolated situation, where a forged document is received into a collection and only ten years later does it show up as a forgery, then, in all probability, the criminal statute of limitations has run out.

Alan Gribben: Is there a working definition of an appraiser? I am a scholar who has specialized in three or four authors. I am familiar with various collectors throughout the country who periodically send me unsolicited descriptive lists of their books and sometimes even offer to fly me out to see a collection. They usually want valuations for insurance purposes, or they want some statement by an expert in the field.

I know the market prices of those books because I read the catalogues all the time, and I even go to a few auctions and book fairs. I never know quite what to do, so I immediately send them a list of qualified bookdealers. Sometimes these collectors say they are not comfortable with a bookdealer, and they want me to do [the valuation] since I have seen their collection. They just want me to give them an estimate. Am I making myself legally liable if I get involved in this type of thing?

Donald Malouf: These are for insurance purposes?

Alan Gribben: Usually, although occasionally someone is getting ready to give a collection to a library and wants me to give an appraisal.

Donald Malouf: For insurance purposes I know of no statutes, at least locally, that would create a problem. The requirement for signing the IRS form is that one holds oneself out to the public as an appraiser, or performs appraisals on a regular basis. Thus, because of a person's qualifications as described in the appraisal, he or she is qualified to make appraisals of the type of property being valued. If the items are something that are only appraised infrequently, and you only do an appraisal once every three years, that might be considered as a regular basis.

Marie Malaro: Having attended a few hearings before the 1984 statute was passed, I know that the Internal Revenue Service absolutely refused to get into a position of defining the term "qualified appraiser," taking the approach that it would only censure those who had clearly done improper appraisals. If you are aware of the kind of information the IRS looks for in an appraisal, and you feel comfortable in answering those questions, I do not think the IRS is going to hassle you about whether or not you are an "appraiser." They are interested in why you value an item at a certain amount—can you give comparable sales, for example?—and they want to know that you have done your homework.

Alan Gribben: An even more uncomfortable situation is that, in the last year, I have discovered three forgeries in what people have sent me and I have indicated my opinion. Again, I have been quick to state in writing that I am not a bookdealer, and that these items should be taken to a qualified bookdealer. This has caused ripples when they have been indignant and have gone back to the bookdealer. I might add that, in a couple of cases, I have seen these books come up again on the market, at the same price, after I have pointed out that they are forgeries. There has been no checking with any other expert. The dealer simply has given the person his money back and the book comes back onto the market.

Am I getting myself into deep water if I continue to point out that I am not a bookdealer but am a scholar who specializes in these authors?

Marie Malaro: There are several criteria. I am used to dealing with curators who are asked to provide appraisals and are frequently asked to do so as part of their jobs. I believe there is slim chance of liability (1) if you are not accepting money for this service, (2) if you clearly state that this is only your opinion, and (3) if you further state that the person should not rely on this opinion if the intention is to enter into a sales transaction.

If you are getting paid, normally one expects that you will have done your homework, that is, you will have put down the facts. If you have done these things and you have made it clear you are stating your opinion, I still believe you are fairly safe. The troublesome cases I know of were when people clearly did not do their homework, or they were foolish enough not to couch their valuation in cautionary terms such as this was the best they could do—an educated guess—based on the facts at hand, and that the valuation could not really be definitive.

Donald Malouf: When Mr. Davis cited the case of the man at a cocktail party who ventured an opinion as to value and later was sued, it proves that you really do need to qualify, and re-qualify, what you are telling a person.

Tom Taylor: I believe the statute of limitations on forgery does not begin until the forgery is discovered.

Marie Malaro: It might be a civil action, too, as distinct from a criminal action.

Donald Malouf: I was speaking principally to the federal criminal statutes, since Tom Taylor pointed out earlier that the forgery could go undetected for a period of time.

Marie Malaro: The discovery rule would be used: when would a reasonable person have realized an item was a forgery? Perhaps this would be more of a test for a civil action. We have to be clear whether we are talking about a civil or a criminal claim.

Richard Landon: I have a question about legal title. Many of us buy, or are given, books or manuscripts. When we acquire them we assume legal title. We also assume that the person who is either selling, or giving, them to us has legal title. We do not always, or perhaps we seldom, require this actually to be written. One does not ask, every time a book is purchased from a bookseller, or accepted from a donor, that they provide a document stating explicitly that they have the legal right to sell, or give, us that book or manuscript. Secondly, if an institution is given a forgery in what seems to be good faith, that is, the donor believes the document to be genuine but it turns out to be a forgery, where does the legal title in the forgery lie?

Tom Davis: When you purchase a book or document from a person and he gives you an invoice which states you paid $500 plus sales tax, that is all the proof of ownership you need for legal title. If it turns out that the item is stolen, I believe you would have clear cause of action to go against the dealer to recover your money, providing he is solvent. If you buy something of value and pay a high price, certainly it is better to deal with a solvent, rather than an insolvent, dealer!

As far as the title is concerned, if the item in question is a stolen manuscript and the true owner of that manuscript can prove his ownership then, under certain circumstances, even though you had no idea it was stolen, the owner can recover the item. For example, in Texas or in Indiana, a bona fide purchaser for value can never take title to such goods, even though he is totally innocent. The ultimate owner of the goods is able to claim them.

Richard Landon: What about legal title of forgeries?

Marie Malaro: It is not a question of title with forgery. The person who gave you that piece of paper had title to the paper. It is a question of whether you really want to get title, because the item is not what it was represented to be. There is no question of title: the question is whether or not the paper is authentic. In other words, you clearly own that piece of paper, but the paper is not, say, the Texas Declaration of Independence, so you would have a cause of action against the person who gave it to you.

If a library receives an item in good faith from a donor and the library then discovers that item is a forgery, it cannot turn around and sue the donor for civil damages until it proves it has suffered damages. But this is not the case, because a donor gave the document, so the library does not have a cause of action against that donor. The only course of action is to go back to the donor and state you think something should be done about this situation. The library staff might ask the donor if he or she wants to work with them to find out where this document came from. Most of the time, this does not happen.

I think there are some interesting questions, even under the uniform commercial code, if you purchased a forgery. It is sometimes very difficult to prove something is authentic unless you know who the creator was and know for certain he created the item. If the creator is unknown or long dead, it is only an educated guess. It can be very difficult to go back to a dealer if he or she was acting in good faith. Sometimes major art dealers take out insurance and automatically take questionable things back to protect their reputations because these can be very iffy situations.

Tom Davis: I am interested in something that was not addressed in the Cypriot mosaic case. If an institution receives stolen mosaics, does that institution have an affirmative duty to try to return them to the rightful owners? It certainly would have a duty to hold on to the mosaics in question and not pass them on to someone else unless the circumstances were fully revealed.

Marie Malaro: Ethically, the collecting organization certainly would not want to sell something as authentic if it knew this were not the case. In the case of receiving stolen property, many collecting organizations are in a situation in which, years ago, they acquired property that is now claimed to be stolen. Thus, the collecting organization is in a somewhat ambiguous position. They have an obligation to their public to defend, as best they can, title to assets. On the other hand, they have an ethical responsibility to return material that might belong to someone else. The collecting organization will probably want to look at the statute of limitations question.

Consider if an item is stolen from one library and that institution does nothing to notify the police or the public. Eventually, the material ends up with a dealer who does not know the provenance and who, in time, sells the item to a party who gives it to another organization. If the library from whom it was stolen then comes to that organization and wants the item returned and some twelve years or so have passed, I would perhaps raise the statute of limitations question. In fact, the first institution puts the second one in the difficult situation by its negligence and usually the

Floor Discussion III

law prevents a negligent party from going into court for relief. The second institution may have no legal or ethical responsibility to return the item to the original institution, and perhaps I would advise the second institution not to return the item.

David Farmer: Let me cite a wonderful example of just such an instance. We heard yesterday about the infamous T. J. Wise, who had access to books in the British Library. It turned out that, in the 1920s, he was selling to John Henry Wrenn in Chicago originally imperfect copies of books which he had made "whole" by removing leaves from books in the British Library. Those copies are now at the University of Texas. In a gesture of magnanimity, Chancellor Harry Ransom once considered returning the stolen leaves to the British Library until he was reminded by the executors of the Wrenn Estate that the terms of the acquisition by the University of Texas forbade the selling of any books or parts of books in the Wrenn Library.

Session IV:
Dealer/Donor/Institutional Relations

DON CARLETON, Chair
Barker Texas History Center, University of Texas

JENKINS GARRETT, Collector and Attorney
Considerations of the Collector/Donor

GEORGE A. MILES, Beinecke Rare Book and
Manuscript Library, Yale University
Expectations of the Institution

JENNIFER S. LARSON, Yerba Buena Books
Obligations of the Dealer: U. S. Perspective

ANTHONY ROTA, International League of Antiquarian Booksellers
Obligations of the Dealer: International Perspective

Discussion from the Floor

Forged Documents:
Considerations of the Collector/Donor

Jenkins Garrett

After having the experience of participating in a history course taught by Dr. Walter P. Webb in 1932 at the University of Texas, I developed an abiding fascination and interest in the history of Texas and the major part Texas has played in the development of our nation. For many years, this Webb-inspired interest fueled a rather regular purchase of books relating to that subject. These purchases were made solely for the purpose of acquiring knowledge and information about the history of Texas and its relationship to the development and growth of the United States. These years I call my "reading years." This very innocent and enjoyable period of reading developed, by some unexplained process, into a compulsive drive to help build a foundation for a research library in north Texas in which Texas history scholars, students, and other readers like myself might find similar rewards.

In 1974, my wife and I donated our collection to the University of Texas at Arlington, a gift which constituted the beginning of the university's present division of Special Collections. Since that date, we have continued our interest in, and support of, the acquisitions program and in the activities of Special Collections at UT Arlington.

First, let me focus attention on forgeries from the eyes and emotions of the collector. A collector is a separate breed from the reader, librarian, or scholar. I submit it is impossible to formulate a meaningful definition of the collector for the simple reason that collectors exist in countless numbers, varieties, and types. Nevertheless, I believe there are at least three factors common in all true collectors: (1) he or she gathers or collects library material with some unity of purpose, and without this unity of purpose, the result is a mass of oddities; (2) a sense of joy or undefinable inward compensation is experienced when finding a rare item compatible with the purpose of one's collection; and (3) there is a great sense of pride and of kinship between the collector and the individual items which make up the collection.

Understanding these common traits of the true collector—purpose, joy, pride and kinship—opens a window by which one can sense the deep hurt and feeling of betrayal when an item in one's cherished collection is suspected, questioned, or actually determined to be a forgery. This negative feeling is magnified if the item questioned is among the rarest of one's possessions, such as the Texas Declaration of Independence.

The sense of betrayal is directed to oneself, as well as to all who have had a part in the deception. I believe the first feeling sensed is one of frustration concerning one's own shortcomings in not being more careful in determining the provenance or in observing the obvious deficiencies of the item. A corollary feeling of isolation develops when the collector recognizes an inability to be protected from the one, or ones, who created the forgery and from those participating in the deception. Personally, I do not know a collector, regardless of how informed he or she may be as to subject matter, who possesses the technical background sufficient to detect other than the most crude forgeries.

It must be recognized that when a rare item is offered to a collector which is considered "a pearl of great price," the normal defenses tend to fail and the primary force which takes over is the desire to close the purchase quickly before the item is offered to another collector. In the auction room the pressure is intensified.

Let me relate an example of such a circumstance. A number of years ago (I believe it was in the early 1980s), when I was in Houston attending a conference, I dropped in on an auction being held at William Simpson's auction house which had a reputation of regularly offering extremely rare Texana. The auction was in full progress when I arrived. Shortly thereafter, the auctioneer held up a broadside which, he assured the audience, was the only copy known to exist. This caught my eye, because it appeared to be identical to a broadside I had purchased several years earlier which had been represented to me by the dealer as the only known copy of that document! The broadside in question (Streeter No. 1635) announced a $200 reward for the apprehension of a prisoner, Bartolomé Pagés, who was accused of offering General Santa Anna an avenue of escape from his Texian captors. It distressed me to hear that another "only known copy" existed. I entered into the bidding because I thought it appropriate to acquire this other "only known copy" so that I might own both.

Much to my surprise, there seemed to be little interest in the Bartolomé Pagés with the exception of one large fellow sitting in the back of the room. He stopped bidding early in the game, and my bid of $200 bought the item. I was most surprised to be able to acquire it with such a low bid, especially since the cost of the first "only known copy" had been seven to eight times that figure. Upon returning home, in a cursory examination of the just-purchased document, I observed that the printed area was slightly smaller than that of my first "only known copy." However, the possibility of Texas historical material being contaminated by forgery did not occur to me. I thought this second document was probably a variant produced by the primitive printing methods existing in Texas in the 1830s. Last year, when many Texas broadsides began to be questioned, a subsequent detailed examination convinced me that I had acquired a twenty-four carat forgery. Note that all of the elements which produced a near-willing victim were present: (1) the item was deemed important to my collection; (2) there was an immediate compulsion to acquire the second "only known copy"; and (3) no thought was given by me to the possibility that a purportedly reliable auction house would offer a forged document. Certainly I knew of the great forgeries of the past, but I had never associated forgery with the paper trade that I had known and been a part of in Texas.

From the outset of my collecting years, Nancy Taylor of Fort Worth and Hubert Fletcher of Salado, both veteran Texas rare book dealers and lovable human beings (neither of whom are now with us), taught me that it was nearly impossible to build a meaningful library without the aid and advice of a committed bookdealer. Out of the recent forged Texas documents fiasco, I experienced my first disappointment in the conduct of some dealers. Possible fraud or negligence arising out of cash register considerations seemed to be present. I do congratulate those dealers who have dedicated themselves to the identification and location of forged documents in order that this mess might be cleared up and, at least as far as the forgeries so far identified, might prevent further contamination of the holdings of dealers, collectors, and institutions.

What I have said is not an indictment of all dealers. My early-taught concept of a necessary collector/dealer relationship I still support wholeheartedly. My wife and I will continue to work with and through dealers in acquiring material for ourselves and for Special Collections at the University of Texas at Arlington, and we will encourage that institution to do the same.

The recent forgery epidemic in Texas has directed our attention to single page broadsides. However, it must be remembered that multiple page print and manuscript material likewise might be the work of a forger. We are reminded of the forged Hitler diaries, composed of some sixty-two books, and the forged autobiography and the will of Howard Hughes, to name just three. The extensive length and involvement of such materials would, by all logic, eliminate such creations as possible forgeries. Yet history has proven that the audacity, the subject matter, the length, and the complexity of a project, together with the imagination and the ingenuity required of a forger, present no limits, provided the rewards are deemed by the forger to justify such endeavors. As has been pointed out earlier in this conference, since ancient times forgers have been with us and their presence will haunt generations yet unborn. (Incidentally, last month I encountered a warning given in the first century A.D. by the Apostle Paul in his Second Letter to the Thessalonians not to be "shaken in mind" by letters "purporting to come from us.")

Therefore, a collector seeking "pearls of great price" must be diligent. One must familiarize oneself as much as possible with the characteristics of original documents and manuscripts of the period being collected. If an original is available, it is most important to compare each word and letter and, in the case of manuscripts, the sweep of the pen as well. For the collector unskilled in the technical aspects, the greatest safety lies in diligently establishing the provenance of an item. The fact that it has been in a related family's possessions for many years always gives the collector a comforting feeling. In the final analysis, I would suggest that the collector's protection is dependent upon the exercise of cautious judgment, based on one's own experience, together with the advice of dealers and technicians in whom one has confidence.

As we shift our focus to the considerations of the donor, we must realize that forgeries introduce entirely new factors. In the instance of the collector/forgery relationship, only the collector's frustrations are involved. However, when that collector donates forged material to an institutional library, it is at that point that the donor/institution and the donor/Internal Revenue Service relationships come into play. It is easy to see that the donor's frustration and feeling of betrayal are magnified when an item donated to his or her institution of choice is found to be a forgery. Regardless of how close the donor/institutional relationship may be, the donor is immediately on the defensive with the institution, the Internal Revenue Service, and the public. The donor well may feel called upon to prove innocence of any wrongdoing.

Embarrassment to the donor and the institution particularly is aggravated in situations in which the donation, upon its presentation, received public expressions of gratitude and pride. Again, there arises in the donor a feeling of personal negligence for not having detected the forgery before its presentation to the institution. As a matter of fact, some months ago, after a news story in a local newspaper told of a questioned document being found in the Special Collections at the University of Texas at Arlington, an insensitive local news reporter asked me, "Did you check out the forged item before giving it to U.T.A.?" I considered my answer accurate and logical, but I detected that, in the reporter's estimation, I was deemed unforgivably negligent.

One of the points the planning committee for this conference suggested I cover in my remarks was what the collector/donor should do if a forgery, or questioned document, is discovered in his or her collection, or is among items already donated to an institution. I offer three basic suggestions:

1. Before any action or remedy is pursued, the collector should consult his or her attorney or, in the case of the donor, consult the attorney for the receiving institution. The discussions by the very knowledgeable attorneys in yesterday's conference sessions outlined the complexity of the matters involved in forgery situations and the problems and dangers attendant in seeking either civil or criminal remedies. At all times, the distinction between forgery and theft must be recognized.

2. Should a deduction equal to the asserted value of a gift be claimed by the donor on his or her federal income tax return, the donor should disclose this fact immediately to the professional responsible for preparing the income tax return. It may require a timely amendment to the tax return for the year in which the claim for deduction was made.

3. A description of the questioned document should be reported to the Antiquarian Booksellers Association of America directly, or to a dealer who is a member of ABAA. This association has established a Committee on Questioned Imprints to give special attention to questioned documents and to assemble a list of such items which is made available to dealers, collectors, and institutions.

My wife and I continue to be committed collectors and donors. We find most dealers honest and devoted to their trade. Maybe it takes, in the words of the title of the March 1989 *Texas Monthly* article, "Forgery, Texas Style," to cause dealers, collectors, and institutions to renew their diligence in guarding against such a fiasco happening again in Texas, or elsewhere.

Mindful of the excellent papers and discussions we have heard at the Houston conference which expose the many foibles of the paper trade, I submit that collecting can be both a great and, at the same time, a perilous adventure.

Dealer/Donor/Institutional Relations: Expectations of the Institution

GEORGE A. MILES

When I began work at Yale's Beinecke Rare Book and Manuscript Library in 1981 my experience with rare books and documents came entirely from the readers' side of the service desk. My knowledge of the antiquarian book trade was nil, but I soon learned, as all Yale curators do, of the vital role that book scouts, dealers, and collectors have played in building our collections. From 1701 when ten Congregational ministers met in Branford, Connecticut to donate their books for the purpose of organizing what became Yale College, through the late nineteenth and early twentieth centuries when Yale men Henry Stevens and Henry Wagner helped create the field of Americana, to the modern era of Edward Eberstadt & Sons, William Robertson Coe, Peter Decker, and Frederick Beinecke, the Yale University Library has relied upon the antiquarian book world to nourish and sustain it. When that trade is wounded, as it has been by the recent forgery scandals, the future of Yale's collections is endangered. All of us at Yale, therefore, appreciate the efforts of Pat Bozeman and the other members of the conference committee in organizing this meeting.

Perhaps it was a recognition of Yale's close and abiding ties to the antiquarian book trade which led Pat and her committee to ask me to address the topic of institutional expectations of dealer, donor, and institutional relations. It is a topic which I have been wary of approaching, for the idea of expectations seems to me both ambiguous and explosive. The *OED* defines expectation as both "a preconceived idea with regard to what will take place," such as expecting that Houston is hot and humid in July, and as "what one looks for or requires as one's due," such as expecting that my three sons behave for their mother in my absence. Since, as all parents know, what does happen often bears little resemblance to what one believes ought to happen, discussions of expectations frequently become occasions for moralizing about past disappointments. I hope to avoid that trap and will focus upon the future of the antiquarian trade in Americana and how American research libraries and their professional staffs, in particular their curators and bibliographers, might conceive their role in that trade.

My focus ignores a variety of issues which might concern a university's development officer or legal counsel, as well as the agenda of foreign institutions of all sorts. My training and experience, however, prepare me to speak best from the perspective of an Americana collection, and the events which gave rise to this conference, while they have implications for the antiquarian book trade at large, occurred principally in the Americana trade in this country. Let me close my preliminary remarks with the observation that, although I have exchanged ideas with colleagues at rare book and manuscript collections around the country, a full survey of their opinions was beyond my means and inclination. My comments, therefore, ought not be regarded as a précis reporting the "expectations" of the profession at large but rather as the considered personal opinions of a single curator.

For the last thirty years the antiquarian book trade in Americana has been a remarkably competitive field, marked by low barriers to entry for dealers, a broad national market accessible to new as well as older firms, and few proprietary secrets. The open, egalitarian character of the trade emerged as a consequence of the explosive growth of state university systems throughout America during the 1960s. The creation of new campuses and the transformation of two-year junior colleges into institutions granting graduate degrees created an unprecedented demand for out-of-print books and other research materials. Government support of public and private higher education underwrote a rapid expansion in the antiquarian trade allowing many former "book scouts" as well as new entrepreneurs to enter the retail market. At the same time, established firms enjoyed unprecedented success.[1]

The Americana trade continued to prosper throughout the 1970s. Reductions in federal support undermined the acquisition programs of some institutions, but the soaring energy costs of the decade had different implications in different parts of the country. While many eastern universities, including Yale, encountered financial difficulties, western schools in regions endowed with large deposits of oil, coal, and natural gas enjoyed windfall revenues which enabled them to continue their aggressive expansion. In like fashion, many people who lived in those regions prospered and found collecting local history a respected, enjoyable way of displaying and validating their wealth. Although some institutional customers began to reduce their acquisitions and some subfields such as early American imprints fell into quiescence, Americana values in general continued to increase throughout the decade. Indeed, as Gordon Ray observed, it was a time when "many dealers would rather have [had] their capital in goods than in currency."[2] The appreciation of their stock made it easy for new or smaller dealers to finance their operations, and the trade expanded even as individual institutions suffered problems.

The Americana trade of the 1960s and 1970s was nourished not only by government dollars and inflationary trends but also by several broadly held, poorly examined assumptions about the character of the field. The first assumption was exemplified by books like *Gold in Your Attic*[3] which suggested, implicitly if not explicitly, that important, authentic Americana could be found easily by anyone with half an interest. A second assumption shared by most institutional and private collectors as well as dealers was that Americana, especially printed Americana, was what it appeared on its surface to be, that is to say, authentic. Finally, there was a general belief that almost anyone could and would recognize the few bad apples that might appear.

Like most of the unspoken assumptions upon which we base our personal and professional lives these ideas had some basis in reality; they were at least half-true. First, compared to most rare book and manuscript fields, Americana has been abundant. Just as the glut of books disgorged by European libraries in the aftermath of World War II began to disappear and scarce came to mean rare in most book fields, the dispersal of Thomas Streeter's unprecedented collection of Americana between 1966 and 1969 and of the stock of the firm of Edward Eberstadt & Sons less than a decade latter brought numerous important works of Americana onto the market.[4] Second, Americana has, until recently, been relatively free of such scandals as the John Payne Collier and T. J. Wise affairs. Finally, the linguistic and bibliographical skills required to work with Americana are far less arcane and abstruse than those demanded by early printed books and foreign literature.

Encouraged by optimistic projections about the continuing availability of authentic documents and concerned primarily with supporting historical rather than bibliographical research programs, most Americana curators spent the last three decades thinking more about the textual content and price of their acquisitions than about the technique and history of their production or the identity of the men and women who sold them. Individual and institutional collectors continued to value original documents, especially first editions, but more as icons whose importance derived from their association with great events than as artifacts whose physical properties helped reveal the character of those events. In this respect, librarians seem to have joined their faculty colleagues in the tendency which Bill Joyce discussed in Session II of this conference to devalue source criticism. Clearly there have been exceptions. For instance, Hugh Amory of the Houghton Library at Harvard has recently installed an exhibit and published a catalog entitled *First Impressions: Printing in Cambridge, 1639-1989* based on the premise that "Where books come from, not just what they are, continues to matter to us."[5] Nonetheless, Amory's project, like the unusually intense scrutiny to which Mark Hofmann's fabrication of *The Oath of a Freeman* was subjected a few years ago, seems an exception that clarifies the broader pattern of contemporary Americana collecting as a field driven by greater concern for subject than object.

In such an atmosphere dealers needed neither lengthy professional pedigrees, nor prestigious Madison Avenue or Post Street addresses, nor a listing in the social register to sell to institutions. Nor did their stock have to be in beautiful condition. If they had the right titles, in serviceable condition, at reasonable prices, they could sell them. The Americana trade flourished and many talented, enthusiastic bookmen with relatively little capital or formal training contributed to some of this country's great collections, often helping to define new sub-fields and making possible many ethnic studies, labor history, and popular culture programs.

For the better part of a quarter century, Americana dealers and curators presided over a golden age of institutional collection building whose accomplishments will be unmatched for many decades. The Hofmann and Texas document scandals have, however, finally made us confront the untrue halves of that era's optimistic assumptions about Americana. First, attics around our country contain far more dross than gold. Such exceptional discoveries as a unique copy of the first edition of Rachel Plummer's captivity narrative ought to remind us how ephemeral our documentary heritage is and not encourage us to believe that caches of the Texas *Declaration of Independence* remain to be uncovered. Second, the Americana trade, if not scandal-ridden, has never been naive or innocent. Sophistication and facsimile perfection are not inventions of the late twentieth century. Nineteenth century collectors and dealers frequently repaired and made whole imperfect copies of important books and pamphlets. Many such items continue to circulate, and while they often make useful reading copies, they have lost much of their original artifactual value and are most interesting bibliographically for what they reveal about nineteenth century book trade practices. Finally, as the Hofmann and Texas cases demonstrate, facsimilists and forgers are frequently skilled artists whose work can withstand not only superficial investigation but also careful scrutiny by specialists. These scandals remind us that building a collection of important, authentic Americana requires patience and skill, not just enthusiasm and money.

The forgeries likewise remind us that the meaning of a document lies not only in its text but also in its origins and that questions about its physical characteristics and provenance are intrinsic to its historical, as well as bibliographic, research value. Rare book librarians and archivists have always acknowledged this idea, but for the last thirty years they and the auction houses, dealers, and private collectors of Americana have downplayed, if not ignored, its implications. Many of us have encountered documents which leave us uneasy or suspicious, but few of us are intellectually prepared or have access to the necessary tools to address our concerns systematically. The recent scandals have increased our sensitivity to potential mischief, but we remain without the training or technical expertise to protect ourselves. And so, just as ship captains rely upon the specialized knowledge of local pilots to help them navigate hazardous or poorly chartered waterways, most of us involved with the Americana trade will, over the next few years, depend upon recognized bibliographic and forensic experts to help us avoid the shoals of fabrication and facsimile.

As dealers, collectors, and institutions place increasing importance on technical expertise, the egalitarian aspects of the contemporary Americana trade will be undermined. Knowledge of printing processes, of historic typefaces, or of the chemical composition and physical properties of nineteenth century papers and inks, for example, is neither as widely distributed nor as easily obtained as knowledge of American history, its primary documents, and their prices. Specialized knowledge will allow, indeed encourage, dealers to differentiate themselves, and the creation and nurture of specialized professional reputations will provide great competitive advantages to some individuals and firms.

This trend was borne home to me by a recent incident at Yale. A few weeks ago, a well known Western Americana dealer offered us a collection of Streeter period Mexican broadsides. The dealer and I knew each other personally, and his firm has enjoyed an impeccable national reputation for many decades. Nonetheless, he felt compelled to attach Tom Taylor's endorsement of authenticity to the documents. When long established firms with outstanding reputations feel compelled to seek expert verification, smaller, newer, or less well known firms will find it increasingly difficult to retail expensive manuscripts, broadsides, and ephemera. Only those collectors and curators who have full confidence in their own judgments will be willing to purchase such items without carefully considering the credentials of their source. I do not mean to imply that only certified students of printing history will be able to sell Americana, but a dealer's reputation for bibliographical and technical expertise, not to mention integrity, has become as important a consideration as the titles in his or her stock in determining the clients he or she can attract and the prices these dealers can expect to receive. Depending upon your point of view, dealers will be able to charge a premium or will be forced to offer a discount to their customers.

The creation of a multi-tiered market in Americana also may be stimulated by other developments related to the renewed interest in bibliographic verification. As institutions and private collectors place greater emphasis upon physical examination and analysis, consideration periods will probably drag out and expensive items will sell slowly. The capital resources of individual firms will become more important, and smaller dealers may find that other dealers are far more accessible and attractive customers than institutions. The prices offered by other dealers may not represent full retail value, but sales will be completed in timely fashion and payment promptly received. The ranks of the "scouts" will increase while the number of retail dealers will diminish.

Such a scenario is not unprecedented in the history of the rare book trade, not even in the traditionally egalitarian field of Americana. Think of the ways Henry Stevens, Edward Eberstadt & Sons, and Wright Howes dominated the market in their eras. Nor would such a market necessarily be detrimental to institutional needs. Although institutions as a class have, for the last thirty years, funded and driven the Americana market, individual institutions have had little influence within it. The principal challenge for dealers since the 1960s has been not to sell but to find Americana; customers, being abundant, have had to take what they can get. To the extent that differential pricing reflects the impact of customer demands for greater service, a less egalitarian market may be one in which institutions can exercise greater flexibility and exert greater influence in their acquisition decisions. The darker side of the scenario is, of course, that reputations are not always earned and often persist when they are no longer appropriate. To the extent that reputation alone, rather than service and performance, drives the market, institutions will suffer from oligopic pricing and a reduced pool of potential suppliers with whom they might do business.

In the long run, it seems improbable that the technical expertise upon which an oligopic market might rest could remain as specialized as it is today. The publication of Mark Hofmann's confession, of the ABAA's List of Questioned Imprints, of George Throckmorton's appendix in *Salamander,* and of Hugh Amory's study of Stephen Daye's typefaces represent the beginning of a process of public revelation and discussion of which this Houston conference is a part. As Tom Taylor and the American Antiquarian Society disseminate their findings concerning Texas documents and *The Oath of a Freeman,* the market will begin to come to terms with most of the recent forgeries.[6] Questions will remain, just as they do about the Wise forgeries, but over time their character will become more academic than practical. As the current scandals are exposed and analyzed, dealers and curators are likely to assess their own bibliographic skills and to begin to remedy the deficiencies they discover. The education of buyers and sellers of Americana will not occur in a few months or even a few years, but it is unreasonable to assume that Americanists are incapable of the bibliographic sophistication that characterizes the field of modern literature. More experienced, skilled dealers will begin to appear at the same time that curators develop the ability to distinguish real from reputed expertise. Although a return to the halcyon days of the 1960s is improbable, the market will gradually become more open and competitive.

Ultimately, as the excitement and furor over the current scandals fade, and as their violent and tragic aspects become more remote, their lessons will become less immediate and powerful. In the absence of dramatic forgeries, bibliographic investigation, thrust into the limelight by a crisis of confidence, regrettably will again come to be seen as a legitimate but recondite field of scholarship, and people will forget that some documents are simply too good to be true. Then, when an intense intellectual or emotional longing to possess some aspect of our heritage develops that the normal processes of the Americana trade are unable to satisfy, someone with knowledge of or position in the trade will abuse it. A scholar, a dealer, a collector, a librarian will, for reasons only partially explained by monetary considerations, fabricate or distribute fraudulent items. Eager to satisfy its insistent consumers, the book world (dealers, librarians and collectors alike) will initially accept the fakes as authentic. Their eventual discovery will trigger a period of recrimination and self-examination not unlike the last few years, and a new name or names will be added to the list that includes Ireland, Collier, Wise, and Hofmann.

My pessimism about the ability of participants in the antiquarian book trade to eliminate or suppress the human tendency to invent that which it wants but cannot find is intended neither as an indictment of the trade nor as an excuse for it to ignore its responsibility to investigate the specific character and extent of the current scandals. In dealing with each other the various components of the trade cannot, however, arrive at reasonable expectations of appropriate behavior without acknowledging that the forgery of documents seems to be principally an episodic problem which festers when we allow our enthusiasm for rarity and discovery to overwhelm our judgment. In the end, forgeries and fabrications, like all confidence schemes, succeed because we want to believe that which we know we should doubt; the problem is not simply one of dishonesty but also one of self deception. It is, for example, hard to conceive how anyone who did not desperately want to believe in the authenticity of a common nineteenth century promissory note marked with a simple "X" alleged to have been made by the famous illiterate mountain man Jim Bridger could be convinced to pay $10,000 for it, yet Mark Hofmann succeeded in selling not one but multiple copies of such a note. The avarice or gullibility of a victim does not absolve the con man of his culpability, but it does suggest that for institutions (or any other members of the Americana trade) to invoke that modern day Diogenes, Billy Joel, and suggest that "honesty is all [they] ever ask" is naive and inadequate.

Consider, for example, what most institutions regard as their due from dealers or auction houses who aspire to do regular business with them. As suggested earlier, most Americana curators around the country base their acquisition decisions on judgments about particular items, not about who offers them. Nonetheless, if a dealer or auction house wants curators carefully to consider their catalogues on a regular basis, we expect them to have sufficient knowledge of American history and its documents to separate the unusual from the commonplace and the significant from the merely rare. We expect them to find such documents regularly, to distinguish fakes from authentic pieces, and to acquire clear title to them. We expect these dealers to appreciate the full range of research potential in their documents so that they make the correct choice

Expectations of the Institution

about when or when not to repair them, and when or when not to break up a collection. We expect them to handle items in such a way as to protect them from damage or deterioration until they reach our hands. We expect them to fully describe their documents, physically and intellectually, in order to permit us to evaluate what they offer. Additionally, in the case of dealers, we expect them to know our collection development policies and research agenda well enough to appreciate the importance to us of less expensive as well as major pieces and to help us find the former as well as the latter. And, finally, we expect dealers to have a sufficient appreciation for both the history of the trade and of institutional collecting patterns to permit them to establish reasonable prices and to select appropriate institutions to whom to offer particular items. Clearly, honesty is an implicit expectation in any exchange between institution and vendor but, as this summary suggests, an enduring professional relationship entails far more.

The relationship between institution and donor is, if anything, more complex, particularly if the donor is a long-standing friend and major collector. The ideal donors of books and manuscripts (as opposed to those who offer money) have the same skills and perspective we expect of dealers. In addition, we expect of them the virtually impossible generosity and grace to surrender not only title but also responsibility for and control over documents they have spent a lifetime of sacrifice and effort collecting. In return, we offer them little more than a tax deduction, our profuse thanks, and a promise that in contributing to an institutional library they come as close to sharing immortality as is possible in our world.

Given our expectations of others in the trade, institutional curators and bibliographers ought to expect much of ourselves. A foremost expectation should be that we appreciate the bookmen and bookwomen, be they dealers, auctioneers, or collectors who embody the qualities just described, for they are the people who make it possible for libraries to become far more than any single curator or set of staff members could possibly find time to make it. We ought also hold ourselves to the same standards of knowledge and selflessness we expect of them. In this regard, it seems clear that institutions must be cognizant of the role of theft in the production of at least some of the Texas forgeries and of the ways theft distorts the trade in general. Our obligation to protect our collections extends not only to the donors who have entrusted them to us, but also to the dealers whom we expect to find additional things for us. Timely reporting of stolen and missing items and fair replevin practices are the obligations we incur when we demand that dealers avoid trafficking in stolen goods.

Perhaps our foremost expectation of ourselves is that we accept responsibility for thoroughly investigating the origins and character of the items we acquire by purchase or gift. Unless we are willing to abdicate our professional status we cannot place the onus for our poor acquisition decisions upon vendors and donors. When we fail to ask ourselves whether something is too good to be true, whether out of the vague hope that our suspicions are groundless or from fear of embarrassing a dealer or donor, we open the door to forgers. If they enter, we must share the blame and disappointment.

Taking responsibility for our acquisitions does not mean that Americana curators and bibliographers should serve as warranty agents for the scholarly world. In the end, it is only possible to prove that a document is a forgery, not that it is genuine, and many documents of uncertain or fraudulent origin may be of great interest to scholars. It is both arrogant and imprudent for librarians to assume principal responsibility for consigning such pieces to the waste pile, especially when their decision not to retain and preserve a document may prevent later generations of scholars from re-examining the controversial judgments of their predecessors.

The history of the Vinland Map, now at Yale's Beinecke Library, illustrates how contentious investigations of authenticity can be. Initially hailed in 1965 as a crucial fifteenth century document providing the earliest graphic evidence of the twelfth century Viking explorations of North America, the map was soon criticized by a variety of scholars as a modern fabrication. In 1974 an analysis of the map's inks appeared to confirm the charges, and most people assumed that the map could safely be considered an intriguing hoax. In 1985, however, the Crocker Historical and Archaeological Project staff at the University of California at Davis re-examined the map employing new analytic techniques; their report contradicted the 1974 study in virtually every detail. Neither the Crocker team nor the Yale Library claims that the recent analysis "authenticates" the map, but it seems unlikely that it can any longer be regarded as a proven hoax.[7]

The Vinland Map represents an unusually controversial case, but nearly every major Americana research collection contains important, intriguing items of uncertain origin which stimulate valuable research. The only foolproof protection against acquiring fakes and fabrications is not to acquire anything, and the more ambitious and aggressive we are in building our collections, the more likely we are to encounter dubious documents. Our responsibility is not mindlessly to bar our institutional doors against them but to ask whether their potential value is sufficient to warrant the expense of their acquisition. Our principal questions of these, as of all our major acquisitions, ought to be not simply "Is it real?" but rather "Is it valuable? Will it benefit scholarship? Is its research potential commensurate with its expense?" Asking these questions should help us temper our own emotional attachment to the rare icons of our heritage with the recognition that they can too easily become false idols whose pursuit distorts our values and clouds our judgment. Then, perhaps, we can do a better job of avoiding the self-deception upon which most forgers depend.

References

1. A classic account of the antiquarian book trade in this era is Gordon N. Ray. "The Changing World of Rare Books." *Papers of the Bibliographic Society of America* 59 (1965): 103-141.
2. Gordon N. Ray. "The World of Rare Books Re-examined." *The Yale University Library Gazette* 49 (1974): 77-146.
3. Van Allen Bradley, *Gold in Your Attic* (New York: Fleet Publishing Corp., [1958]).
4. The bulk of Streeter's collection is described in the auction catalogs published by Parke-Bernet Galleries, *The Celebrated Collection of Americana formed by the late Thomas Winthrop Streeter*, 7 volumes plus an index volume, (New York: Parke-Bernet Galleries, Inc., 1966-1970). For an account of the Eberstadt sale by one of

the principals see John H. Jenkins, *Audubon and other Capers: Confessions of a Texas Bookmaker* (Austin, Texas: Pemberton Press, 1976), 105-120.

5. Hugh Amory, *First Impressions: Printing in Cambridge, 1639-1989* (Cambridge, Massachusetts: Harvard University, 1989).

6. *Mark Hoffman Interviews*, ed. Ronald Vern Jackson, (North Salt Lake: A.I.S.I. Publishers, 1987); Linda Sillitoe and Allan D. Roberts, *Salamander: The Story of the Mormon Forgery Murders* (Salt Lake City: Signature Books, 1988); Hugh Amory, *Steven Day's First Type* (Cambridge, Massachusetts: Printed at the Meriden-Stinehour Press for the Houghton Library, 1989); *The Judgement of Experts: Essays and Documents about the Forgery of the Oath of a Freeman*, ed. James N. Gilreath, (Charlottesville, Virginia: University Press of Virginia, 1990). No publication date has been announced for Tom Taylor's study.

7. For a recent summary of the discovery and investigation of the Vinland Map see Laurence C. Witten II. "Vinland's Saga Recalled." *The Yale University Library Gazette* 64 (1989): 11-37. The notes to Witten's article include references to virtually all of the major earlier studies.

Obligations of the Dealer: The U.S. Perspective

JENNIFER S. LARSON

> When regard for truth has been broken down or even slightly weakened, all things will remain doubtful.
> —*St. Augustine*

> If we could first know where we are and whither we are tending, we could better judge what to do and how to do it.
> —*Abraham Lincoln*

The Antiquarian Booksellers Association of America (ABAA) was founded in 1949, and chief among its stated objectives was to uphold the status of the antiquarian book trade and maintain its high professional standards. The steadily increasing membership now approaches 450, and has over the years encompassed an ever-broader range of bookseller, from the come-one, come-all secondhand dealer who makes no pretense to expertise and whose entire stock is regarded by wise customers as offered "with all faults," to the paragon of erudition trading only in the most valuable books, fully researched and accurately described.

There are, as one might expect, differences of opinion within the Association as to the wisdom of casting the net so wide, and as to what precisely are the guidelines and principles members are expected to uphold. Some members behave as professionals of the highest caliber, while others seem to function as indiscriminate entrepreneurs or agents between buyer and seller. Is the ABAA a trade association, its *raisons d'etre* the publication of a directory and sponsorship of book fairs? Or should it, as its constitution implies, aim for something higher?

More to the purpose at hand: what, in fact, did the nation's antiquarian booksellers as a group do in response to the three major groups of questionable items which have surfaced in recent years: Mark Hofmann's forgeries, the Texas fabrications and facsimile reprints, and spurious early American imprints? What should have been done, or might have been done, or would have been done if possible; and is there anything that now can be done to prevent such disasters from happening again?

My personal interest in the subject of forgery became acute towards the end of 1985, when the career of Mark Hofmann, a young and relatively unknown dealer in rare documents, began to be discussed in the trade in hushed and scandalized tones. The sensational case of this confessed forger of Mormon documents, literary autographs, and Americana was of riveting, but largely academic, interest. With the perpetrator in custody and his dealings scrutinized by reporters, investigators, and indeed the entire Mormon community, one assumed that the complete history of his fraudulent documents had been, or would soon be, fully exposed.

There were eventually three full length books written about Hofmann, extensive periodical and newspaper coverage, and a transcript of his interviews with prosecutors, which seemed to provide support for widespread confidence that all of the forgeries had been identified and removed from the marketplace.[1] Although several ABAA members had been involved, there was no suggestion of any misconduct on their part, and apparently no purpose to be served by ABAA involvement of any kind.

Nearly a year after Mark Hofmann's guilty plea, I was asked, on December 30, 1987, on behalf of an insurance company, to examine the books and related materials damaged in The Jenkins Company fire of the preceding September. At that time, I had heard no rumors regarding forged Texas documents. My January 1988 examination of the damaged, but largely intact, Jenkins materials turned up a number of what I felt to be questionable items. Among them were three broadsides that, unbeknownst to me, already had been identified by W. Thomas Taylor as existing in spurious copies; there was a fourth document unknown to Taylor at that time.

Telephone calls to colleagues led me to Taylor, whose work in progress was by that time no secret to those in the know in the field of Texana. He was generous in sharing his research with me. His willingness to get involved, to lend moral support, and to provide testimony if need be, came at a time when I felt as though the integrity of the entire trade in antiquarian books was in jeopardy.

As with the Hofmann case, however, it appeared as though, through Taylor's dedicated efforts and his intention to research and write a book, the truth eventually would be established and justice would be done. In early April 1988, John Jenkins acknowledged to Tom Taylor what had previously been denied: that Taylor's work was sound and his conclusions valid that numerous Texas documents had been faked. Local press coverage immediately followed, together with an alert sent out by the Southwest Chapter of ABAA, listing by Streeter and Winkler numbers the items believed to exist in copies not genuine (see Appendix I). Again, it seemed as though the situation, though deplorable, was well in hand.

It was not until September 1988, four months later, that it began to dawn on me that the problem of spurious documents was not being adequately addressed by the community of dealers. In that month, Tom Taylor addressed a letter to ABAA leadership in which he called for an investigation by ABAA counsel, requiring members to account for the provenance of any spurious documents they might have handled. Taylor's emphasis was on the importance of identifying any members who might be guilty of misconduct, with a view toward taking steps to censure or expel them from the organization.

While many others were completely in sympathy with this objective, and wrote letters seconding Taylor's, it struck me that although the ABAA already had in place a Standards and Ethics Committee with jurisdiction over complaints about members, there was no mechanism by which the trade and the book world at large could be alerted to spurious items in the marketplace. A clearinghouse to collect and disseminate information would help to curtail

The Dealer: U.S. Perspective

future sales of items that had been identified as fraudulent, would act as a general warning to alert the community to the types of items susceptible to being faked, and ideally would act as a deterrent to those tempted to create and market future deceptions.

There was a precedent for this clearinghouse notion in a parallel effort attacking the similar and often interrelated problem of theft, which had been addressed by ABAA in like fashion, working with the Rare Books and Manuscripts Section of the American Library Association, Daniel and Katharine Leab of BAMBAM (Bookline Alert — Missing Books and Manuscripts), the Society of American Archivists, and the Manuscript Society. The goal of establishing methods of alerting the trade to specific items known to have been stolen had a parallel in the unmet need to notify the trade of items known to exist in spurious copies.

Through the grapevine, I also learned in September 1988 of a deceptive reprint of an unrecorded 1858 Kansas broadside recently offered for sale, which is headed "To the People of Kansas. Jim Lane Begging for Sympathy." The need to spread the word systematically, not only in the trade but among collectors and in the academic world, seemed increasingly pressing. Further information turned up yet another problem: an apparently recently manufactured Pennsylvania document, purportedly printed in 1777, and vague rumors of additional reprinted eighteenth century American documents which had been appearing on the market in recent years. These items represented an entirely new category of fake, and, to my knowledge, no one was investigating these problems.

Furthermore, in-depth coverage of the Hofmann case in publications such as *The Book Collector* and *Maine Antique Digest* had raised some doubt that, in fact, the situation had been adequately addressed with regard to identifying all of Mark Hofmann's forgeries. That there was reasonable ground for this suspicion became abundantly clear to me in the next few months as I entered into voluminous, but largely one-way, correspondence and conversations with some of the researchers, librarians, investigators, as well as associates of Hofmann.

At its meeting in November 1988, the ABAA Board of Governors took prompt action on the report of John Curtis, chairman of the Standards and Ethics Committee, and created a Committee on Questioned Imprints charged with compiling a list of suspected items to be distributed to the entire membership.[2] The list also was to be circulated to related professional associations and to selected librarians, and its availability advertised. A liaison was to be established with law enforcement authorities. Information regarding the sources for questioned items was to be solicited for consideration and action by the Standards and Ethics Committee.

Thus, there were two separate ABAA committees with distinct but complementary responsibilities: the newly-established Committee on Questioned Imprints, consisting of Tom Taylor, Dorothy Sloan, John Curtis, Elizabeth Woodburn, and me, charged with identifying and publicizing the existence of spurious imprints, and the already existing Standards and Ethics Committee, comprising John Curtis, Elizabeth Garon, Douglas Harding, Doris Frohnsdorff, Edwin Glaser, and Louis Weinstein, entrusted with receiving and acting upon complaints relating to the conduct of ABAA members.

I think it appropriate to point out that according to Standards and Ethics Committee chair John Curtis, no single aggrieved private collector or librarian registered a complaint with that committee regarding the sale, or attempted sale, of any specific forgery. The actions of the ABAA were, to this extent, self-policing and were hampered severely by the fact that the very people with the most pertinent and useful information at hand — the victims themselves —were not the ones who came forward. The ones who did register specific complaints were members of the trade and, in a handful of cases, librarians and collectors who were concerned in a general way, but had no specific complaint to register.

Incidentally, there are myriad reasons for this silence on the part of the victims, which is typical of forgeries in all fields. My initial surprise at this has been tempered by reflection upon some of the compelling motives to reticence: fear of legal repercussions in the form of lawsuits over libel and defamation of character; a natural disinclination to admit one has been deceived; the extreme rarity of successful prosecution in fraud cases of this type; the unpleasantness of the role of complainant; the difficulty and expense of proving an item not genuine, borne by its questioner; and the impossibility, once one has acknowledged the inauthenticity of an item, of ever attempting to sell it as genuine, or "possibly genuine."

For the next month, building on the groundwork laid by Tom Taylor, and through the tireless efforts and superb cataloguing skill of Dorothy Sloan, a preliminary report on questioned imprints was compiled. The work was assisted immeasurably by the cooperation of a number of individuals and institutions, including, in addition to the many Texas institutions and private collectors who aided Tom Taylor: Georgia Barnhill and Sidney Berger, the American Antiquarian Society; James Gilreath, the Library of Congress; George Miles, Yale University; James Green, the Library Company of Philadelphia; Steve Ferguson, Princeton University; Curt Bench, Benchmark Books (formerly of Deseret Book); Linda Sillitoe, one of the authors of *Salamander: The Story of the Mormon Forgery Murders*; and George Throckmorton, the forensic document examiner who provided the vital pieces of information that cracked the Hofmann case.

This invaluable assistance was deeply appreciated; however, not everyone was so forthcoming. It was discouraging for me recently to look over my files of unanswered correspondence with some of the investigators and librarians in Utah. One of the investigators is quoted in the *Maine Antique Digest* as saying that there remain $500,000 worth of Hofmann fakes still in circulation (not including, presumably, the alleged fabricated *The Oath of a Freeman*). I was unable to obtain any basis for this figure or any information of any kind as to what these items might be. The people who are holding these documents have not come forward, nor have those who had access to the material seized from Hofmann assisted us in our efforts to remove any outstanding fraudulent material from the marketplace.

To digress briefly: the problem of permanently removing a spurious item from the marketplace remains a frustrating one. Questionable items are identified, only to reappear elsewhere as genuine. In France, authorities have

The Dealer: U.S. Perspective

the legal right to seize and retain proven forged works of art, resulting in a massive storage problem. Similarly, the British Goldsmiths' Company possesses the right to confiscate spurious objects in its area of expertise. Apart from counterfeit currency and stamps, there is no legislation in this country to permit such actions with regard to printed and manuscript merchandise.

On the contrary, there is a thriving trade in forged documents, knowingly bought and sold as forgeries. Some of Thomas J. Wise's spurious pamphlets now command higher prices than they would if they were genuinely what they were purported to be. It has been whispered that some of Mark Hofmann's forgeries are currently changing hands at prices ranging from several hundred to several thousand dollars. Indeed, I have been asked by a member of the trade whether I could offer for sale copies of any of the faked Texas broadsides. The response to my purely academic query as to the contemplated asking price: "A couple grand." Subsequent calculations of the cost of faking the fakes ended in the realization that there easily would be plenty of room for profit all around.

To return to the work of the ABAA Committee on Questioned Imprints, the possibility exists that all of Hofmann's printed forgeries have come to light through: the charges brought against him, the items referred to in David Hewett's coverage in *Maine Antique Digest*, the Addendum to Alvin Rust's *Mormon and Utah Coin and Currency*, and similar sources. This is adequate cause to doubt that, in fact, this is the case. For example, Con Psarras of KSL Television in Salt Lake City obtained a copy of a negative that had allegedly been ordered by Mark Hofmann. It was an inscription, apparently in Mark Twain's hand, reading: "None genuine without this signature on the bottle: Yrs truly, Mark Twain, Mch 1886." This was supposed to be the text of a printed whiskey label endorsement by Mark Twain. I have not been able to have this information confirmed or denied by any official source, despite multiple inquiries.

A more chilling consideration arose toward the end of 1988, when a diabolical scheme occurred to me: one that I was able to determine Hofmann had carried out at least once. It is known that he cleverly introduced his manuscript forgeries in such a way that one forgery would subsequently be used to lend authenticity to another. In addition, I have been able to confirm that he created a printed forgery which he inserted into an institutional collection, simultaneously stealing the genuine copy. Not only does this accomplish a theft with a dramatically reduced likelihood of detection, but it also establishes the forgery as a copy of seemingly long-standing provenance, thereby setting it up as the standard whereby other forged copies may be validated. With regard to printed forgeries, this technique does not appear, to my knowledge, in the Hofmann literature.

I wrote in some alarm to the librarian in charge at this institution, hoping for some information as to the extent of Hofmann's substitutions and a list of suspect items. The pattern Hofmann established with his printed forgeries, as one might expect, was to create multiple copies which then were sold to a variety of purchasers. The same pattern reasonably could be presumed to be characteristic of his substitution/thefts; thus, there was cause for concern about other possible printed forgeries, circulating unrecognized in the marketplace, and an urgent need to know what they were.

In reply, I received a courteous acknowledgment of the outstanding problems, gratitude for the ABAA's efforts, and a statement to the effect that no information will be forthcoming since the process of checking everything will take a long while. My purpose is not to criticize this caution or to make light of the tremendous amount of work required to undo this insidious damage. Rather, the intention is twofold: to alert other librarians to this potential problem, and to illustrate the obstacles and difficulties encountered by the ABAA Committee on Questioned Imprints in its efforts to identify and publicize deceptive imprints.

More problems arose over the Revolutionary War broadsides. Few dealers, when confronted with an item they believe is not genuine, do more than decline to purchase it. It was difficult for us to compile information about specific items and specific sales. We were able to obtain some general information about several imprints through dealers and librarians and, gradually, we built up a list. Our work in this area is sadly incomplete and suffers from the lack of a competent and thorough researcher to run these problems to the ground, as Tom Taylor is doing in Texas.

Nevertheless, despite these inadequacies, the ABAA Committee on Questioned Imprints realized the importance of distributing the list as soon as possible. The preliminary report consisted of an eight-page, short-title list of thirty-two items, and a detailed questionnaire for the reporting of additional items. A cover letter stressed the earnest desire of the committee to add to this list if it proved necessary and urged that information regarding sources of questioned imprints be referred to the ABAA Standards and Ethics Committee. The preliminary report was reviewed by counsel for ABAA and circulated in December 1988 (see Appendix II).

Since the distribution of that list, little progress has been made in the area of identifying other spurious documents. This is attributable to an almost complete lack of participation on the part of the antiquarian book community at large. One ABAA member submitted report forms identifying two additional colonial broadsides; another provided provenance for an additional copy of a listed item; one institution provided information on an unlisted item; and another institution provided locations of suspect copies of Texas broadsides already identified. These newly submitted items, together with some older deceptive facsimile reprints reported to the committee since the initial mailing as well as several printed documents associated with Mark Hofmann about which very little is known, have been compiled and appear herein (see Appendix III).

The paucity of these additions to the original list is surprising. Either the recent problems were quashed at one quick stroke, or there are spurious items which remain undetected, or there are people who would prefer not to inquire too closely into the nature of their documents or who choose not to share what they know. That there is widespread apathy on the subject as well is at once astonishing, mystifying, and deplorable.

The original ambitious project of attempting to compile a list of all potentially deceptive facsimile reprints has been abandoned, partly because of the above-mentioned lack of support. Another reason is borrowed from Heidegger, who objected to gossip on the grounds that it tends to pervert genuine understanding by making us think that we already know everything.[3] What is called for, we came to realize, is not a comprehensive attempt to list all deceptive reprints, which will of necessity be incomplete and therefore misleading, but meaningful efforts to alert and educate all members of the book community: dealers, collectors, and librarians. The ABAA's financial support to the Houston Conference on Forged Documents was approved by the ABAA Board of Governors in this spirit.

What about the other half of the ABAA effort, that of determining whether the organization has an obligation to take action against any of its members? There have been allegations, publicly and privately, that the ABAA has failed miserably in this regard, particularly with respect to the Texas situation; that the organization tolerates wrongdoing on the part of its members; and even that (this charge is made "off the record") the ABAA is involved deliberately in attempting to hide and distort the truth. These charges relate to the perceived failure of the ABAA to determine whether any member was involved in knowingly selling forgeries or, failing that, whether any ABAA member was so negligent or so ignorant as to require official action.

There can be little doubt that there have been some people in the organization who have had an interest in attempting to ignore, deny, and isolate the forgery problem. Those individuals have not, in the long run, had their way; and through the efforts of an outspoken few and the vast silent majority of honest ABAA members, some of these people have seen the wisdom of a different point of view. Personally, I am content with this. It is neither warranted nor useful to accuse the organization as a whole for the ignorance, greed, pathological behavior, or guilty secret knowledge of a few of its members; and those who level such charges, in my opinion, reveal more about themselves than they do about the organization they attack.

What actions, in fact, were taken by the Standards and Ethics Committee? The gauntlet, as we have seen, was thrown down by Tom Taylor in September 1988 in a letter calling attention to the Texas problem and offering to make available the provenance of the documents that he was able to trace. The committee did not, in fact, ever request this information from him. The ABAA Board of Governors met in Boston in November of that year and adopted the Standards and Ethics Committee's recommendation to form a separate committee to list and publicize the recently questioned imprints. The preliminary report and list was prepared entirely by mail and by telephone, reviewed by counsel, and widely disseminated by ABAA within six weeks.

The Committee on Questioned Imprints finally met in San Francisco in February 1989. The primary concern was to decide whether it would be appropriate to turn over to the Standards and Ethics Committee any information regarding provenance that had been gathered in the course of our research. We had no knowledge of what that committee was doing, and we knew that it had not requested any further information from Tom Taylor as a result of his September letter. Our meeting was attended by all members of the committee except Elizabeth Woodburn, together with several ABAA board members. It was decided that such action would be appropriate, and it was agreed that Taylor would send full details about the provenance of the Texas documents to the Standards and Ethics Committee, while I, as archivist, would provide the sketchy details about any other questioned items that had come to our attention, insofar as any ABAA member was involved.

Taylor made his report to the Standards and Ethics Committee in March 1989. The report raised serious questions about either the expertise, the competence, or the ethics of ABAA member John Jenkins, who had handled a large number of the questioned documents. Acting on this report, John Curtis, in a telephone conversation with Jenkins late in March, indicated that the committee would require a full accounting of the origin of each of the items in question. Jenkins agreed to cooperate fully, but he was found dead in April, without having complied with the committee's request.

On February 28, 1989, the committee of the International League of Antiquarian Booksellers adopted a resolution expressing concern about the Texas broadsides, urging action towards identifying and punishing those responsible, and requesting that the ABAA president report on the matter when the presidents of all the member associations of the League convened in Switzerland the following September. That report, prepared by John Curtis, stated in part that "Some troubling questions regarding Mr. Jenkins' involvement in all this still exist; however, it is not clear that any definitive answers can be found after Mr. Jenkins' tragic death."

While it is undeniably true that Mr. Jenkins no longer can answer directly to the charges against him, it is also true that a document exists that provides a better understanding of what course his defense might have taken. This document is a three and a half page memorandum, dated November 2, 1988, which is addressed by John H. Jenkins to the ABAA Board of Governors and concerns the subject of the questioned Texas broadsides. It appeared six months after the fakes had been exposed publicly, and after Tom Taylor had, in a lecture before the Friends of the University of Texas, stated that of thirty-five spurious items then identified, twenty-two were traced to The Jenkins Company, nine to William Simpson, and five to Dorman David.[4] Clearly, in November 1988, John Jenkins was aware that questions were in the air regarding his involvement; the fact that he addressed a memorandum to the ABAA Board of Governors indicates his recognition that some sort of a response was in order.

The existence of this memorandum was leaked, as such things generally are. The Northern California Chapter of ABAA at three of its quarterly meetings has engaged in sometimes heated debate regarding the legitimacy of the Board of Governors holding this memorandum in confidence. In December 1988, a motion failed to pass. In March 1989, the following motion passed:

> The Northern California Chapter of the Antiquarian Booksellers Association of America requests that the ABAA Board of Governors asks John Jenkins for permission to distribute to the membership of the ABAA Jenkins' letter to the Board on the Texas forgeries.

No written response to this motion was received from the board. An informal, verbal report was received to the effect that it did not consider the request appropriate. At the June quarterly meeting of the Northern California Chapter of the ABAA, the motion again passed, slightly altered, requesting that the Board of Governors distribute the letter without seeking any further permission. Again, a verbal message from one board member suggested that the response of the board was that those members who wished to see the Jenkins memorandum should address their requests directly to The Jenkins Company.

Is the ABAA Board of Governors or its Standards and Ethics Committee equipped to judiciously determine whether or not someone has knowingly sold forgeries? I think not. A person suspected of criminal behavior in this country is entitled to be charged and tried in a court of law with all of the cumbersome but necessary machinery of rules of evidence and testimony. The errors and injustices that occur in the absence of such due process stagger the imagination. Wild discrepancies occur even when unbiased witnesses to a vehicular accident give testimony; when preconceived notions, ignorance, ineptitude, inaccurate memory, emotions, and money are involved, the possibilities for error proliferate.

It is infinitely to be preferred to allow some crimes to go unpunished than to take action against anyone based on hearsay; and it is a fact of life that many crimes, particularly white-collar crimes, are essentially beyond the reach of the law. Among these crimes, that of passing forgeries poses special and very difficult problems, because the law requires that intent to defraud be demonstrated. It must be shown not only that spurious items were sold, but that the seller knew that they were spurious.

This is not to say that the ABAA must content itself with no higher standard than that of proudly proclaiming that all its members are unindicted, so far as is known. While it may not be in the power of such an organization to establish intent, it is well within the realm of possibility to determine incompetence or negligence, not to a legal standard, but to the generally recognized standards of the antiquarian book trade. It may be fairly said that the ABAA's Standards and Ethics Committee showed no great zeal for this difficult task in the case of the Texas broadsides; however, once the basis for some of the allegations was placed before the committee, a serious effort was underway towards arriving at a deliberate and fair conclusion.

The recent spate of spurious imprints has contributed to a highly-charged climate of rumor and innuendo, described by *Texas Monthly* editor Gregory Curtis as "the surprisingly Machiavellian world of antiquarian bookselling." [5] The resulting atmosphere of suspicion and distrust, shocking and alien to most of us in the book community, has fostered an all-too-human readiness to convict in our minds certain individuals based on wholly inadequate evidence; this is not to say, of course, that adequate evidence does not exist. Detailed and specific information is in the hands of only a very few people, most of whom, for a variety of reasons, are not in a position to share publicly what they know. In an ideal world, charges would be brought, evidence presented, depositions taken, witnesses cross-examined, and a judgment reached. This is not an ideal world.

I would like to suggest that the ABAA is in a position similar to that of a nineteenth century cancer patient. An operation is clearly called for, yet it is not known precisely where the tumor is nor how many cells are cancerous. The necessary diagnostic and surgical tools are not available. The operation has never been done before; there are no textbooks to use as guides. The members of the family cannot agree as to what is to be done, although most acknowledge that healthy cells would certainly be damaged if all who despise the disease are allowed to begin hacking at will. Nevertheless, no reasonable person can deny that the problem is only a tumor, not a systemic disease, that most of the patient is perfectly healthy, and certainly should live and prosper.

In the final analysis, it will not be the failure to instantly cut out this tumor that will be important, but the actions now taken to ensure, insofar as it is possible, that such a growth does not occur again. The ABAA is in a position to render fraudulent documents, misrepresented or defective merchandise, horrendously overpriced material and the like much more difficult and dangerous for its members to market. The efforts of past presidents Edwin Glaser and Louis Weinstein to revise and update the association's ethical guidelines will be critical in this regard.[6]

If the new guidelines are detailed and specific, they will go a long way towards rebuilding the organization's image among those with whom it has been damaged by recent events. If the guidelines are general and vague, they will do little to encourage confidence that the ABAA intends to set any minimum standard expected of its members, with a view to enforcement of said standard. It is quite true, as stated by Michael Alan Weinberg in an article calling for a strong professional organization of autograph dealers, that "the community of. . .dealers is only as sound and reputable as the least competent and ethical dealer which it knowingly permits to function unchallenged in its midst."[7]

Another method by which the ABAA can hope to forestall future forgery problems is through education, both of its members and the public at large. The usual advice dispensed to a collector concerned about forgeries is to make certain he or she purchases only from trustworthy dealers. The obvious problem with this plan is that people often err in their judgments of the character and reliability of others. Furthermore, anyone not capable of determining authenticity is hardly capable of weighing the qualifications of someone who professes expertise. In addition, even the most honest and knowledgeable dealer occasionally will make a mistake.

The only wholly satisfactory answer is to foster awareness and expertise on the part of the trade and the buying public alike, and it is to be hoped that the ABAA will, in future, play an increasingly active role in this regard. A welcome step in this direction has been taken by the Southern California Chapter of ABAA and Muir Dawson, who will be coordinating an exhibit highlighting "Forgeries, Fakes, and Facsimiles" at the ABAA Bookfair in Los Angeles in February 1990. This exhibit is aimed at educating the eye and mind of all book people.

Unaddressed by ABAA has been the problem of permanently preventing spurious items from reappearing in the marketplace, only to be mistaken again for originals. As a book with facsimile leaves changes hands, the fact that some of the leaves are reprinted sometimes fails to be transmitted. The problem is so serious in the coin world that for years the American Numismatic Association has condemned wholesale the buying and selling of counterfeit and altered coins of any kind, even when full disclosure is made. This extreme is unwarranted in the book trade; however, a cooperative effort among librarians and the international trade to devise acceptable methods of permanently marking facsimile leaves and documents would be a useful undertaking.

In the light of the ease with which forgeries have been created, the new technologies on the horizon which will result in fraudulent documents being increasingly difficult to detect, the seemingly inexhaustible supply of credulous buyers, and the extreme difficulty of successful prosecutions, it is all the more incumbent upon the trade to take every possible action to protect the marketplace from fraudulent material.

In the opinion of many, the ABAA has been caught napping by recent events. It is hoped that this record of the actions taken and not taken will provide interested persons with the facts with which to make a fair determination in the matter, and will, more importantly, provide lessons for the future. The ABAA is at a critical juncture in its history, at which it can make a leap towards ensuring that ABAA membership is genuinely an assurance of ethics and expertise in the antiquarian book trade, living up to the ideals with which the association was founded. Or, it can choose to function at the level of its description in the current edition of *The Encyclopedia of Associations*: "Dealers of rare and out-of-print books. Sponsors annual regional international book fairs. Publications: *ABAA Membership Directory*, annual. Conventions/meeting: annual...spring, New York City."[8]

If we are to learn anything at all from the disasters of recent years, let it be to refuse to wallow in self recrimination and cynicism and to shun the accusatory judgments of persons who possess no facts or will not commit their remarks to writing. Those who would accuse the ABAA of failing to clean house would do well to consider how extraordinarily unpleasant it is to an honest, struggling dealer to witness the continuing prosperity of a colleague he or she knows, or suspects, to be crooked. There are certainly still some members of ABAA who are impostors; in the absence of written complaints and proof the only acceptable stance is a steadfast adherence to the ethical principles which we all know to be consistent with the highest standards of the antiquarian book trade. To me this means, among other things, support of the ABAA and its ideals. The elect "are to be saved for trying, not for succeeding; whereas the reprobate are eternally damned, not for failing, but for not trying."[9]

References

1. Linda Sillitoe and Allen Roberts, *Salamander: The Story of the Mormon Forgery Murders* (Salt Lake City: Signature Books, 1988); Robert Lindsey, *A Gathering of Saints: A True Story of Money, Murder and Deceit* (New York: Simon and Schuster, [1988]); Steven Naifeh and Gregory White Smith, *The Mormon Murders. A True Story of Greed, Forgery, Deceit, and Death* (New York: Weidenfeld & Nicholson, [1988]); Nicolas Barker. "A Scandal in America." Parts 1 and 2, *The Book Collector* 36 (Winter 1987): 449-470 and (Spring 1988): 9-28; David Hewett. "The Mark Hofmann Story." *Maine Antique Digest* 14 (July, 1986): 1C-7C; David Hewett. "New Evidence of Fake Americana Surfaces in Utah." *Maine Antique Digest* 15 (February, 1987): 12A; David Hewett. "Mark Hofmann: A Boy and His Chemistry Set Gone Bad." *Maine Antique Digest* 14 (November, 1987): 1D-7D; David Hewett. "Wrapping Up the Mark Hofmann Case." *Maine Antique Digest* 16 (December, 1988): 24C; and Office of Salt Lake County Attorney. Mark Hofmann Interviews. Transcripts, Supplements and Exhibits. (North Salt Lake: A.I.S.I. Publishers, 1987), 541, 31 plates.

2. There has been some criticism of the selection of the phrase "questioned imprints" by the committee, as opposed to the more familiar term, "forgery." "Questioned documents" is a phrase well established in law enforcement circles, where it is recognized that use of the word "forgery" implies that intent to defraud is present.

3. Sissela Bok, *Secrets: On the Ethics of Concealment and Revelation* (New York: Pantheon Books, [1982]), 90.
4. W. Thomas Taylor, abridged version of a talk given to the Friends of the University of Texas, September, 1988, [10].
5. Gregory Curtis. "Forgery Texas Style." 17 *Texas Monthly* (March, 1989): 179.
6. [Louis Weinstein], *Guidelines for the Antiquarian Booksellers Association of America* (New York: Antiquarian Booksellers Association of America, 1982).
7. Michael Alan Weinberg. "The Autograph Dealer in the Years to Come." *AB Bookman's Weekly* 83 (May 22, 1989): 2268.
8. *Encyclopedia of Associations, 1990.* 24th edition. (Detroit: Gale Research, [1989]), no. 8499.
9. Perry Miller, *The New England Mind: The Seventeenth Century* (Cambridge, Massachusetts: Harvard University Press, 1967), 384.

Appendix I

W. THOMAS TAYLOR
Printers • Publishers • Antiquarian Booksellers

April 10, 1988

Dear Colleagues:

The Southwest Chapter of the Antiquarian Booksellers' Association of America would like to inform you of the fact that a large number of broadsides relating to Texas, and purportedly dated between about 1820 and 1865, are forgeries, or in some cases complete fabrications. These documents have been in circulation since about 1970. In most cases there is a relatively simple way to detect the forged copies, and if you presently have, or have had, copies of these documents, please feel free to call me for this information. The documents so far proven to be bogus are:

> Streeter 7, 11, 64.1 (a fabrication--there are no genuine copies), 88, 89, 112.1 (another fabrication), 165, 185, 1082, and one document by Thomas J. Rusk, dated April 23, 1836, and headed "Glorious News," which is another fabrication, not in Streeter.

In addition, I have reason to believe that copies of the following may have been forged, and would appreciate information regarding any copies that you may know of: Streeter 114, 151, 178, 875, and 1246.

In the post-Streeter period, there is reason to believe that the following may have been forged: Winkler (Checklist of Texas Imprints) 202 and 935, both relating to Sam Houston.

I do not believe that the above list will prove to be at all complete, and I would welcome information or inquiries regarding any broadside related to Texas dated between 1820 and 1865 which does not have a proveable provenance before 1970. Thank you.

Yours sincerely,

W. Thomas Taylor

1906 Miriam, Austin, Texas 78722 • 512-478-7628

Appendix II

Questioned Imprints: A Preliminary Report

The ABAA has been increasingly concerned with the growing number of questioned imprints which have been recently reported by a variety of recognized experts. For this reason we are publishing a list of imprints questioned to date. The newly appointed ABAA Committee on Questioned Imprints will continue to compile information on similar items as necessary.

The resulting register of questioned imprints will include in its scope any printed item which is a reprint, facsimile or fabrication that might be mistaken for a genuine original. The list which follows represents only the beginning of an ongoing project. Additional bibliographical information, locations, or corrections regarding any item on this list would be appreciated.

The Committee is using the term "fabrication" to refer to an imprint of which no genuine copies are presently known. On the advice of legal counsel the phrase "alleged fabrication" is used in the enclosed list. The term "facsimile" will be applied to an exact copy of a genuine original. The term "reprint" indicates an imprint which in general follows the appearance of the original but is not an exact imitation. Owners of questioned imprints of which recognized originals exist are advised to take steps to authenticate their copies, if possible by comparison with a genuine copy. Only in the case of alleged fabrications should all copies be treated with suspicion.

We hope that anyone who has knowledge of any questioned imprint will report it to us on the enclosed form, filling out any part or all of it. Plans to make the results of this process and our research generally available are being formulated. Inquiries about individual items will be welcomed by the Committee and should be addressed to Jennifer S. Larson, Chairman, ABAA Questioned Imprints Committee, c/o Yerba Buena Books, 882 Bush Street, San Francisco CA 94108, phone (415) 474-2788. Any information regarding the source of any questioned imprint on the enclosed list should be referred to John R. Curtis, Jr., Chairman, ABAA Ethics Committee, The Bookpress, Ltd., P. O. Box KP, Williamsburg, VA 23187.

ABAA Questioned Imprints Committee:
Jennifer S. Larson, Chairman
John S. Curtis
Elisabeth Woodburn (consultant)
W. Thomas Taylor
  1906 Miriam, Austin TX 78722   (512) 478-7628
Dorothy Sloan
  P. O. Box 49670, Austin TX 78705   (512) 477-8442 / 477-8602

Questioned Imprints

ALLEN, Augustus Chapman. The town of Houston. [Text begins]: Situated at the head of Buffalo Bayou, is now for the first time brought to public notice... [Signed in type at end]: A. C. Allen, J. K. Allen. No place or date, but represented as Columbia, Texas, 1836. Broadside. 23 x 14 cm. (9-1/16 x 5-1/2 inches). Streeter 112.1. Alleged fabrication, printed in 18 point Linotype Bodoni, which did not exist until 1918.

AUSTIN, Stephen F. Notice. [To colonists in Austin's Colony. Text begins]: Each Emigrant who has removed to this Colony... [Signed and dated at end]: S. F. Austin, Town of Austin, 20th November, 1829. [San Felipe de Austin: Printed by G. B. Cotten, 1829]. Broadside in two columns. NOTICE in very large type at top, decorative horizontal bar between heading and text, vertical bar with diamond devices separating the two columns of text. 19.5 x 24.5 cm. (7-5/8 x 9-5/8 inches). Streeter 11 (genuine copy illustrated on p. 41; genuine copy at General Land Office, Austin, Texas). Facsimile.

AUSTIN, Stephen F. [Printed form of permit authorizing individuals to settle in Austin's Colony, reading]: By Stephen F. Austin, Civil Commandant of the Colony forming on the Colorado and Brassos Rivers in the Province of Texas: Permission is hereby granted to _____ to emigrate and settle in the Colony forming by me, under the authority and protection of New Spain, at the points above stated. Said _____ required to comply with the general regulations hereunto annexed. General Regulations relative to the Colony... [five regulations]. [New Orleans, 1821]. Broadside. 25 x 20 cm. (9-7/8 x 7-7/8 inches). Streeter 1082 (genuine copies at Yale and Univ. of Texas at Austin). Facsimile.

BAKER, Moseley. Letter from Gonzales to the Standing Committee of San Felipe. [Text begins]: Gonzales, 8th March, 1836. Gentlemen, On day before yesterday I arrived here... Our own situation is critical--too weak to advance, and insufficient to protect this place--and daily expecting two thousand cavalry to attack us... [Signed in type]: Moseley Baker, Captain. [Addressed to]: John R. Jones, Thomas Gay, Wm. Pettus, Committee. [At end]: Published by order of the Committee, February 10, 1836. [San

Felipe de Austin: Printed by Baker & Bordens, 1836]. Broadside in two columns. 24.9 x 20 cm. (9-3/4 x 7-7/8 inches). Streeter 114 (genuine copies at Univ. Texas at Austin and Texas State Library). Facsimile.

BOWDOIN, James. [Heading]: Commonwealth of Massachusetts. By His Excellency James Bowdoin, Esquire, Governour of the Commonwealth of Massachusetts. [rule] A Proclamation. [Text commences]: Whereas information has been given to the Supreme Executive Commonwealth, that on Tuesday last, the 29th of August... within this Commonwealth, a large concourse of people... assembled at the Court-House in Northampton, many of whom were armed with guns, swords and other deadly weapons... Boston: Printed by Adams and Nourse, Printers to the General Court, September 2, 1786. Folio broadside with large seal at top. 36 x 25 cm. (14-1/16 x 9-3/4 inches). Evans 19789. Genuine copy at Massachusetts Archives, State Library, Boston. Facsimile.

BRIDGER, Jim. Printed promissory note completed in manuscript. S[alt] L[ake] C[ity], Utah Territory, 1852. 8.6 x 20 cm. (3-3/8 x 7-7/8 inches). With purported signature of Jim Bridger signed with his "x" plus two other signatures. Throckmorton, George J., "A Forensic Analysis of Twenty-one Hofmann Documents" in Sillitoe & Roberts, Salamander (SLC: Signature, 1988), pp. 549-50. Facsimile.

CLAYTON, William. The Latter-Day Saints' Emigrants' Guide... St. Louis: Mo. Republican Steam Power Press--Chambers & Knapp, 1848. 24 pp. 18.5 cm. (7-5/16 inches) tall. American Imprints Inventory (Missouri) 577. Graff 751. Howes C475. Jones 1166. Plains & Rockies IV:147 (locating genuine copies at Huntington Library, San Marino, California; Yale; Newberry Library, Chicago; Harvard; New York Public Library, New York City). Facsimile and reprint copies exist, both containing only one signature (see Plains & Rockies for collation of genuine copy).

[COLUMBIA JOCKEY CLUB]. Columbia Jockey Club [cut of race horses. Text begins]: The Races over the Columbia Turf will take place on the 4th Monday in May ensuing in the town of Columbia... [Last paragraph reads]: Gentlemen at a distance wising [sic] to enter horses, and procure stables, will do well to address the proprietor J. H. Bell, Esq. [sic] or the Secretary of the Club. [Signed in type at end]: A. C. Ainsworth Sec'y. Columbia [Texas], April 11, 1835. Streeter Broadside. 23.5 x 13.5 cm. (9-1/4 x 5-3/8 inches).

64.1 (locating the Yale facsimile copy). Alleged fabrication, printed in 12 point Linotype Century, which did not exist until 1896.

[COUNCIL OF SAFETY]. In Council of Safety, Lancaster, 21st October, 1777. Whereas divers of the inhabitants of this commonwealth, not regarding their duty to the State, but renouncing their allegiance thereto, and disclaiming the protection thereof, have wickedly joined themselves to our unnatural enemies, giving to them aid and assistance... [ending]: By order of the Council of Safety, Thomas Wharton, jr. President. [printed rule of diamonds and dashes] Lancaster: Francis Bailey, 1777. Broadside. 33 x 15 cm. (13 x 5-7/8 inches). Evans 15529. Genuine copy at Library of Congress. Facsimile.

[CURRENCY (DESERET CURRENCY)]. B. Young will Pay the Bearer Ten Cents in Deseret Currency... No place or date, but represented as Great Salt Lake, ca. 1858. Printed scrip note in the denomination of 10 cents. 2.7 x 7.8 cm. (2-1/16 x 3-1/16 inches). With purported signature of Brigham Young at lower right. Rust, fig. 94. Alleged fabrication.

[CURRENCY (DESERET CURRENCY ASSOCIATION)]. Deseret Currency Association will pay the bearer... in Live Stock... Great Salt Lake City, Utah Territory, 1858. 8 printed scrip notes in denominations of $1, $2, $3, $5, $10, $20, $50, and $100. Approximately 6.2 x 12.2 cm. (2-1/2 x 4-7/8 inches). Each with signature in lower left corner, date in lower right corner, and printed or purported written signature of Brigham Young at lower right, manuscript serial number at upper left. Rust, figs. 86-93. Throckmorton, George J., "A Forensic Analysis of Twenty-one Hofmann Documents" in Sillitoe & Roberts, Salamander (SLC: Signature, 1988), p. 543. Of the $1, $2, and $3 denominations facsimiles exist; remaining denominations are alleged fabrications.

[CURRENCY (SPANISH FORK COOPERATIVE INSTITUTION)]. Spanish Fork Co-op Institution Will Pay to the Bearer... in Merchandise. No place or date, but represented as Utah, early 1850's. Small scrip note set: 3 printed notes in denominations of 5 cents, 10 cents, and 25 cents. Approximately 5.1 x 9.5 cm. (approximately 2 x 3-3/4 inches). Manuscript initials at bottom crossed out by hand with two horizontal lines. Only known genuine example issued by "Spanish Fork Co-operative;" forgeries read "Spanish Fork Co-operative Institution." Rust, figs. 203-206. Throckmorton, George J., "A Forensic Analysis of Twenty-one Hofmann Documents" in Sillitoe & Roberts, Salamander (SLC: Signature, 1988), pp. 541-2. Alleged fabrication.

[CURRENCY (SPANISH FORK COOPERATIVE INSTITUTION)]. Spanish Fork Co-operative Institution Will Pay To the Bearer ... In Merchandise Retail. No Place or date, but represented as Utah, early 1850's. Rainbow scrip note set: 4 printed notes in denominations of 10 cents, 25 cents, 50 cents, and 1 dollar, each denomination printed in a different color--red, blue, green, and yellow, on grey-colored card stock. 6.3 x 9.9 cm. (2-1/2 x 3-7/8 inches). Manuscript number and signature at end of each note. Rust, figs. 207-210. Throckmorton, George J., "A Forensic Analysis of Twenty-one Hofmann Documents" in Sillitoe & Roberts, Salamander (SLC: Signature, 1988), pp. 541-2. Alleged fabrication.

[DELAWARE PILOTS]. To the Delaware Pilots ... [from] The Committee for Tarring and Feathering ... To Capt. Ayres of the Ship Polly, on a Voyage from London to Philadelphia, Sir ... Philadelphia, Nov. 27, 1773. Philadelphia, Nov. 27, 1773. Folio broadside. 33.4 x 20.3 cm. (13-1/8 x 8 inches). Evans 12942. Hildeburn 2941. Genuine copy at Library Company of Philadelphia; Facsimile.

GARCIA, Lt. Col. D. Luciano. [Circular in Spanish of the Junta gubernativa of the Province of Texas announcing the arrival of Lt. Col. D. Luciano Garcia in this capital, and his assumption of the office of governor. With heading]: Junta Gubernativa de la Provincia de Texas, [Text commences]: El Gefe Superior Político de estas Provincias Brigadier D. Felipe de la Garza ... [San Antonio de] Bexar, July 8, 1823. One page of 4 pp. folder printed on page [1]. 19.5 x 16 cm. (7-3/4 x 6-1/4 inches). Streeter 7 (genuine copies at Yale; General Land Office, Austin, Texas; Univ. Texas at Austin). Eberstadt, Texas 162:326 (illustrated on p. 94). Facsimile.

HOUSTON, Sam. Army Orders. [Text begins]: Head Quarters, [sic] Camp near Beason's, March 2, 1836. The Chairman of the Committee of Safety at San Felipe, will take immediate measures as will arrest the deserters from the army ... [At end]: In a few days I hope to have force sufficient to capture the enemy before he can reach the Guadaloupe. [Signed in type]: Sam Houston, Commander-in-Chief. [San Felipe de Austin; Baker & Bordens, 1836]. Broadside. 25 x 14.5 cm. (9-7/8 x 5-3/4 inches). Streeter 151. Facsimile.

HOUSTON, Sam. Proclamation by the Governor of the State of Texas ... [ordering an election to be held February 23, 1861, to approve or disapprove the Ordinance of secession]. [Austin, February 9, 1861]. Broadside. 50.5 x 23.5 cm. (19-7/8 x 9-1/4 inches). Parrish, Confederate Imprints 4213. Winkler & Friend 202 (genuine copy at Univ. of Texas, Austin). Facsimile.

[HOUSTON, SAM]. The funeral ceremonies of the late Gen. Sam Houston will take place at the family residence, this evening Monday 27th instant, at 4 o'clock. The friends of the family and the public, are respectfully invited to attend. Huntsville, July 27, 1863. Broadside. 10.2 x 16 cm. (4-1/4 x 6-1/3 inches). Parrish, Confederate Imprints 5397. Winkler & Friend 935 (locating only the photocopy at Univ. of Texas, Austin). Facsimile.

[KANSAS]. To the People of Kansas. Jim Lane Begging for Sympathy. [small rule followed by text in two columns, commencing]: The Notorious Gen. Jim Lane has issued an address to the People of Kansas, in which he gives an account of the killing of Colonel Gaius Jenkins ... [at end]: TRUTH IS MIGHTY AND WILL PREVAIL. [Kansas, 1858]. 23 cm. (9-1/8 inches) tall. Broadside printed in two columns with heavy blank rule between columns. Genuine copy at Yale. Facsimile.

[MAID OF IOWA]. Maid of Iowa ... No place or date, but represented as Nauvoo, early 1840's. Printed steamboat ticket, with purported signatures of Joseph Smith, also Brigham Young or Emma Smith. Alleged fabrication.

[NAUVOO AGRICULTURAL AND MANUFACTURING ASSOCIATION]. The bearer is entitled to One Share, of the Capital Stock of The Nauvoo Agricultural and Manufacturing Association ... No place, but represented as Nauvoo, 184[1]. Printed stock certificate. 7 x 19.4 cm. (2-3/4 x 7-5/8 inches). With eagle and 2 circular decorative devices at left, beehive at top center, 3 signatures (including Joseph Smith) below, and date, amount and serial number provided in manuscript. Rust, fig. 40. Alleged fabrication.

[NAUVOO MUSIC ASSOCIATION]. The Bearer is entitled to One Share of the Capital Stock of the Nauvoo Music Association ... Nauvoo, 1843 & 1845. Printed stock certificate. Approximately 7.8 x 19.4 cm. (3-1/16 x 7-3/4 inches). With eagle and two circular devices at left, bearing signatures at end, and date, amount, and serial number provided in manuscript.

Two issues: $500 dated June 5, 1843 & $1000 dated January 10, 1845. Rust, figs. 36 & 37. Alleged fabrication.

[OATH OF A FREEMAN]. The Oath of a Freeman. [text begins]: I AB being (by Gods providence) an Inhabitant, and Freeman, within this Iurisdictio [sic] of this Common-wealth, doe freely acknowledge my selfe to bee subject to the governement thereof.... No place or date, but represented as Cambridge: Stephen Daye, Massachusetts, 1638. Broadside within ornamental ruled border. 15.6 x 10.7 cm. (6-1/8 x 4-1/4 inches). Illustrated following p. 150 in Robert Lindsey's A Gathering of Saints (NY: Simon & Schuster, 1988). Throckmorton, George J. "A Forensic Analysis of Twenty-one Hofmann Documents" in Sillitoe & Roberts, Salamander (SLC: Signature, 1988), pp. 546-547, 549. Alleged fabrication.

[PROTESTANT CHURCH AT GALVESTON]. A Public Meeting. [Text commences]: At a large and respectable meeting of the citizens of Galveston and subsequent to a meeting convened for public worship, the following proceedings took place: On motion of Col. Turner, Gail Borden Jr. Esq. was called to the Chair, and C. H. Winkle Esq., appointed Secretary... Resolved, That a subscription be created in this place for the purpose of obtaining funds for the creation of a Church, for Public worship in this city.... Galveston, April 8, 1838. Broadside printed in two columns. 20 x 20 cm. (8 x 8 inches). Alleged fabrication. Under magnification this imprint appears to be a photocopy of an article taken directly from the April 18, 1838, issue of the Telegraph and Texas Register (first newspaper published at Houston; copy of this issue available at the Texas State Library in Austin). The type is unaltered from its newspaper appearance except that the dateline of "Galveston, Sunday, April 8th" has been moved to appear at the end of the questioned imprint instead of under the headline.

RUSK, Thomas J. Glorious News! Headquarters, Army, April 23. We met Santa Anna on the 21st inst.; we attacked him with 600 men; he had about eleven hundred with two howitzers. We entirely routed his whole force, killing about half and taking the remainder prisoners... [Signed in type at end]: Thomas J. Rusk, Secretary of War. Nacogdoches: D. E. Lawton, Printer [1836]. Broadside. 18 x 12 cm. (7-1/4 x 4-7/8 inches). Alleged fabrication, printed in 12 point Linotype Century, which did not exist until 1896.

[TEXAS]. Declaracion del Pueblo de Tejas, Reunido en Convencion General. [Text begins]: Por cuanto el general Antonio Lopez de Santa Ana, [sic] asociado con otros gefes militares han destruido por medio de la fuerza armada las instituciones Federales de la Nacion Mejicana, y disuelto el pacto social que existia entre el Pueblo de Tejas y las demas partes de la confederacion Mejicana, el buen Pueblo de Tejas ... Declara Solemnemente ... [Signed and dated at end]: B. T. Archer, Presidente [and two columns with names of delegates from twelve municipalities] P. B. Dexter, secretario. Sala de la Convencion en San Felipe de Austin, 7 de Noviembre de 1825 [i.e. 1835]. San Felipe de Austin: Baker y Bordens [1835]. Broadside in Spanish. 32.5 x 19.5 cm. (12-5/6 x 7-3/4) inches. Streeter 88 (genuine copies at Yale; Library of Congress; Univ. of Texas at Austin, Texas State Library). Facsimile.

[TEXAS]. Declaration of the People of Texas, in General Convention assembled. [Text begins]: Whereas, General Antonio Lopez de Santa Ana, [sic] and other military chieftains, have, by force of arms, overthrown the Federal Institutions of Mexico and dissolved the social compact which existed between Texas and the other members of the Mexican Confederacy; now the good People of Texas ... Solemnly Declare ... [Signed and dated at end]: B. T. Archer, President [and followed by two columns with names of delegates from twelve municipalities] P. B. Dexter, Secretary November 7, 1835. San Felipe de Austin: Baker & Bordens [1835]. Broadside. 31.5 x 19.3 cm. (12-3/8 x 7-5/8 inches). Streeter 89 (genuine copies at Univ. of Texas at Austin and Yale). Facsimile.

[TEXAS] Texas! [Ornaments]. Emigrants who are desirious [sic] of assisting Texas at this important crisis of her affairs may have a free passage and equipments, by applying at the New-York and Philadelphia Hotel, on the Old Levee, near The Blue Stores. Now is the time to ensure a fortune in and: To all who remain in Texas during the War will be allowed 1280 Acres. To all who remain Six Months. 640 Acres. To all who remain Three Months, 320 Acres. And as Colonists, 4600 Acres for a family and 1470 Acres for a Single Man. New Orleans, April 23d, 1836. Broadside. 25 x 26 cm. (9-7/8 x 10-1/4 inches). Streeter 1246 (genuine copy at Univ. Texas at Austin). Facsimile.

[TEXAS]. Unanimous Declaration of Independence, by the Delegates of the People of Texas, in General Convention, at the Town of Washington, on the Second Day of March, 1836. [Text begins]: When a government has ceased to protect the lives, liberty, and property of the people ... [At end]:

We, therefore, the delegates [sic] ... of the people of Texas, in solemn convention assemble ... do hereby resolve and declare, that our political connection with the Mexican nation has forever ended, and that the people of Texas do now constitute a Free, Sovereign, and Independent Republic .... [Signed in type]: Richard Ellis, President [and 49 members of the Convention]. San Felipe de Austin [1836]. Broadside in four columns. 40.5 x 33.2 cm. (16 x 13-1/4 inches). Streeter 165 (genuine copies at Yale; Texas State Library; Univ. of Texas at Austin). Streeter, Americana Beginnings 60. Genuine copies illustrated in Streeter Sale (Vol. I, p. 257, State A) and Burns catalogue (State B). Facsimile.

[TEXAS WAR DEPARTMENT]. War Department Columbia, November 30, 1836. General Orders. [Text begins]: It has been reported to the president by general Felix Huston, commanding the army of Texas, that the Mexicans are engaged in active and formidable preparations for the immediate invasion of Texas.... [Signed in type at end]: By order of the president, Wm. G. Cooke, Acting Secretary of War. [Columbia: Printed at the Telegraph Office, 1836]. Broadside. 20.5 x 16 cm. (8-1/16 x 6-1/4 inches). Streeter 178 (entry from Texas State Library, Austin copy, now apparently missing; no genuine copy now available for inspection, but Yale has a photostat). Facsimile.

THOMSON, Charles. Philadelphia. In Congress, Thursday, September 22, 1774. [Text begins]: Resolved, That the Congress request the Merchants and Others, in the Several Colonies, not to send to Great Britain any Orders for Goods.... [Signed in type at end]: Charles Thomson, Sec. [Philadelphia: Printed by W. and T. Bradford [1774]. Broadside. 16.2 x 21.5 cm. (16-3/16 x 8-1/2 inches). Evans 13702. Genuine copy at Harvard. Facsimile.

TRAVIS, William Barret. To the Citizens of Texas. [Text begins]: Commandancy of the Alamo, Bejar, Feb. 24, 1836. Fellow-Citizens, I am besieged by a thousand [sic] or more of the Mexicans, under Santa Ana. [sic] I have sustained a continual bombardment and cannonade for twenty-four hours, and have not lost one man.... [Signed in print]: Victory or Death, W. Barret Travis, Lieutenant-Colonel Commandant. [Followed by]: P. s. The Lord is on our Side. [Signed in type at end]: T. San Felipe de Austin: Printed by Baker & Bordens, 1836. Broadside. 25.2 x 19.5 cm. (10 x 7-3/4 inches). Streeter 185 (genuine copy at Yale). Facsimile.

-8-

150

12/06/88

Appendix III

Questioned Imprints: Addenda to the ABAA Preliminary Report

BOWDOIN, James. [Seal] Commonwealth of Massachusetts. By His Excellency James Bowdoin, Esq. Governour of the Commonwealth of Massachusetts. A Proclamation. [Text begins]: Whereas by an Act passed the sixteenth of February instant, entitled, "An Act describing the disqualifications to which persons shall be subjected who have been, or may be guilty of Treason, or giving aid or support to the present Rebellion, and to whom a pardon may be extended".... [Signed in type]: John Avery, jun. Secretary. Boston: Printed by Adams & Nourse, Printers to the General Court, [1787]. Broadside, approx. 17-1/4 x 12-3/8 inches. Evans 20510. Facsimile.

[CLEMENS, Samuel Langhorne]. (In printed facsimile of autograph): None genuine without this signature on the bottle: Yrs Truly, Mark Twain Mch 1886. Whiskey label endorsement? It is not known whether any forged copies exist.

[CONFEDERATE IMPRINT]. To the People of Western Virginia. [Text begins]: The Army of the Confederate States has come among you to expel the enemy, to rescue the people from the despotism of the counterfeit State Government imposed on you by Northern bayonets, and to restore to country once more to its natural allegiance to the State. [Signed in type]: Maj. Gen. Loring. Charleston, Va., September 14, 1862. Broadside, approx. 9-1/2 x 4 inches. Parrish & Willingham 1529. Reprint.

COTTON, John. Spiritual Milk for Boston Babes. 14 pp. Boston, 1684. It is not known whether any forged copies exist.

[COUNCIL OF SAFETY]. In Council of Safety, Philadelphia, December 2, 1776. [Text begins]: Resolved, That it is the Opinion of this Board, that all the Shops in this City be shut up.... By Order of Council, David Rittenhouse, Vice-President. Philadelphia: Henry Miller, 1776. Broadside, approx. 2-1/4 x 3-3/4 inches. Evans 15023. Genuine copy at Historical Society of Pennsylvania. Facsimile.

[CURRENCY]. One Dollar. Nauvoo, Illinois. This Certificate will be received by the City of Nauvoo as One Dollar.... Nauvoo: L. Robinson, Stereotyper and Pr., 184-. Approx. 7.5 x 16.8 cm. Facsimile?

[Dust Jackets]. The First Edition Library has issued, to accompany its fine facsimile editions, full color and potentially deceptive reprints of the original dust jackets for For Whom the Bell Tolls, the Great Gatsby, and Of Mice and Men. While the volumes themselves are clearly marked, 2,500 copies of each of these jackets were printed without identification. Subsequent dust jackets will be identified by the First Edition Library logo, F.E.L., which will appear at the center bottom of the back flap of the jacket.

LANCASTER COUNTY, PENNSYLVANIA. Extracts from the Votes and Proceedings of the Committee of Observation for the County of Lancaster. At a Meeting of the said Committee, held at the Court-House...on the 16th and 17th Days of June, 1776. James Burd, Esq; in the Chair. [Text begins]: Resolved, That it be recommended...to all the Inhabitants of the County of Lancaster...immediately to provide themselves with Good and sufficient Firelocks.... [Signed in type]: William Barton, Secretary. Lancaster: Printed by Francis Bailey, [1775]. Broadside, approx. 16-1/4 x 10-3/8 inches. Evans 14142. Facsimile.

NAUVOO, ILLINOIS. Broadside supporting candidacy of Joseph Smith, Jr. for Mayor. It is not known whether any forged copies exist. Fabrication?

NEW YORK (CITY) COMMITTEE OF OBSERVATION. [Text begins]: The following Persons were mentioned in the Committee of Observation, as proper to be elected for a General Committee.... [Signed in type at end]: Isaac Low, Chairman. New York, April 28, 1775. Broadside, 46 x 31 cm. (18-1/16 x 12-1/8 inches). Bristol 4074. Genuine copy at the New York Society Library. Facsimile.

NORTHWEST TERRITORY. Laws of the Territory of the United States North-West of the Ohio: Adopted and Made by the Governour and Judges, in their Legislative Capacity, at the Session Begun on Friday, the XXIX Day of May, One Thousand Seven Hundred and Ninety-five, and Ending on Tuesday the Twenty-fifth Day of August following: with an Appendix of Resolutions and the Ordinance for the Government of the Territory. By Authority. Cincinnati: W. Maxwell, 1796. [225] pp. 4to. Evans 30916, locating genuine copies at John Carter Brown Library, Library of Congress and New York Public Library. Facsimile.

NORTHWEST TERRITORY. Laws of the Territory of the United States North-West of the River Ohio Adopted and published at a Session of the legislature begun in the Town of Cincinnati, County of Hamilton and Territory aforesaid upon the 23d day of April in the year of our Lord 1798 and continued by adjournments to the seventh day of May in the same year. By Authority. Cincinnati: Edmund Freeman, 1798. 32 p. Evans 34257. Facsimile.

PENNSYLVANIA GAZETTE. Many issues exist in facsimile copies dated 1730s – 1780s. Reported copies vary in size from originals approx. 15-20%. Precise measurements of leaf size and information as to watermarks found in genuine copies given in C. William Miller's Benjamin Franklin's Philadelphia Printing, 1728-1766, Philadelphia: American Philosophical Society, 1974.

PUTNAM, Israel, Major General. Headquarters, Philadelphia, Dec. 13th, 1776. [Text begins]: The General has been informed that some weak or wicked Men have maliciously reported that it is the Intension [sic] and Wish of the Officers and Men of the Continental Army to burn and destroy the City of Philadelphia.... [Philadelphia: John Dunlap, 1776]. Broadside, approx. 4-1/2 x 5-3/4 inches. Evans 15181. Genuine copy at the Historical Society of Pennsylvania. Facsimile.

151

SCHMITZ, E.E., Mayor. Proclamation by the Mayor. [Text begins]: The Federal Troops, the members of the Regular Police Force, and all Special Police Officers have been authorized to KILL any and all persons found engaged in looting or in the commission of any other crime. [San Francisco]: Altvater Print, April 18, 1906. Broadside, approx. 21.5 x 12.3 cm. (sans serif body type) or approx. 21.6 x 12.4 cm. (serif body type). Two apparently genuine issues, plus a facsimile reprint of the issue with serifed body type. Genuine copies at The Bancroft Library.

THOMSON, Charles.. In Congress, June 6, 1778. [Text begins]: Resolved, That the Resolution of Congress of the 2d of June, relative to the Subsistance Money to be allowed to Officers in the Continental Service, be extended to all Militia or other Troops which may from time to time be called into the Continental Service, or which may be raised in pursuance of a special Resolution of Congress. [Signed in type]: Charles Thomson, Secretary. York-Town: Printed by John Dunlap, [1778]. Broadside, approx. 7 x 5-1/2 inches. Evans 16127. Facsimile.

WELLS, FARGO & CO. $1850 Reward! [Text begins]: This is for the Special Information of Gold Buyers, Officers and Wells, Fargo & Co's employees only, and not for posting. San Francisco, Aug. 17, 1875. Broadside, approx. 10 x 7 inches. Facsimile.

The Texas Forgeries.
Obligations of the Dealer:
The International Perspective*

ANTHONY ROTA

I rather suspect that I was asked to speak at the Houston Conference on Forged Documents for two reasons. The first is that I have the honor to be *pro tempore* President of the International League of Antiquarian Booksellers, and the second is that I am known to get very hot under the collar about abuses such as those which form the subject of our present deliberations.

I am a fourth generation bookseller. Bookselling and, for that matter, book collecting, are in my blood. Soon after I joined my father at Bertram Rota Ltd. we came across a sophisticated copy of a modern first edition (in fact, first edition sheets removed from a soiled binding and put into an immaculate binding case from a slightly later printing in a crude and misguided attempt to increase the value). Even now, thirty-seven years later, I still remember the intensity of my father's anger as he explained to me what had happened and why. Speaking perhaps of private rather than institutional collecting, he said that we booksellers made the rules and also acted as referees. If we cheated, everything became meaningless. It is because the forger, or forgers, of the Texas documents and those who knowingly trafficked in them were, in effect, setting my life's work and my father's life's work at nought that I hope a special circle of Dante's Hell is reserved for them. If their punishment were to be devised by the eponymous emperor in Gilbert and Sullivan's Mikado, whose "object all sublime" was "to make the punishment fit the crime," they might perhaps be condemned to an eternity of attempting to collate an endless supply of imperfect incunabula.

Their offense was no "caper." It was not just a peccadillo: it was, in bibliographical terms, a sin.

It is not so much the forgers' illicit financial gain which weighs heavily with me: it is the fact that they were thumbing their noses at what I imagine every one of us holds dear, indeed sacred, and were, by their antics, attempting to make buffoons of us all.

It gives me no pleasure to report that two booksellers on this side of the Atlantic, in what seemed to me an attempt to sweep the affair under the carpet,

---

*This paper was written expressly for and delivered at the Houston Conference on Forged Documents and appears under the same title and in slightly revised form in *International League of Antiquarian Booksellers Newsletter* Anton Gerits, ed. (Hilversum, The Netherlands: I.L.A.B.) 43 (April, 1990): 2-18.

asked why I was getting so excited about the matter and why the International League of Antiquarian Booksellers was seeking to become involved in what they saw as essentially a local problem. John Donne had the answer for them when he said that "No man is an island." That is as true in the world of bibliography as it is in the world-at-large. Happily my colleagues on the committee of the International League take the same view. The market for Texas documents may be a narrow and highly specialized one, having little immediate or obvious relevance for dealers in London, Paris or Vienna, but the world of rare books is built on confidence, on trust, on expertise and on integrity, and anything that chips away at that fabric is bad news for us all. For example, when, in the 1930s, T. J. Wise was exposed as the forger of nineteenth century pamphlets spuriously dated to suggest that they were rare first printings of works by widely collected authors, the whole collecting world suffered from the scandal.

The Texas forgeries are not the disease: they are only a symptom of it. The disease is greed: the desire to make easy money from the credulity of others. It is a disease which flourishes in the dark. Turn a strong enough light on it and it will wither and die. That light is publicity. Once buyers become aware that clever forgeries exist, they will be on their guard and, if I may mix my metaphors a little, the door will begin to close on the forgers' access to quick and easy profits. Try to hush up the affair, try to pretend that nothing is wrong, and the disease will flourish.

In the trade in rare books and manuscripts, recently the subject of the Rare Books & Manuscripts Section's conference in Cambridge, England, confidence is everything: confidence in the integrity and expertise of those with whom one does business, confidence in the integrity of material, and confidence in the structure of prices and values.

I hope to demonstrate that this confidence is a web spun worldwide. Tug at one strand and the rest moves a little; snap it, and the whole may sag. There is little direct connection between the sale of a forged document in Paris, Texas and the price of illuminated manuscripts in Paris, France, but there is a thread that links them. That thread is confidence.

We are told that the present affair caused one collector to stop purchasing Texas imprints altogether. The loss of at least one important collector in Texas and a sharp decline in interest in, and prices for, Texas material may, at first, do no more than damage dealers in Texas. But they may not then be able to support the market in Americana generally and their dealings with their counterparts in, say, New York and California may dwindle. Thus, the whole of the American trade can be affected and, in consequence, its dealings with Europe damaged.

This is bad enough, but far worse is the risk of a spread of forgery to other specialized markets around the world. That is why we must condemn what has happened in this State, do all that we can to discover how and why the forgeries occurred, and do our utmost to see that life is made difficult for those who might think of following in the Texas forgers' track.

I want to play my part in bringing about a trade response to the present troubles which will leave confidence stronger rather than the contrary.

The International League of Antiquarian Booksellers is a federation of seventeen sovereign and independent national associations spread across the globe. Europe is very strongly represented, of course. One of the largest associations is in America, and there is a young and thriving association in Canada. We have a member in Brazil, as well as associations in Australasia and Japan. In all, the League represents approximately fifteen hundred dealers in rare books and manuscripts. The national associations vary enormously, one from another, not only in size but also in nature. In some countries it is usual for member firms to trade widely across national boundaries; in others it is not. On the continent of Europe some member firms sell not just by retail but by auction as well, thereby encountering a different and additional range of problems, some of them relevant to our subject today.

In some nations our members quite frankly represent the elite. In others—and perhaps this is the nub of the matter—to exclude, or to attempt to exclude, would-be members is to run the risk of being sued for restraint of trade.

The motto of the League is *Amor librorum nos unit*, and it is indeed the love of books which unites us. I can tell you that at our international gatherings we seldom reach 100 percent agreement on anything else! What I want to stress is that to establish one single definitive voice for the League is no easy task.

It goes without saying that the League seeks to further the highest standards in antiquarian bookselling, in matters of expertise as well as ethics. The League's constitution does not permit the central body to interfere in the internal affairs of a member association, but if a problem spills over into the international arena then, at least during my presidency, that is another matter. Be that as it may, the League simply does not have, for example, the power to insist that a national association expel or otherwise discipline a given bookseller. We can exert moral pressure—and we do—but we have to accept what we are told about the legal constraints in given countries.

In Amsterdam in February 1989, at its first meeting after news of the Texas scandal broke, the I.L.A.B. committee, drawn from seven nations including the United States, unanimously passed the following resolution which was widely promulgated:

> The committee of the International League of Antiquarian Booksellers learned with concern of the forging of various printed and manuscript documents relating to the history of Texas. Mindful of the League's role as the upholder of the highest standards of integrity and of expertise, the committee welcomed the prompt response of the Antiquarian Booksellers Association of America and urges the ABAA's board of governors to do all in its power to aid the identification and punishment of those responsible for the betrayal of the ideals which are close to the League's heart. To that end the committee of the League asks the president of the ABAA to give a further report on the matter when the presidents of all the member associations of the League meet in Switzerland in September.

What happened in Switzerland I shall reveal shortly.

In my field of English and American literature of the last hundred years, it has (so far) always seemed pretty easy to identify forgeries. Similarly, I never saw the late Peter Croft, author of *Autograph Poetry in the English Language* (1973), one-time head of the Manuscript Department of Sotheby's in London, and late Librarian of King's College, Cambridge, in doubt for long about the authenticity or otherwise of a manuscript. A notoriously short-sighted man, he used to make his decisions about authenticity after the merest (and disingenuously casual) glance; only if his opinion was questioned (and it seldom was) would he remove his spectacles, hold the document close to his eye and examine it carefully in order to produce reasons for the correctness of his initial diagnosis—for correct it was always proved to be.

Now it appears that we are sailing into stormier waters. Not just the forgers of the Texas documents, but also Mark Hofmann, who produced the fake Mormon material, have shown us that a casual glance, supported by the instinctive reaction that comes with experience (useful though that may be), is often no longer enough.

Making forgeries that will pass more than the most cursory examination requires a considerable investment of time and skill. It always used to be the case that the rewards available to potential forgers in the world of rare books and manuscripts were not large enough to be tempting. Those who had the disposition to forge in the first place, and who had the technical knowledge and skill to go with it, therefore concentrated, thank goodness, on the production of such things as counterfeit banknotes. It is only in these last years, which have seen steep rises in the prices commanded by rare books and manuscripts, that serious criminals have turned their attention to our world.

This means that the dealer must constantly strive to increase his or her expertise. It is not sufficient merely to sell things in good faith: one needs to be sure of what one is selling. If there is the least doubt, then outside specialist advice should be sought. I know that this is the firm conviction of Ms. Jennifer Larson. Doubtless, she will be preaching it inside the Antiquarian Booksellers Association of America, just as I shall be in the League at large.

Yet it must be remembered that booksellers are not trained scientists. In his informative talk, Dr. Antonio Cantu, with his talk of "spectrophotometric analysis" and of "extractability curves," left me in no doubt about that. Moreover, I am not convinced that even science has all the answers. For example, is the Vinland Map genuine or not? As Mr. George Miles has indicated, science has yet to give a final and definitive verdict. What is more to the point is the question of logistics: one cannot submit every $100 letter to carbon dating!

What should the responsible dealer do if a customer seeks to return an item on the grounds of its questionable authenticity? The ideal policy is always to take back, unhesitatingly and for a full refund, anything with which the customer is not completely happy—and to do so without qualification, whether one thinks the customer is right or whether one thinks the customer is wrong, without any kind of time bar. In normal circumstances most of the best dealers are prepared to do this. This is not just altruism on their part, it is good business. The difficulty is that any published terms of business have of necessity to be more restrictive.

When, for example, things have been sold in good faith and in the light of the best scholarship available at the time, the honest dealer could be put to quite unwarranted financial hardship by having to accept returns without any time limit whatsoever. Difficulties arise in particular when costly items and long periods of time are involved. Imagine, for example, a $10,000 document sold ten, or even twenty, years before. Start to calculate the compound interest and you will see what I mean. The United States law on the buyer's so-called "loss of profit" also has a bearing on this. There are further complications when the dealer is not acting on his own account—i.e. first as buyer and then as seller of something that was, for a period, his or her own property—but when, instead, he or she is acting as agent for the previous owner and is selling on commission. For the dealer to carry the entire burden in a situation when he or she is unable to seek redress from the owner (which might well have been an estate), his or her trouble is great indeed.

In this regard, I have recently examined the published conditions of sale of five British firms of auctioneers, all of whom of course are normally agents, rather than sellers of their own property. All impose a time limit on returns and have to be given proof that the material concerned is "a deliberate forgery," i.e. "made with intent to deceive." The time limits vary from a generous five years at one end of the market down to a ludicrously short seven days at the other.

Returning to the I.L.A.B., I am happy to be able to bring you some positive news. At its September meeting in Switzerland, the League received a detailed report on the Texas affair from the president of the American association. He listed the various actions and initiatives taken by the ABAA and followed by giving an undertaking to send the League's committee updated reports as the ABAA's Security and Ethics Committee gives further consideration to the affair. The League hopes that a full account of the ABAA's actions will, subject to legal considerations, be given the widest publicity at the earliest practical opportunity.

The League itself is now preparing a revised and strengthened edition of its Compendium of Usages and Customs, which sets out guidelines on ethical and professional behavior. In a new initiative the League is preparing a form of warranty for use at book fairs sponsored by the League and its affiliated associations. It is also intended that the warranty be printed in the catalogues and displayed in the bookshops of affiliated dealers. In matters of speed the League perhaps can be likened to the proverbial "mills of God," but a draft of the warranty and the new edition of the Compendium will be put before the committee at its 1990 spring meeting in Milan. If approved, it will then go before the General Assembly at the League's Congress in Tokyo in October 1990. This is a slow process, but unless we have full consultation and the agreement of all parties, the documents we are drafting will not have maximum power.

I bring you a plea from the League to aid us in helping you. In regard to the Texas forgeries, the Antiquarian Booksellers Association of America has said that its hand would have been strengthened greatly if even one collector or one librarian (i.e. someone outside the trade) had made a written complaint to the association, stating that he or she had bought, from an ABAA member, an item which proved to be spurious. Such a complaint has yet to be made.

What would have been even more helpful, of course, would have been a lawsuit brought by a purchaser against a vendor. But, for reasons of their own, the buyers kept their heads below the battlements, even though, as I said earlier, one was so sickened by the affair that he gave up collecting forever.

Nobody likes to admit that he or she has been made a fool of. That is the strongest weapon in a confidence trickster's armory. No librarian wishes to have to tell administrators that precious funds have been spent on a forgery.

Likewise, no librarian likes to upset a donor by saying that his or her gift was spurious; nor does one like the trouble and expense of going to law. But the silence and the inaction of the buyers cost us all dear in this case.

In a recent publication on security in libraries,[1] the British Library urged librarians everywhere to look a similar problem squarely in the face. Urging the dropping of euphemisms, it said, "Call theft theft. Call thieves thieves." Hear! Hear! The International League of Antiquarian Booksellers urges you to adopt the same approach to forgery. And let us offer a word of thanks and praise to those who, in the face of a campaign to say nothing, had the courage to organize this conference.

I am the final speaker on this program and therefore should particularly have liked to close with an optimistic message. What I seem to have told you is how the book trade establishment's hands are tied in seeking to deal with the occasional miscreants that might be found in our ranks. I have explained the practical limitations on what most of us would like to do. Nevertheless I can find words of comfort. Let us not forget that it was a bookseller, Tom Taylor, who, being suspicious of some of the Texas documents, put an enormous amount of time and effort into proving—to his own considerable financial disadvantage—that the documents were indeed forgeries. What he did was in the best traditions of the trade. Also, let us not forget that most booksellers are decent men and women, proud of their calling and anxious to be able to go through this life holding their heads high. That, I suggest, is the buyer's best protection. Lastly, let us not forget that over the centuries book and manuscript forgeries have been a very small problem indeed.

During this last decade when the rapidly rising value of materials has made it more worthwhile for the forger to go to great lengths to perfect his artifacts, we have seen a growth in the number of forgeries coming onto the market. Perhaps by the very fact that the Houston conference has focused attention on the problem there will be a growing awareness of it. If so the incidence of forgery will certainly fall.

References
1. British Library. National Preservation Office, *Security Guidelines* (London: National Preservation Office, 1989).

Floor Discussion IV: Dealer/Donor/Institutional Relations

Donald Farren: I wonder if Mr. Rota would say something more about the movement for bookdealers to provide a warranty. This is an interesting development which has wide implications, although certainly this sort of thing would not be the solution to our problems. The solution rests on the sense of trust and integrity of all involved: the trade, purchasers, and collectors. Is this practice related to what I believe is beginning among antique dealers who vet items displayed at shows? Also, is there any relationship between the movement in the book trade with practices in the wider antiquities market?

Anthony Rota: In my country, we have had over thirty antiquarian book fairs sponsored by the Antiquarian Booksellers Association of Great Britain. Almost from the first one we had a vetting committee. As a condition of entry, one cannot rent a booth without agreeing to abide by the decision of this committee, which is not open to question and is not required to state its reasons. The president of the Antiquarian Booksellers Association and any two committee members chosen to act as assessors on any particular object are able to form an opinion and may ask an exhibitor to remove an item from display. The committee is not required to state that they disagree with the dealer's description of an item, nor are they required to say the item is a forgery. The vetting committee is not constrained by the threat of legal action because the exhibitor has signed a waiver, and if asked to remove something, he or she is obliged to do so.

When I was president of ABA, someone came to me and pointed out that what was offered as a William Wordsworth letter was, in fact, a letter in Dorothy Wordsworth's hand. I went over and had a quiet word with the exhibitor and he said to me, "William, Dorothy—it's all the same." That attitude is, I think, on the way out.

The warranty is a document in draft. Speaking personally, I believe the Islamic Law should be followed with regard to book theft, and I feel the same way about forgeries. This draft warranty will not be as strong as I would wish—I would never be able to get such a version through a committee meeting of the International League of Antiquarian Booksellers, let alone a general assembly. The draft is subject to revision, but I am very pleased to say that the idea, and the first text, came from a member of the Antiquarian Booksellers Association of America.

Pat Butler: I have listened with great interest to the discussions of how forged documents have been identified. What is going to happen to these forged documents? As one trained on the graduate level in furniture history, one of my most important experiences was to study fakes, and to learn about past mistakes which institutional curators—the experts—had made. I hope those institutions which have forged documents will not destroy or dispose of them, but will make them available so all of us may learn more about the process of forgery.

Jennifer Larson : I applaud those sentiments. One of the frustrating problems the trade faces is having an item identified by a dealer as spurious, or possibly spurious, only to have the owner repeatedly offer it until a credulous buyer finally is found. We would like to have some method by which these items could be permanently removed from the market place and have them put in teaching collections. As you are aware, there is a thriving trade in forged items which are knowingly bought and sold as forgeries. I believe the British Goldsmiths' Company has obtained the legal right to seize and retain fraudulent items in their area of expertise, and fraudulent coins are not sold legally in this country. This is a frustrating problem for book and manuscript dealers. I would like to see the international trade and the academic community devise methods of permanently marking items in some acceptable, yet indelible, way so they are not returned to the market simply to deceive people once again.

Alan Gribben: Forged items do not need to have "fake" stamped across them in red letters as much as they need to be described precisely in print, noting their location, so they may be traced more readily.

I have just completed a wide survey showing what has happened to the libraries of American authors. I found that, when compilations have been done, it has been a common practice of the compiler to omit any books that looked at all suspicious or fraudulent. They believed they were doing a service by leaving those out, though they planned to authenticate the others. My own two-volume survey [*Mark Twain's Library: A Reconstruction*. Boston: G. K. Hall, 1980], as well as a few other surveys, have gone to great lengths to list every book that was claimed as an association copy and to give the compilers' opinions regarding accuracy. I have received numerous thanks from dealers and others who otherwise might not know that a skeptical eye should be cast on a particular book. If forgeries can be described in some readily accessible print source, I believe this would be the best way to protect all of us in the future.

David Hewett: As a point of information, I want to make sure everyone knows that, after Mark Hofmann's trial, the Hofmann materials were returned to those people from whom they were seized. The prosecutors in Utah told me all those materials were to be returned to their owners. Whether they chose to sell, trade, or mount them on the wall was up to those individuals. The *Maine Antique Digest* made an effort to print a list of those pieces and to illustrate them where possible, but there was a lot of material seized by the police and stored in a warehouse.

Pat Bozeman: I am reminded of the phrase, "We are only as sick as the secrets we keep." It is up to all of us to continue in our efforts to expose forgeries.

Eric Wolf: Several speakers have said most dealers are honest. I think all but a very tiny fraction are indeed honest. My confidence in dealers has not been destroyed because of these forgeries; if anything, it has been increased

Floor Discussion IV

through a conference such as this and some of the actions we have heard about.

Richard Landon: I believe I can speak for everyone here when I congratulate the people who organized this conference. It has been extraordinarily interesting and useful, with a kind of passionate commitment exhibited that most academic conferences do not have. The people here—speakers and participants—care about these matters in a way that transcends the academic considerations of forgery and the faking of documents. I believe the international implications are extremely important as well. I can, in fact, speak on behalf of the Rare Book and Manuscripts Section of the International Federation of Library Associations which is planning a program in Stockholm in 1990 that will focus specifically on theft and security. I believe that a program on matters of forgery and questioned documents would be most appropriate. Although there is a temptation sometimes to confuse the problems of theft and security with the problems of forgery, they often do seem to go hand in hand. I will attempt to make known to the international community—particularly the European community— what has taken place at this Houston conference and how important this is in an international sense, to every institution, collector, and dealer around the world. Many early inhabitants of Texas regarded themselves as genuine pioneers; the group of Texans who organized this conference in 1989 may also regard themselves as genuine pioneers.

Dora Guerra: On behalf of other special collections librarians who hold forgeries in their collections, I congratulate everyone involved in planning this conference. We are all caught in the shocks and aftershocks of what has happened recently in Texas, and it is reassuring to be with our colleagues and to learn more about what we might do about these forgeries which have touched our lives.

Stuart Frank: It seems to me that the University of Texas has been stung and graduates of the University of Texas, in effect, run this state. There are highly-placed alumni all over Texas, among them collectors and bookdealers who have been damaged. If law enforcement agencies have not been interested in this issue and their response has not been satisfactory, there is one major institution, the University of Texas, that stands for the honor and the intellectual and spiritual well-being of this fine state. The University of Texas is not the same as a lone voice of an Austin bookdealer calling out from the wilderness, nor is it a bunch of effete intellectuals who bandy about with their precious treasures. I think there is a lot of untapped power at the University of Texas which could draw the attention of those officials who should be interested in these forgeries. How many Texans work for the FBI and the Secret Service? Most of the prosecutors, law enforcement agents, and the people with real power and influence in this state probably were educated right here in a great university that has been a victim of forgeries. I do not understand the lack of action. I commend the University of Houston for taking the first step by bringing this all to light and getting us all down to Houston to participate in this conference.

William A. Moffett: As president of the Association of College and Research Libraries, I must express the appreciation of librarians and curators across the country to the organizers of this conference and to the participants for airing so comprehensively the subject, and for giving a lot of people assignments for follow-up. I am sure that my colleagues in the Rare Books and Manuscripts Section of ACRL—Bill Joyce and others—can speak more pointedly to the interests of the rare books people, but all of us are very much indebted to the conference planners and speakers. I am particularly grateful to Jennifer Larson and Anthony Rota for their efforts. They continue to prod the booksellers' associations and to sustain those organizations' interests in tightening the apparatus for policing the profession and for bolstering confidence in the profession. This is needed, and it can be recognized there is a problem without having to make apologies to all the honest dealers.

I was reminded of this recently when I interviewed the convicted book thief, James R. Shinn, whose systematic looting of libraries prompted the 1983 Oberlin Conference on Theft. Shinn noted, rather smugly, that, although he had actively fenced the books he had stolen across the country through dealers—some of whom were ABAA members—not a single one of them had come forward to discuss those interactions. Obviously, there is a need for this kind of gathering, and we very much appreciate the dedication of those who organized the Houston Conference on Forged Documents.